Julian Hight

www.britainsancientforest.co.uk

For Charlotte, Jake, Harry and Pops and for John, who first suggested I write this book.

Than a tree, a grander child earth bears not.
What are the boasted palaces of man,
Imperial city or triumphal arch,
To forests of immeasurable extent,
Which Time confirms, which centuries waste not?

From *Sylva Britannica* by Jacob George Strutt, 1822

Britain's Ancient Forest – Legacy and Lore

ISBN: 978-0-9932906-2-6

First published in the United Kingdom in 2019 by Julian Hight

Volume copyright © Julian Hight 2019
Text copyright © Julian Hight 2019
Images copyright © Julian Hight 2019 (except where stated)
The moral rights of the author have been asserted.

All rights reserved. No part of this publication may be reproduced, stored in a retrieval system, or transmitted in any form or by any means, electronic, mechanical, photocopying, recording or otherwise, without the prior written permission of the copyright owner.

A CIP catalogue record for this book is available from the British Library.

Design and artwork by Julian Hight: www.julianhight.co.uk
Edited by Felicity Laughton

Printed in Europe by Imago on paper sourced from sustainable forests.

For further information, or to order this book direct from the publisher visit the website: www.britainsancientforest.co.uk

Contents

Introduction	4
Britain's forest – a history	8
Directory of forests	16
Forest flora and fauna	270
Appendices	
Sponsors	297
Bibliography	298
About the author, picture credits, roll of honour	299
Index	300

Introduction

Forest

- *tract of mingled woodland and open uncultivated ground; a district chiefly devoted to the purposes of the chase, subject to its own laws, courts and officers; once a royal forest; typically owned by the sovereign and partly wooded, kept for hunting and having its own laws.*
- *ORIGIN from Latin foris, meaning 'outside.'*

From *The New Gresham English Dictionary,* 1931

The word 'forest' in a modern sense, conjures a picture of dense woodland, supported by a long-held belief that Britain was blanketed with trees, an isle where the ubiquitous squirrel could scurry from John O'Groats to Land's End without ever setting foot on the ground. However, the original word conveyed an altogether different meaning to that which it conjures up of today.

Derived from the Latin *foris*, meaning outside, from early medieval times 'forest' could include meadow, grass, bog, marsh and woodland, wood pasture and even entire villages – land that was fit for the hunt and under jurisdiction of forest law. These tracts of land were reserved solely for the pleasure of the king and his retinue. Heavy fines for poaching – including the death penalty in the 12th century – cutting timber and 'assarting' land for agriculture, were issued to offenders of forest law, drawn up to protect the royal game and the *verte* – the green habitat where they lived. The law was upheld harshly by appointed foresters and often resented by the local people.

Opposite: The author in his prefered habitat, 2016

Britain is one of the least wooded countries in northern Europe with around 13% woodland cover; however, it is thought to be blessed with the highest number of ancient trees. Millennial oaks stand in remnant deer parks, wood pasture and historic manorial estates, vestiges of a once-thriving and now deeply declining worked medieval treescape, where trees were afforded the time and space to reach giant proportions, some of which date to the Norman Conquest and beyond.

Growing up on a housing estate in Surrey, I was lucky to have 3.23ha (eight acres) of woodland behind my garden. As well as playing in the street, as kids we played in the woods – climbing trees, building camps and staging pitched fir-cone fights. It instilled in me a love of nature and trees and woodland in particular. Not far away stood the old dodders of Windsor Great Park – scores of ancient oaks, gnarled, hollow and twisted – living links to a rich history, hotspots for biodiversity – a legacy of William the Conqueror. As a boy those trees fired my imagination; what must they had witnessed and what stories could they tell?

Then, about 15 years ago, I stumbled across a Victorian photograph of Sherwood Forest's Major Oak – arguably Britain's most famous of the species. I had visited as a child on a school trip 30 years previously, and remembered vividly its connection to tales of Robin Hood and his merry men, and the wonder I had sensed standing beside its huge, cavernous trunk. I revisited and photographed the Major Oak in its present state, and was immediately struck by the fact that in the century between the two photographs, there was almost no perceivable change in the shape, size and character of the tree. Estimated to be between 600 and 1,000 years old (impossible to date accurately due to its lack of internal growth rings),

INTRODUCTION

I considered the photographs good visual evidence supporting the idea that the tree could credibly reside at the upper end of the age estimate, and be a millennial oak.

That one photograph inspired me to travel throughout Britain to seek out our largest and oldest trees, to photograph them and tell their stories. Led in the first instance by archive photographs and engravings, after five years the project manifested itself in my first book, *Britain's Tree Story*.

Since then, my passion and curiosity for ancient trees has taken me around the globe on a photographic odyssey to capture the tales of 100 of the great survivors of the tree world across 39 countries: from 3,500-year-old giant sequoias and twisted, dwarf-like bristlecone pines in California – the oldest known trees on the planet – to the venerable, hollow millennial oaks and prehistoric yew trees of northern Europe; from ancient olive trees in the Mediterranean – still producing harvestable fruit after two millennia or more – to the upside down, sacred baobabs of Africa and Australia and towering kauris of New Zealand. All that and even the God-inhabiting cedars, camphors and cherry blossoms of mountainous, magical Japan, eventually culminated in my second tome: *World Tree Story*.

It became clear to me that ancient trees survive thanks to their economic, religious or cultural value. They have earned their keep from communities who have lived amongst them, and have provided food, shade, fuel and timber. They have acted as meeting places over generations, in mutually beneficial partnerships that endure for millennia, sometimes outliving empires that rise and fall around them.

Stories attach themselves to the trees to the extent that some achieve God-like status – even enshrining spirits, becoming shrines themselves, such as in India and Japan – and I have no doubt the same was once true in Britain on a grand scale.

Their prospects may appear grim, and the great challenge is to try and secure their survival. Ancient trees are a dying breed, deprived of the succession and continuity which traditionally supported the mutually beneficial human/sylvan relationship that existed prior to the era of modern forestry plantations. Thankfully, volunteer groups such as the Ancient Tree Forum are championing the cause. A thousand-year-old tree cannot be replaced overnight; that kind of longevity requires 15 or more human lifespans, which, when viewed in tree terms, takes us back to a time before the thawing of Britain's last ice age.

For this book, I continued to tour Britain, searching for vestiges of its ancient forest, told from the perspective of surviving ancient trees – some of which were part of the landscape a millennium or two ago – living links not just to Britain's forest, but also to its rich and vibrant history.

INTRODUCTION

THIS PAGE: The Ankerwyke Yew, under whose branches in 1215 Magna Carta is thought to have been sealed by King John, 2015

OPPOSITE: The Ankerwyke Yew in 1845, illustrating its unchanging character in over a century, supporting the case for its longevity

Britain's forest – a history

A forest is a certen territorie of wooddy grounds and fruitfull pastures, priveledged for wild beasts and foules of forest, chase and warren, to rest and abide in, in the safe protection of the king for his princely delight and pleasure.

From *Manward's Forest Laws*, 1598

Coming in from the cold

Britain hosts between 20 and 30 native species of tree. Exactly how many is open to conjecture, depending on the precise definition of tree (when does a shrub become a tree etc). A native tree is defined as a species that colonised our island between 12,000 years ago (when the great ice sheets of the last ice age started to melt), and 8,000 years ago when the land bridge connecting Britain to the European mainland was flooded by rising sea levels. Tree seeds were carried on the wind and via birds and animals, along with other native species of flora. Herds of grazing animals as well as their predators and nomadic people all had an effect on the spread and development of Britain's treescape from the earliest times.

The wildwood

The first trees to arrive were birch and willow (which remain pioneer trees on recently cleared land), followed gradually by pine around 7500BC, then oak, hazel and alder. Next came elm, lime and beech, and by 4000BC, Britain is considered to have established its 'wildwood' – a term coined by ecologist Oliver Rackham to describe Britain's woodland cover prior to major human intervention.

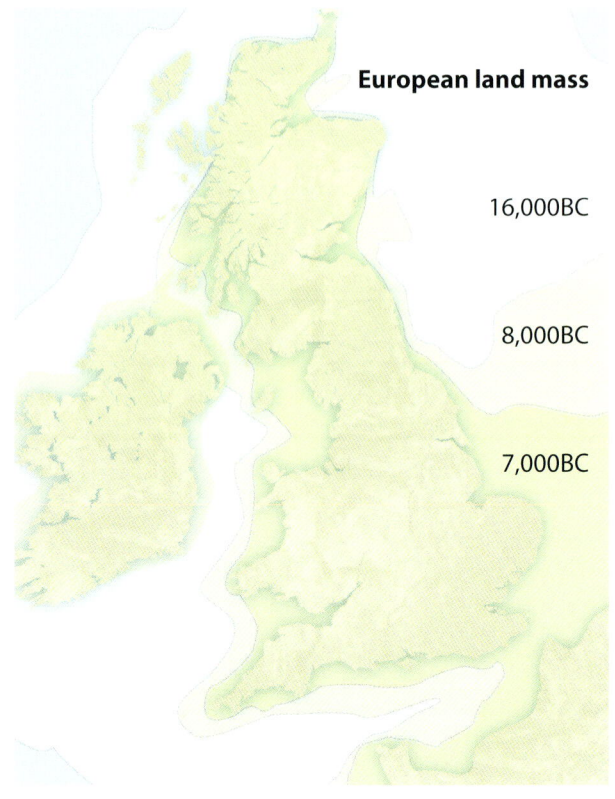

European land mass

16,000BC

8,000BC

7,000BC

An understanding of how Britain's vegetation appeared at this time can be gleaned from various sources, and are interpreted as various scenarios.

Pollen grains, which can survive indefinitely preserved in mud or peat, provide a record of the species that were common at any given time. Pollen, however, cannot reveal the true density of tree cover, as some tree pollens are wind-blown and others rely on insects. For instance, the wind-pollinated oak deposits a far greater pollen footprint than the insect-polinated lime, thus distorting the overall picture.

Frans Vera presented a view different to the long-held dense-canopy woodland picture, by suggesting a more open landscape that was shaped by large herbivores, who naturally grazed the landscape. This scenario suits Britain's broadleaved trees such as oak and elm – light-loving trees that thrive in an open-grown environment.

Fossil beetle records reveal further evidence. Certain beetles (such as the violet click beetle) live only in decaying oak wood, their presence suggesting a landscape that included old, large oaks. In support of that scenario, the presence of dung beetles suggests a more open, grazed landscape.

Ancient submerged woodlands around the coast of Britain tell us what trees were growing there around 6,000 years ago, as do fallen trees preserved in ancient bogs and peat.

BELOW: Ancient submerged tree stump at Borth, 2019

From hunter-gatherer to farmer

Natural glades created by fallen trees, the effect of fungi, insects and occasional fires were kept open by grazing herbivores, which limited regeneration.

From the earliest times, people also played a part. Neolithic oak trackways provide evidence for early woodland management dating from 3800BC. But it was the advent of farming, well established as a way of life in Britain by 3000BC, that saw more drastic changes in the landscape. A move from a hunter-gatherer lifestyle to a more settled farming subsistence necessitated land clearance, and the exclusion of grazing animals, to yield a successful crop. It coincided with a dramatic decline in Britain's elm population. Whether this was caused by disease or clearance by people is unclear; it may well have resulted from a combination of both.

Invaders and settlers

The introduction of farming in Britain appears to have followed the arrival of people with new ideas migrating from the Middle East. Migrations continued, with each subsequent arrival impacting on the landscape, whether by peaceful movement of people or invasion. Celts, Romans, Saxons. Vikings and Normans all had an effect on Britain's treescape. Land clearance for the plough, town development, military and industrial purposes and active woodland management all played a part.

The combined picture suggests a patchwork, mosaic landscape consisting of cultivated land, woodland, wood pasture (open-grown trees), grassland, marsh, bog and scrub, all liable to constant change as each culture stamped its own identity on the country.

Royal Forests

In 1086, William I commissioned the Domesday Survey to ascertain exactly what land, stock and dues he had gained following the Norman Conquest 20 years earlier. Using the survey as a basis, Oliver Rackham calculated that Britain then had around 15% wooded cover. That equates broadly to our current 13% cover. So, 1,000 years ago, far from being blanketed in dense woodland, it seems much of Britain was an open, treed landscape.

William was a keen hunter. On ascendance to the throne, he established Royal Forests all over his kingdom to satisfy his indulgence. The Saxons had Royal Forests in place together with a system of laws, but William greatly expanded on these, both in terms of acreage and rules and regulations.

Huge tracts of land were put under 'forest law'. Estates, farms, even entire villages were incorporated, restricting local people from interfering with the 'venison and vert' (game; mainly deer and trees and greenery – their habitat), which belonged to the king.

Penalties for poaching or the felling of trees were harsh and were upheld by appointed 'verderers'. Cases were heard at 'swainmotes', forest courts.

William's successors expanded the forest system, sometimes including entire counties, as happened in Essex, Cornwall and Devon. By the 13th century, a quarter of the country was classified as Royal Forest.

The original definition of forest was not land covered in dense woodland, but simply land under forest law. It derived from the latin *foris* meaning simply 'outside', and referred to land within its jurisdiction. 'Forest' included woodland, wood pasture, grassland, marsh and bog. I use that definition when describing forest in this book, and refer to 'woodland' when describing close-canopy.

Charter of the Forest

In 1215, King John was pressured into sealing Magna Carta – probably near the shade of the monumental Ankerwyke Yew at Runnymede.

The closest Britain ever came to a bill of rights, it offered protection to the barons from false imprisonment and upheld church rights, yet did little for the rights of the common people.

Two years later, John's son and heir, Henry III, sealed the Charter of the Forest, which set out freedoms and liberties and, re-established rights of access to the Royal Forest that had been gradually eroded since the Conquest.

The charter gave ordinary people the chance to make a living from the forest as they always had; such was its importance in everyday life.

Medieval forest

The medieval period saw coppicing increase as more land was taken for agriculture. Wood pasture was still common, but some of it was converted into coppice to maximise wood production.

In 1349 the Black Death devastated the human population, reducing it by a third, and thereby relieving pressure on the country's woodland.

When Henry VIII dissolved the monasteries between 1536 and 1541, much of the land previously held by the Church was sold off to favoured individuals, benefitting new lords of the manor all over the country. Some of those manors are still held by the same families that took control of them 500 years ago; Longleat is an example. There was an increase of Deer parks under Henry, such was his love of the chase.

Hunting later declined as a royal pasttime and parts of the Royal Forest were disafforested, snapped up by the lords, who were eager to enlarge their estates.

Coppicing and pollarding

Sustainable wood is nothing new. People have been cutting wood from trees and harvesting their fruit for thousands of years. Recently, a tree stump carbon dated to 5000BC showed clear signs of pollarding, the practice whereby a tree's branches are cut every eight to 20 years above head height to prevent grazing animals from devouring the regrowth. Not only does pollarding provide a sustainable source of timber, it also promotes regrowth and can be partly responsible for supporting the longevity of ancient trees.

The practice of pollarding – a legacy which provides us with so many of our ancient trees today – lapsed around 200 years ago when coal largely replaced wood for heating. Sites such as Burnham Beeches, saved by the City of London Corporation in 1890 for 'the recreation and enjoyment of the people', still practices traditional pollarding, maintaining many wonderful trees in the process, including the ancient Druid's Oak (see page 160).

Coppicing is the practice of cutting trees at ground level. Hazel, oak and ash all take to being coppiced, and regrow to form new shoots, which can be cut in cycles depending on the thickness of wood required. Coppicing, however, unlike pollarding, requires fencing or hedging to keep grazing animals from devouring the regrowth.

In Somerset, 'stoggles' were formed, where the trees were cut at chest height to protect their regrowth from grazing pigs. Adding 'standards' to coppice – leaving selected trees to grow tall for timber – emerged by the late Middle Ages.

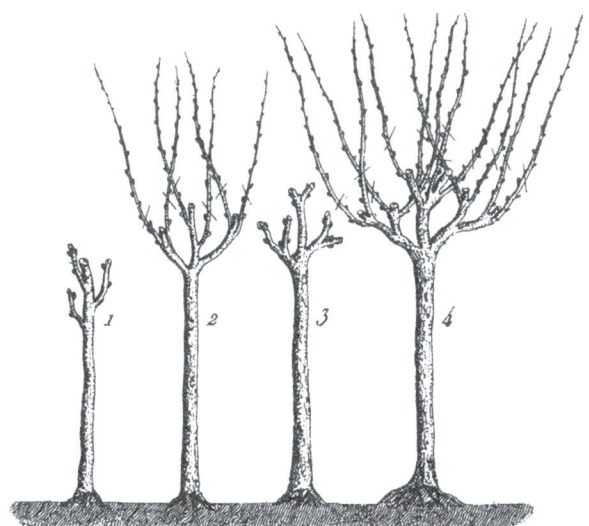

ABOVE: Pruning fruit trees over four years, c1850

ABOVE: The Westonbirt Lime, estimated to be 2,000 years old, is still coppiced on a 20-year cycle, 2016

Wood Pasture

Frequently mentioned as *Silva pastilis* in the Domesday Survey, wood pasture was once common across Britain. Open-grown trees, often pollarded for wood or shredded for animal feed, provide shade and shelter for grazing animals. Many ancient trees survive as relics of wood pasture, as they have done since the wildwood.

ABOVE: Wood pasture, Somerset, 2016

Parkland

Early parks catered for deer from the 11th century, when the Normans added fallow deer to the native red and roe. They were 'emparked' with a bank and ditch and a cleft wooden park pale or wall to keep the deer from straying. Emulating and often enclosing wood pasture, open-grown trees offered cover for the deer whilst providing open ground for the chase.

The 18th century saw a new-age of country-house parks designed by landscape gardeners such as Lancelot 'Capability' Brown and Humphry Repton. They introduced sweeping views, lakes and follies and planted trees while retaining veterans as part of the vista, emulating wood pasture and parkland.

Enclosure

Between 1604 and 1914, enclosure acts were passed allowing land owners to enclose common land. While they may have already owned it, enclosure restricted access to people who had previously held rights of common for fuel and grazing.

The 19th century saw enclosures accelerate. In 1850, 405ha (1,000 acres) of Epping Forest was enclosed by the Manor of Loughton. With little forest left, the people of Epping followed the lead of a labourer, Thomas Willingdale, and opposed the enclosure. Supported by the Commons Preservation Society, it took until 1881 before Queen Victoria declared the forest open to the public, paving the way for the removal of other enclosures across the country.

Forestry

The 19th century saw the rise of commercial plantation forestry. Bearing no resemblance to Britain's native forest, and of little benefit to wildlife, non-native, densely planted conifers laid out in rows served as a quick-growing cash crop.

After the First World War, following severe depletion of Britain's timber supply, in 1919 the British Government established the Forestry Commission to expand Britain's forests. Plantations sprung up around the country on fields, heaths and agricultural land, utilised in the Second World War.

It was not until the 1950s that plantation forestry grew at the expense of ancient native woodland, shading it out at best and removing it at worst.

Britain may have 13% woodland cover today, on a par with medieval cover, but only 2% is ancient native woodland: Britain's unique, natural, irreplaceable rainforest.

Commercial forestry – along with Germanic fairy tales – has redefined our understanding of the word 'forest', from a patchwork, mosaic, open-wooded landscape to that of a dense, dark, terrifying wood.

Rewilding

The current trend towards rewilding – the restoration of wildlife areas through the re-introduction of lost species and connectivity of landscape – has gathered pace.

Rewilding projects such as those at Knepp Castle have shown how the idea can work. The introduction of grazers such as red deer, longhorn cattle and Tamworth pigs and leaving the land to restore itself, without chemical intervention and little planting, has seen the return of many key species. Knepp now hosts the country's largest population of purple emperor butterflies, where before there were none. After all, a successful biodiverse forest is not just about trees, but about all the species that have developed to coexist there.

A nation built from forest

Tales of Druids worshipping in sacred groves are deeply imbedded in the British consciousness. They stem from Roman sources, notably Pliny's first-century *Natural History*, yet a strictly oral tradition means no Druidic records survive, their customs shrouded in mystery.

However, Shinto worship of ancient trees in Japan – where spirits or *kami* are believed to reside and similar beliefs such as those held by tribespeople of the Amazon, leave little doubt in my mind that comparable observances were once held here.

Britain's shipwrights selected timber from trees with natural 'knees' that were still growing and were ideal for a ship's bow or A-Frame for a pitched roof. Sometimes it was just the required branch that would be removed. Huge lengths of oak taken from Sherwood Forest to construct the roof of St Paul's Cathedral following the Great Fire of London still hold firm after almost 450 years.

Elizabeth I, concerned at the decline of mature oaks needed for shipbuilding, ordered a considered replanting. Many ancient oaks survive from this period, such as the giant 'Queen Elizabeth Oak' at Cowdray Park in Sussex. A tree of the same name stood at Hatfield Park where the Virgin Queen, was informed of her imminent accession to the throne following Mary's execution in 1558.

In the 18th and 19th centuries, bark stripped from oak trees was exploited for its high tannin content to tan animal hides. The oak tannin was also ideal for use in the production of barrel staves for wine casks.

Charcoal burners lived and worked in oak woods to supply fuel to iron works. Around 300 trees a year were required in charcoal form to fire a smelter, which equates to around 4ha (10 acres) of oak wood consumed for the purpose per annum.

Historically, acorns provided 'pannage' – a common right for fattening swine – still observed in the New Forest each October and November. Although poisonous to ponies, acorns ground into meal were used to make bread in times of hardship and, prior to farming, provided a natural staple.

BELOW: Rewilding at Knepp Castle, West Sussex, 2018

Literature, legend and lore

Trees have been celebrated in literature over the centuries, most famously by Shakespeare and Wordsworth among many others.

Oak galls – growths resulting from the tree's reaction to gall wasps laying eggs on it – provided the main ingredient for ink that fuelled the writers' pen. It was used to scribe historic documents such as Magna Carta – still legible over 800 years after it was written. Oak apples came to symbolise the 1664 Restoration of the English monarchy, traditionally celebrated on May 29th – Oak Apple Day. The Restoration is indebted to the Boscobel Oak in Shropshire, as it was in the tree's branches that the young Charles II hid from pursuant Parliamentarian forces, allowing him to keep his head on his shoulders, unlike his father.

In search of giants

Pinning an age on Britain' ancient trees is problematic. Without a known planting date, counting annual growth rings is the only way to accurately confirm lifespan. Decay and hollowing, shedding heartwood in a symbiotic relationship with fungi and invertebrates, creating compost for the tree itself, leaves only the more recent growth rings.

Alongside established age-estimators, such as those provided by John White, historic records, art and archive photographs offer supporting evidence and visual dating. Oaks trees can show little change in shape and character in over a century, lending credence to their great longevity.

Ancient legacy

Ancient trees offer considerably more habitat than younger trees. Oak leads the way, supporting at least 500 species, more than any other British tree. Some invertebrates are found only in their decaying wood. Ancient trees are biodiversity hotspots, havens for wildlife.

According to the Woodland Trust Ancient Tree Inventory, 120 ancient oaks stand at over 9m (29.5ft) in circumference. It is no accident that their legacy endures. They survive in historic deer parks, forest remnants, wood pasture and commons, beside ancient roadways, on village greens and in hedgerows – former worked treescapes and ancient meeting places.

A similar number of yew trees – Britain's longest-lived tree – can be found mainly, although not always, in Britain's churchyards. Now rare in woodland groves, yew once featured more prominently outside the safety of the church wall.

Descendants of Britain's original wildwood, these ancient trees paint a picture at odds with the long-held perception of a country once covered in dense woodland. Britain's broadleaves are light-loving trees that thrive in an open-grown environment. Part of an historic, patchwork landscape, their longevity could place them less than ten generations from the end of the last ice age when they first colonised our islands 10,000-12,000 years ago.

Future forest

Climate change has undoubtedly affected Britain's trees. They flower earlier year on year, and grow larger at higher elevations than before.

Diseases imported on trees grown abroad are also making their mark, with Chalara ash dieback threatening to consume Britain's ash population.

But loss of biodiversity – cited in a 2019 UN report as equally devastating to our future as climate change – is in danger of being overlooked. Planting projects to offset carbon dioxide need to take into account Britain's 'open-grown' nature in order to preserve our unique, native biodiverse flora and fauna.

BRITAIN'S FOREST – A HISTORY

The Drive Oak, Gloucestershire, 2019

Directory of Forests

As depicted in the text

Scotland
		Page
1	The Caledonian Forest	18

England
2	Forest of Northumberland	34
3	Inglewood Forest	42
4	Forest of the High Peak	44
5	Sherwood Forest	48
6	Kesteven Forest	60
7	Needwood Forest	64
8	Charnwood Forest	82
9	Forest of Arden	88
10	Salcey Forest	90
11	Forest of Clun	103
12	Forest of Dean	118
13	Wychwood Forest	124
14	Kingswood Forest	132
15	Forest of Essex	142
16	Burnham Beeches	158
17	Berkshire Forest	144
18	Windsor Great Forest	168
19	Forest of the Weald	190
20	Savernake Forest	196
21	Harewood Forest	201
22	Clarendon Forest	204
23	Grovely Forest	210
24	Selwood Forest	216
25	Blackmore Forest	238
26	Cranborne Chase	234
27	Kingley Vale	238
28	Neroche Forest	242
29	The New Forest	248
30	Dartmoor Forest	254
31	Forest of Cornwall	260

Wales
32	Forest of Snowdonia	100
33	Long Forest	104
34	Borth Sunken Hundred	106

ABOVE: Studley Oak c1850

DIRECTORY OF FORESTS – MAP

FOREST OF CALEDONIA

Great Wood of Caledonia

There are two principal races of the Britons, the Caledonians and the Maeatae... The Maeatae live next to the cross-wall which cuts the island in half, and the Caledonians are beyond them...They can endure hunger and cold and any kind of hardship; for they plunge into the swamps and exist there for many days with only their heads above water, and in the forests they support themselves upon bark and roots...
From *History of Rome, Volume V* by Cassius Dio, c155-c235

Around 9,000 years ago, the ice sheets that had previously engulfed Britain had retreated far enough to allow trees to take root in Scotland. The pioneer species – birch, followed by Scots pine – could both tolerate the colder northern climate (Scots pine in Siberia can persist at -64°C(-83°F), and grows in more countries than any other conifer). In the following millennia, as the temperature warmed and allowed the oak, lime and elm to prosper at the expense of pine in southern Britain, at its northern reaches pine continued to thrive, and formed a vast, temperate rainforest.

Scotland's Caledonian wood was first referenced by Classical Roman writers. Ptolemy and Pliny the Elder both mentioned Caledonia Silva – wood of the Caledonii – presumably named after the tribe of the same name who were based in the Central Highlands.

By around 5000BC the forest had reached its peak – with estimates of its extent in the region of 15,000km^2 (5,792 miles^2). Scots pine dominated, with birch, rowan, aspen, juniper and other hardy pioneers joining the fray. The trees colonised the marshy bogs and swampland across all but the harshest and most mountainous regions, creating a patchwork forest mosaic, a more open landscape than might be expected. The Scots pine is a long-lived tree that needs light and space to grow to its full potential – illustrated by surviving 'granny pines' aged between three and 500 years old.

FOREST OF CALEDONIA

When the Roman Legions arrived, they underestimated the fierce resistance they would face from Pictish tribes, and hastened to build Hadrian's Wall in AD122, followed by the Antonine Wall further north 20 years later.

The Picts continued to wage guerrilla warfare from the forest beyond the walls. It was from this period that tree cover noticeably started to reduce. Emperor Severus experienced 'countless hardships in cutting down the forests, levelling the heights, filling up the swamps', during his failed attempt to conquer Caledonia in AD208.

Arthurian legend depicts Merlin retreating to the sanctuary of the Caledonian woods in madness, which was brought on as a result of the Battle of Arfderydd in AD573.

The Vikings burnt large areas and felled tall pines for their longship masts. Feuding Highland clans burnt their enemies' woodlands – their vital winter fuel stocks.

Elk all but disappeared from the landscape in the Bronze Age, and by the tenth century, brown bear, lynx and reindeer had joined them, hunted to extinction. Wild boar survived into the 13th century, which doubtless had an effect on forest regeneration – their ploughing action on the soil proving beneficial to pine regeneration. The last wolf was shot in 1743, by which time most of the oak woods had been felled. By the mid-19th century, the pines too were decimated, felled to build ships and fuel iron works. In the 20th century two world wars and a Forestry Commission founded to maximise timber all but finished the job.

Regeneration virtually halted; overgrazing by sheep and red deer put a stop to that. Deer overran the diminished pine woods, where they had previously coexisted for thousands of years. Of all former large beasts of Caledonia, red deer have demonstrated the greatest resilience.

Today, perhaps as little as 1% of the former ancient forest remains in 35 isolated locations. Red deer herds are culled to encourage tree regeneration, with several initiatives designed to replenish the great pine forests of old. Crossbills and red squirrel can still be seen, and pine marten, capercaillie and black grouse have been reintroduced. Plans are afoot to add beaver, lynx, wolf and bear to the list, with the aim of re-establishing Caledonia's unique biodiversity.

Seven score heroes, maddened by battle,
To the forest of Celyddon they fled.
Since I Myrddin, am second only to Taliesin,
Let my words be heard as truth.

'Dialogue of Myrddin and Taliesin' from
The Black Book of Carmarthen I, c1250

ABOVE: Scots pine, 1817

OPPOSITE: Red deer stag – 'Monarch of the Glen,' 2018

Where's the thane of Cawdor?
We coursed him at the heels, and had a purpose
To be his purveyor: but he rides well;
And his great love, sharp as his spur,
hath holp him To his home before us.
From *Macbeth* by William Shakespeare, 1606

ABOVE & BELOW: The Cawdor Thorn, c1890 and 2018
OPPOSITE: 200-year-old lime avenue at Cawdor Castle

The Thorn of Cawdor

Cawdor Castle, Nairnshire

The Thane of Cawdor is first mentioned in a charter of Robert the Bruce from 1310, in which William, Thane of Cawdor, was granted the hereditary title in return for an annual payment to the Crown of twelve marks.

The Thane was appointed Sheriff and Constable of Nairn Castle and its lands, which effectively controlled the strategic coastal passage between Inverness and Elgin. The Thane held a smaller fortified family residence at Old Calder about 8km (5 miles) to the south of Nairn. Built on marshy ground, and repaired at the expense of the Crown in 1398, the decision was taken – probably by William's son of the same name – to build a new, improved castle on a safer footing about 1.6km (1 mile) to the south.

Legend holds that Thane William had a prophetic dream that advised him to let loose a donkey, carrying a chest loaded with gold – reserved to pay for the new castle – and to build his new domain wherever the ass set down to rest that evening, securing the future prosperity of the castle.

The donkey wandered on, and came to rest beneath a thorn tree. There the Thane built his castle, and retained the tree forever-more in the castle dungeon and, beside it, the chest; where both remain there to this day.

Historically, the thorn tree was referred to as a hawthorn *(Cratagus monogyna)*, but following carbon-dating analysis was found to be a holly *(Ilex aquifolium)*. The tree died around 1372, probably shortly after the castle tower was built, once the tree had been deprived of light.

As it happens, the ass appears to have chosen well – the roots of the tree cling to solid bedrock – providing a stable foundation for the castle walls. In addition, Cawdor Woods to the south provided a good supply of wood. Its sessile oaks *(Quercus petraea)* are thought to descend from ancient primeval oak forest and host a large variety of lichens.

Holly's thorny leaves were thought to symbolise Christ's crown of thorns, believed to ward off evil spirits, fire and storm, so mystisism is likely to have influenced the decision to build there.

FOREST OF CALEDONIA

Glen Affric Inverness-shire

On first impressions, Glen Affric – the dappled glen – may appear to epitomise the very essence of Caledonian wilderness, and while it displays Britain's largest area of native pine forest, on closer inspection, the glen calls to mind Oliver Rackham's assertion: 'Human activities have been so pervasive that in historic times there have not been many forests on earth (other than on uninhabited islands) never altered by people's activities'.

Glen Affric's long and arduous history is testament to that assertion and its reputation as Scotland's most beautiful glen – a mosaic landscape of river, loch, ancient pinewood, moor and mountain – survives through a mixture of judgement and luck.

From the 15th century, the glen was owned by the Clan Chisholm – a fact prominently displayed on a plaque attached to a boulder at the head of Glen Affric. By the mid-16th century, logs were cut and floated down river to the sawmill at Beauly, then on to Inverness, a growing city hungry for timber.

In the early 19th century, the clan evicted tenant farmers as part of the Highland Clearances, to introduce sheep farming as a more profitable land use. Sporting activities followed – shooting and deer stalking in particular – ans Affric Lodge, built in 1870, hosted visits from Queen Mary, Lady Fanny Spencer-Churchill Lady Glen Affric and her nephew Winston Churchill.

In the 1950s, Loch Beinn a' Mheadhain was dammed to feed a power station at Fasnakyle, raising the water level by some 6m (20ft). The Forestry Commission took ownership of Glen Affric in 1951, and found few remaining pines all under a hundred years old. Regeneration had been halted by over-grazing from introduced sheep and an uncontrolled deer population – formerly kept in check by a now-extinct wolf population. Since 1960, measures have been in place to conserve the National Nature Reserve, and reinstate a wider Caledonian Forest.

From mauve to green to grey to blue,
With golden shafts begot –
The stark and mighty mountains
Enfold the restless loch.
From *Poetry through my life* by Pauline Hight 1934-2010

ABOVE: Glen Affric, c1935
OPPOSITE: Pioneer birch at Loch Beinn a' Mheadhain, 2018
BELOW: Ancient 'granny pine' at Glen Affric, 2018

The Black Wood of Rannoch

Rannoch, Perthshire

Of the 35 recorded remnants of old-growth Caledonian pine forest, the Black Wood of Rannoch – located between the 1,081m (3,547ft) peak of Schichallion and the southern shore of Loch Rannoch's black water – is one of its finest.

The small wood, only 4.8 x 1.6km (3x1 miles), hosts a fine array of ancient Caledonian 'granny pines', birch, juniper and holly. Some measure up to 5m (16.4ft) in circumference, and it is likely they date from the time of the Jacobite Rebellion of 1745. Landlords of the time, the Robertsons, found themselves on the wrong side of fortune supporting Charles Stuart at Culloden – the defining battle of the Jacobites – and surrendered the wood to Commissioners of the Forfeited Estates. The Commissioners stewardship however, effectively safeguarded the Black Wood in that period, by enclosing it with ditches to protect seedlings from grazing, and by planting a new generation of pines.

With most of Caledonia's oak woods gone, relative inaccessibility to the ancient pine woods offered scant protection. Tall, straight pine trunks presented the perfect resource for planks and ship masts, and the loggers moved in.

The Black Wood was no exception and it suffered heavy losses. Felled timber was slung down a network of sluice canals cut into the hillside to the loch below and was floated on to the River Tay via the Tummel. Some trees apparently found their way across the North Sea, washing up on the shores of the Netherlands.

Tragedy almost struck in 1918 when the entire wood was selected for clearfelling to support the war effort. The end of the war in November of that year saved the wood from peril, but the Second World War sanctioned the loss of around 8,000 trees, many felled by the Canadian Forestry Corps.

Since 1947 the Forestry Commission has managed the wood, which has gained SSSI (Site of Special Scientific Interest) and Forest Nature Reserve status. The wood supports a host of native wildlife including red deer – Monarch of the Glen – Scottish crossbill, red grouse, capercaillie, red squirrel and pine marten. There are lichens and fungi, and rare plants such as coralroot orchid and one-sided wintergreen, a flowering plant that obtains half of its carbon via its roots from mycorrhiza networks – which in turn obtain their carbon from the roots of the ancient trees of Rannoch's Black Wood.

BELOW: The Black Wood of Rannoch beyond Loch Rannoch, 2009
OPPOSITE: Ancient 'granny pine' in the Black Wood, 2009

Braveheart Trees

Scotland's past is often remembered in its many landmarks – characters and events woven into the tapestry of the landscape – and historic trees are no exception.

In *Macbeth*, Shakespeare tells of the prophecy that heralded the king's demise, if Birnam Wood should 'come against him'. An ancient hollow oak on the south bank of the River Tay in Perthshire is known as the last oak of Birnam Wood.

A veteran sweet chestnut named after Mary Queen of Scots is reputed to have been planted by her in 1561 – the year of her return to Scotland from France – at Cumbernauld Castle, North Lanarkshire, family home to one of her ladies-in-waiting. Yew, however, is said to have been her favourite tree, and adorned the coin of her realm. An ancient specimen named after her at Crookston Castle, near Glasgow, was felled in 1816. A model of the castle was carved from its wood and is displayed nearby, at Pollok House.

William Wallace, 13th-century warrior and freedom fighter, who embodies the very spirit of Scotland and is fiercely defended by Scots to this day, is remembered in the Wallace Yew and the Wallace Oak, both of which grew on his family estate in Elderslie, Renfrewshire.

No trace of the oak remains – it fell in 1856, its demise no doubt hastened by relic hunters who hacked off its limbs, eager to own a piece of history. Legend has Wallace eluding English forces by hiding in the branches of the tree, along with 300 of his men. It measured 3.65m (12ft) in circumference in 1782, 6.4m (21ft) in 1830 – its branches said to cover an area of 15 Scottish poles, a distance of 85m (278.8ft).

The Wallace Yew remains and stands beside the ruins of his family home. By yew standards the tree is relatively small, the trunk only 4.3m (14ft) around, so it is unlikely to have been planted or even climbed by the hero as folklore suggests. But, like Wallace, the tree had a hard life, damaged from fire and storm, and was already described as ancient in the 1700s.

Whether the trees witnessed these events is impossible to say, but their part in helping to remember and understand Scottish history, culture and place cannot be underestimated.

Above: The Wallace Oak, 1856
Below: The Birnam Oak, 1910

FOREST OF CALEDONIA

On foot arrayed in armour light.
We shall at great advantage fight,
While in the park among the trees
Their horsemen cannot ride with ease.
From The Bruce of Bannockburn by John Barbour, 1375

The Bruce Yews

Loch Lomond, Argyll and Bute

William Wallace's efforts in the battle for Scottish independence paved the way for Robert the Bruce to claim the throne at Scone in 1306, a reign that eventually saw Scotland gain full independence from the English in 1328.

Robert's accession compelled Edward I of England to declare him an outlaw and, following defeat at the Battle of Methven in 1306, Robert fled for the Scottish Ilses with around 200 men. On reaching Loch Lomond, it is said they found a leaky rowing boat, and made their escape across the water – four men at a time. It took 24 hours to ferry the troop over. First to cross were Bruce and his ally Sir James Douglas, who set up under a yew tree near Tarbet on the western shore of the loch to wait for their men. As each contingent approached, Bruce raised their spirits, applauding them for their valour in song and jest from beneath the yew.

ABOVE: Robert the Bruce's Yew, 2017
BELOW: Loch Lomond looking towards Inchlonaig, 1924

Inchlonaig, the 'marsh isle' whose yew trees, it is said, were planted by Robert the Bruce for his archers.
From In Scotland Again by H V Morton, 1933

The tree came to be known as Robert the Bruce's Yew, and to this day it stands perched on a rocky outcrop above the loch. Yews are notoriously difficult to date, the Bruce Yew's hollow 6.27m (20.5ft) multi-stemmed trunk ensures it is no exception to the rule.

Inchlonaig, meaning Isle of Yews, is an island in Loch Lomond clearly visible from Bruce's Yew. It is said to have been planted with yews by order of Robert the Bruce to supply his archers with the best wood for long bows.

In 1663, Sir John Colquhoun replaced the existing dairy herd with fallow deer and converted Inchlonaig to a deer park. Yews were recorded in abundance in the 1590s, 1770 and 1879, and today there are around 800 yew trees on the island. Unlike cattle, horse and sheep, fallow deer suffer no ill effects from grazing the poisonous yew, and still roam the Isle of Yews.

Bruce's penchant for yew is reflected in his order for every Scotsman worth a cow to own a yew-stave bow, whilst he and his men wore sprigs of yew into battle at Bannockburn in 1314.

FOREST OF CALEDONIA

The Gallows Tree
Inveraray Castle, Argyll

Folklore relates how King Malcolm imposed the 'right of pit and gallows' to the baronies of Scotland in 1058, after slaying Macbeth and his stepson Lulach and taking the throne. Hanging trees selected to deal with convicted men became known as 'dule trees' (or dole trees in England), reflecting grief and sorrow (while convicted women were drowned in water pits).

In Scotland, between 1746 and 1810, 22 men were hung and left hanging from the branches until they fell – a warning to others to toe the line.

Two such dule or gallows trees stood together on a raised mound known as Gallows Knoll at Inveraray Castle, between its wooded hills and the shore of Loch Fynne – Scotland's largest saltwater loch. Gallows Knoll itself is believed to mark the remains of a Viking structure.

The current castle was completed in the mid-18th century, but an earlier stronghold dates to the mid-15th century, since when it has remained seat of the chiefs of the Clan Campbell.

Tree planting by the Eighth Earl on the hillsides of Dun Na Cuaiche was first recorded in 1650, was later expanded by his successor and continued by subsequent dukes. Some of the veteran oak, plane and sweet chestnuts are believed to date back to this early period. Today, large parts of the woodland are laid out to non-native forestry plantation.

Sycamore *(Acer pseudoplatanus)*, sometimes referred to as 'plane' in Scotland, was often used as a dule tree – its strong, extending branches ideal for the gallows. However, this was not always the case, and the dule trees at Inveraray were in fact two huge beeches *(Fagus sylvatica)*. In 1741, a vagrant, found guilty of robbery and stouthrief (threatening violence), was the last person to be hung there; he was buried in the slope of the knoll, thus ending the macabre purpose of the trees. By the 1990s, they were gone and only decaying stumps remained. Two copper beeches, planted in their place, would not survive either.

Now farewell light—thou sunshine bright,
And all beneath the sky!
May coward shame distain his name,
The wretch that dares not die!
Sae rantingly, sae wantonly,
Sae dauntingly gaed he;
He play'd a spring, and danc'd it round,
Below the gallows-tree.

From *MacPherson's Farewell* by Robert Burns 1759-96

ABOVE: The Gallows Tree, Mar Lodge, 1884
OPPOSITE: The Gallows Tree, Inveraray Castle, 1914

FOREST OF CALEDONIA

Through the huge oaks of Evandale,
Whose limbs a thousand years have worn,
What sullen roar comes down the gale,
And drowns the hunter's pealing horn?
From *Cadzow Castle* by Sir Walter Scott, 1803

The Cadzow Oaks

Cadzow Castle, Hamilton, Lanarkshire

ABOVE: Oaks and Cadzow's famed wild, white cattle, c1830
BELOW: 7.34m hollow oak on the ramparts of Cadzow's Neolithic earthwork, survived being burnt out in 2017 and 2018
OPPOSITE: Ancient wood pasture oaks at Cadzow, 2018

The Forest of Caledonia rightly conjures images of vast pine woodland, but at its southern and western reaches, tracts of oak were common.

Scotland's finest remnant of ancient oaks resides at Cadzow Forest, high on the western bank of a deep gorge carved by the Avon Water near Hamilton. Around 300 pollarded sessile oaks *(Quercus petraea)* were reputedly planted for David I – King of the Scots from 1124 to 1153. Some may be synchronous with the wooden castle that existed at the time, although dendrochronology found the oldest oak samples tested to date from around 1460. Others were contemporary with the late 16th-century stone 'Castle in the Woods', which now lies in ruin. The oaks appear to have been planted on ridge and furrow, after Clan Hamilton were granted the land by Robert the Bruce, and appropriated it for the hunt from its former agricultural use, creating a new castle and deer park. Treacherous hunting it was too – the steep, wooded gorge presented a challenging terrain.

In 1568 the Hamiltons offered refuge to Mary Queen of Scots at Cadzow Castle following her escape from Loch Leven Castle, an action which saw the Castle at Cadzow sleighted by the Earl of Mar, regent for James VI.

A hunting lodge built on the eastern side of the gorge in the 1730s is now the visitor centre for Chatelherault Country Park. Cadzow cattle – an ancient white breed descended from aurochs and first mentioned in old Irish sagas – have grazed Cadzow's oak wood pasture since the medieval period. One of two remaining British herds, they now graze in the open fields near the visitor centre.

In the mid-19th century, Cadzow Forest attracted the attentions of the 'Cadzow Artists', the likes of Horatio McCulloch, John Chalmers, Alexander Fraser and Samuel Bough who captured the great oaks for posterity in their landscape paintings, some of which can be seen in Scotland's museums and galleries.

FOREST OF CALEDONIA

All these forests are now mere desolote scenes. The trees have disappeared, the game has gone, and their history is in a great measure lost.
From *English Forest and Forest Trees*, 1853

ABOVE: The 'Wizard Tree', near Hexham Forest – wood pasture oaks in the field beyond, 2019

Forest of Northumberland

Northumberland

Northumberland's forest routinely brings to mind an image of Kielder – England's largest man-made woodland – 650km^2 (250 miles^2) of non-native coniferous plantation initiated by the Forestry Commission in the 1920s to provide a quick-growing source of timber. A century later it is the English stronghold of the red squirrel, providing a home to around 50% of the national population. An application to reintroduce Eurasian lynx was declined by the UK government in 2018, putting paid to hopes of reintroducing the species after an absence of 1,300 years.

While little can be found in terms of timber records, the Forest of Northumberland is a good example of forest in its true sense – land reserved for the hunt – and includes high open moorland, much of it now protected as Northumberland National Park.

At least three smaller forests – Rothbury, Lowes and Hexham – contributed to the greater Northumberland Forest, with Rothbury alone having a circumference of around 48km (30 miles).

Northumberland was borderland, with Scotland to the north and the Humber to the south and, as such, saw more than its fair share of battles and land disputes.

Early Viking raids launched from oak longships arrived on the Northumbrian coast in the late eighth century, notably at Lindisfarne Monastery, where many monks were slaughtered, dragged into the sea or taken as slaves. At that time the land was under the Anglo-Saxons, but it was firmly in the hands of Viking chiefs just a century later. Norsemen continued to arrive until September 1066, when Harald Hardrada arrived with 10,000 men hoping to claim King Harold's throne. He was seen off at the Battle of Stamford Bridge, but may have dented the king's army enough to have influenced his downfall less than a month later at Hastings.

Fighting and hunting went hand in hand; it was practised by elite warriors who saw the hunt not only as a means to stock the larder, but also as an opportunity to practice horsemanship and hone their weapon skills.

The Queen & the Robbers

Hexham Forest, Northumberland

Britain's medieval forests were often frequented by outlaws, providing hideouts for gangs intent on blackmail and robbery, most notably remembered in the stories of Robin Hood and his Merry Men.

A 15th-century legend featuring Queen Margaret of Anjou illustrates perfectly the danger of straying from the path at night. Margaret was consort to Henry VI, the red, Lancastrian rose which stood against the white rose of York through the Wars of the Roses, a bitter struggle for power between rival branches of the royal family.

Following the Battle of Hexam in 1464 – which further cemented the Yorkist claim to the throne – Margaret is said to have fled into woods at Hexham Forest with her young son Prince Edward. Lost and frightened, at night they came across a band of robbers, who relieved the Queen of her jewellery. As they started to squabble amongst themselves on how to share the spoils, Margaret took her chance to escape, but before long encountered another robber. Exhausted and desperate, she implored the outlaw to show mercy to the King's son and heir. The robber, taking pity, led the pair to a cave in the forest where they could eat and rest, and saw to their safe return.

In reality, it seems that Margaret was not even in the country at the time, but seeking support and sanctuary in France. The story was popularised in the 18th and 19th centuries, no doubt given gravitas through Dickens' retelling, and is befitting of the Victorian romanticism of the time.

The legend illustrates the dangers of the forest in medieval England, whilst portraying the Queen as the romantic heroine, who uses intellect to her advantage in order to gain the upper hand against adversity in a precarious situation.

So the Queen, with a stout heart, took the little Prince by the hand, and going straight up to that robber, said to him, 'My friend, this is the young son of your lawful King! I confide him to your care'.
From *A Child's History of England* by Charles Dickens, 1853

ABOVE: *Queen Margaret of Anjou with the Prince, Her Son, Stripped of Her Regalia by Robbers in a Wood*, by Richard Cosway, 1742-1821

FOREST OF NORTHUMBERLAND

FOREST OF NORTHUMBERLAND

Warkworth Hermitage

Warkworth, Northumberland

*And now, attended by their host,
The Hermitage they view'd,
Deep-hewn within a craggy cliff,
And over-hung with wood.*

From *Hermit of Warkworth* by Bishop Percy, 1771.

The River Coquet runs through the ancient Forest of Northumberland and retains large parts of its wooded heritage, not least at Warkworth, best known for its medieval castle, which towers above a loop in the river.

Twice unsuccessfully besieged by the Scots in 1327, Warkworth Castle became a seat of the powerful Percy family, with Henry – First Earl of Northumberland – adding an imposing keep in the late 14th century that still dominates the village below.

On the opposite side of the river, remnants of oak wood pasture interspersed with hawthorn and sallow lead down to a wooded valley. Here, around the river loop, just out of site of the castle, can be found one of Northumberland's lesser-known curiosities.

Established at the beginning of the 14th century by the First Earl, Warkworth Hermitage was hewn from the bedrock on the north side of the river bank over two floors: two upper-storey cells with windows carved directly from the rock, and two ground-floor rooms constructed from stone. From the south side of the river the hermitage is well hidden amongst the trees: beech and sycamore and notably several veteran, twisted yews *(Taxus baccata)*, probably planted for their sacred significance at the time of construction some 600 years ago.

A tragic legend tells of Sir Bertram of Bothal, friend to Henry Percy, who accidentally slayed his brother and the love of his life, Isabel, while trying to save her. In penance, Bertram gave up his lands to live and pray at the hermitage in solitude for the rest of his life.

It may have been built as a private chapel for the Earl, and various tenants are recorded as celebrating Mass there under salary, rather than living as hermits.

Apart from daytime visitors ushered in by row-boat across the river, Warkworth Hermitage is now the realm of roe deer and other creatures that frequent the wooded valley.

ABOVE: Warkworth Castle, 2019
OPPOSITE: Warkworth Hermitage, c1850
BELOW: Veteran yews at Warkworth Hermitage, 2019

The Sycamore Gap Tree
Hadrian's Wall, Northumberland

Emperor Hadrian's dictate to construct a political symbol of power marking Britannia's northern limit under the Roman Empire in AD122 resulted in the construction of a wall spanning the width of the country, 117.5km (73 miles), from the Solway Firth to the River Tyne.

At Sycamore Gap – a natural dip in a high ridge carved by ancient glaciers – stands a lone sycamore tree *(Acer pseudoplatanus)*, a veteran maiden measuring 2.85m (9.35ft) around its weathered, lichen encrusted trunk.

Also known as the Robin Hood Tree, after featuring in the 1991 film starring Kevin Costner, it is often described as 'the most photographed tree in Britain'. In 2016 it won England's Tree of the Year competition, seeing off around 200 contenders. Danny Clarke – who I sat with on the panel of judges during the filming of Channel 4's TV programme described the tree as a 'show-off,' having 'placed itself there intentionally'. On my visit, withstanding high winds and rain, although seemingly escaping the brunt of the storm in its secluded hideaway, it appeared to own the landscape; a real survivor.

Pollen analysis at Vindolanda – to the south of Sycamore Gap – suggests that woodland clearance occurred prior to the construction of the wall, probably initiated by native farmers expanding agricultural and grazing lands. By the end of the Roman period, however, large-scale tree-felling occurred. The mammoth task of constructing Hadrian's Wall with its incumbent forts and milecastles required large quantities of timber, resulting in local deforestation, while opening up panoramic vistas, useful for seeing enemies approach.

A lack of pollen ruled out sycamore as being a native tree. It self-seeds so freely it is often described as a weed by gardeners, yet its pollen decays quickly compared to other trees, leaving no ancient record for carbon analysis. For this reason there is a school of thought that argues that sycamore was here all along, not introduced by the Romans, but arriving freely with our other native species.

Our goods and fortunes are ground down to pay tribute, our land and its harvest to supply corn, our bodies and hands to build roads through woods and swamps – all under blows and insults.

Rallying speech attributed to Caledonian Chief Calgacus, from *Tacitus on Britain and Germany*, cAD98

ABOVE: Highland grazers close to Sycamore Gap, 2019
BELOW AND OPPOSITE: The Sycamore Gap Tree, 2019

FOREST OF NORTHUMBERLAND

THE BORDERLANDS

And when he came to Falsehope Glen,
Beneath the Trysting-tree,
On the smooth green was carved plain,
To Lockwood bound are we.

From *The Reiver's Wedding* by Sir Walter Scott, 1820

ABOVE: The Meikle Trysting Tree, 1886
BELOW: The Trysting Tree, Gilsland 2019
OPPOSITE: Hadrian's Wall – once cleared of trees, now home to many veterans, Gilsland, 2019

The Trysting Tree

Gilsland, Cumbria

Gilsland is a village situated on the Northumberland/Cumbria border, to the north side of one of the best-preserved sections of Hadrian's Wall, rugged borderland often described as 'the debated lands'.

The Romans made use of Gilsland's sulphurous spa that bubbles up in the deep valley of the River Irthing. In the 12th century, Henry II seized the area from the Kingdom of Strathclyde, and turned it into a barony comprising almost 40,500ha (100,000 acres). By the 16th century, the Gilsland Barony had passed to William Howard, at a time when the borderlands were renowned for 'reiving', a practice which amounted to cattle theft on a grand scale, accepted by perpetrators at the time as a legitimate way to make a living.

The current spa hotel dates to the 1760s, when it replaced an earlier building at the head of the steep river valley. Remnant, veteran wood pasture oaks stand scattered along the sharp slope towards the river, where, shaded among modern plantation forestry, the largest sylvan survivor stands, close to river bank and the sunken remains of a 16th-century tenement.

Known as the Trysting Tree, the 9.8m (32.1ft) girthed oak *(Quercus robur)* has long been an ancient meeting place. It may have inspired Sir Walter Scott to include a trysting tree in his novel *Waverley*, as he visited Gilsland Spa Hotel and met his future wife there. He certainly had a love for trees, planting great swathes of native woodland on his Abbotsford Estate.

Deriving from old English *trist* or *trust*, trysting trees, common in Scotland and the north of England, were meeting places for clans and warrior bands. By the Victorian era they became romanticised lovers' trysts.

The French *triste* translates as 'appointed place of hunting', and may give a clue to the Gilsland Trysting Tree's origin, as the area was once part of Askerton North Moor Chase, reserved for the hunt.

THE BORDERLANDS

*Shout, yeomen! – the den of tyrants is no more!
Let each bring his spoil to our chosen place of
rendezvous at the Trysting-tree.*
From *Ivanhoe* by Sir Walter Scott, 1819

*By the Nine Gods he swore it,
   And named a trysting day,
And bade his messengers ride forth,
East and west and south and north,
   To summon his array.*
From *Horatius* by Thomas Babington Macaulay, 1842

FOREST OF THE NORTH

This manor has been held by the ancient family of that name from at least as early a period as soon after the conquest.
From *History and Antiquities of Cumberland*
by Samuel Jefferson, 1842

The King's Oak Irton, Cumbria

Set in the foothills of the Western Fells in the Lake District, Irton Hall was home to the Irton family from the reign of Henry I, shortly after the Conquest, and it remained in their hands until 1866, when the family line came to an end. Nothing of the original buildings remains, although the Pele Tower dates from the 14th century.

Following the Battle of Towton in 1461 – an important victory for the Yorkists during the English Wars of the Roses – Henry VI fled to Scotland. Legend has him stopping en route at Irton Hall with his retinue, requesting food and lodging. Unfortunately for Henry, the lord of the manor, John Irton, was a Yorkist and refused him hospitality. Henry withdrew to the lawns in front of the hall where he is said to have set up camp beneath a great oak. Irton's wife, Anne, sympathising with the King, took him food and water, and advised him to head for Muncaster Castle, where Sir John Pennington, a Lancastrian, was also sympathetic to Henry's cause. The next day Henry heeded Anne's advice and left for Muncaster where he was received with open arms. In gratitude, Henry gave Sir John a glass drinking bowl with a prayer that his family might prosper, so long as the glass remained unbroken. Known as 'The Luck of Muncaster', the bowl remains unbroken, as has the prosperity of the family.

In contrast, Irton, furious at his wife's transgression, had her imprisoned in the Pele Tower where she starved to death. A ghostly apparition known as the Grey Lady is said to have haunted the tower and grounds ever since.

The King's Oak still stands, dominating the manor lawns. With a 5.27m (17.3ft) hollow trunk *(Quercus robur)*, its diminutive size perhaps belies its great age, and shows little change in over a century. Surrounded by parkland, it is a lone survivor of oak wood pasture felled by land girls during the Second World War. The story of Henry's visit – true or otherwise – is largely responsible for its survival.

ABOVE: The King's Oak, with the Pele Tower behind, c1906
BELOW & OPPOSITE: The King's Oak, 2019

Chatsworth Park Derbyshire

CHATSWORTH! thy stately mansion, and the pride
Of thy domain, strange contrast do present
To house and home in many a craggy rent
Of the wild Peak; where new-born waters glide
Through fields whose thrifty occupants abide
From *Chatsworth* by William Wordsworth, 1830

The Manor of Chatsworth in Derbyshire has been home to the Cavendish family for 16 generations. First purchased for £600 by Bess of Hardwick – the second most powerful woman in Elizabethan England after the Queen – and her husband Sir William Cavendish in 1549, it includes an extant hunting tower built in 1582. The manor straddles the River Derwent, and sits at the south eastern limit of the former Royal Forest of the High Peak, whose borders were defined in 1286 by four rivers: the Wye, Goyt, Etherow and Derwent.

Originally a hereditary domain of Saxon monarchs, the Royal Forest was divided into estates by the Normans, William I granting custody in 1086 to William Peverel, who governed from his castle perched high on the rocks above Castleton village, 'like the nest of a foul bird of prey'. Peverel's realm included the manor of Chatsworth, named 'Chetesuorde' (Court of Chetel) in the Domesday Survey of 1086.

Described as 'a wild and lawless place' due in part to its remoteness, wolf and wildcat were common in the High Peak during the 13th century, along with bountiful herds of red deer. Forest assizes – courts which tried offenders for breaking Forest Laws – found not only local opportunist poachers, but earls, knights and noblemen guilty of taking large numbers of the king's deer, acts which appear to have been statements of intent on the part of the northern elite, a flexing of muscles to remind the king of their defiance. Similarly, assarts of the forest for arable and grazing were common; punishable by fines, these became a convenient money-raising exercise, akin to collecting rent, seemingly as important to the Crown as preserving land for the hunt.

By the 16th century, red deer were competing for grazing with sheep flocks of the monasteries and tenant shepherds who petitioned Charles I. In 1640 the King divided the forest between them and himself, and had all the deer destroyed. In 1674 High Peak was disafforested.

Right: Chatsworth House 'Seat of the Duke of Devonshire' by J Sadler after Allom, c1836.

ABOVE: Chatsworth Park across the River Derwent, 1818
BELOW: Ancient oak wood pasture in the old park, 2018
OPPOSITE: The largest girthed oak in the old park – possibly two trees fused together on limestone boulders, 2018

The mining of zinc and lead in the High Peak, initiated by the Romans, saw its zenith in the 18th and 19th centuries, simultaneously poisoning the land and people, said to have been 'bellanded'. Wood for smelting tin was also used in abundance – although coppicing would have provided a sustainable source for some of that. Even so, the High Peak appears as one of Britain's less-treed Royal Forests, on a par with Dartmoor.

Within the bounds of Chatsworth Park, however, trees remain in abundance. Stand Wood rises to the crest of the hill behind the house – replete with an Elizabethan hunting tower from where to watch the hunt – gardens and vistas were laid out by Lancelot 'Capability' Brown in 1760 and rare conifers were planted by Sir Joseph Plaxton in the mid-19th century.

The oak wood pasture kept to accommodate herds of red and fallow deer predominates both north and south of the house. Several hundred ancient and veteran open-grown oaks abound, interspersed with occasional grand specimens of sweet chestnut, lime and alder, many of which date back to the time when Bess of Hardwick built her manor house there in 1553. Some of the larger oaks – measuring up to 9m (29.5ft) in circumference – are doubtless older still.

Many of the oaks grow on large limestone boulders that are scatterd across the landscape, their roots sprawling over and cradling the rocks. In fact, the spectacle occurs so frequently as to suggest that the trees have either self-seeded, or were unwittingly planted by jays – who stashed their favoured acorns under boulders as winter fodder and forgot to retrieve the bounty. The fact that some young oaks continue the trend without human intervention strengthens the theory.

The old deer park to the south of the house (one of a few areas closed to the public) hosts the greatest variety of ancient oaks – rare fungi, lichen and invertebrates thrive in the decaying wood and bestowing upon the park SSSI (Site of Special Scientific Interest) and National Nature Reserve status.

For, first, she springs out of two marble Rocks,
 On which, a grove of Oakes high mounted growes,
 That as a girlond seemes to deck the locks
 Of som faire Bride, brought forth with pompous shows
From *The Faerie Qveene* by Edmund Spenser, 1590

Sherwood Forest Nottinghamshire

Rich in history and legend, Sherwood is one the most famed forests in England, if not the world. Immortalised in folklore and film, the forest owes much of its renown to Robin Hood, the mythical folk hero outlaw whose adventures have been told and retold over the centuries.

The forest, originally called Sciryuda (shire wood), was hunted in Saxon times and taken under Forest Law by William shortly after the Conquest. Sherwood offered the ideal landscape for a Royal Forest: sandy soils unsuited to agriculture but ideal for the scattered oak and birch which proliferated across the heathland and wooded areas, perfect cover for animals of the forest hunt.

During the 12th century, Sherwood encompassed most of Nottinghamshire north west of the River Trent, an area shown to have slightly reduced in 1218, following a perambulation ordered by Henry III of an area covering around 40km by 16km (25 x 10 miles) between Worksop and Nottingham.

During the reign of Henry VI (1422-60), wolves and wild boar still roamed the forest. Sir Robert Plumpton, who resided at Wolfhunt Manor, was responsible for the 'winding of a horn and chasing wolves'.

Sherwood remains one of the top sites in the UK for ancient oaks, the most recent survey listing 997 of them, 410 of which are alive and 250 of those in good condition. That leaves 587 dead trees – important biodiversity hotspots that provide habitat for saproxylic fungi, lichen and the 316 species of beetle that have been found to live there – dependent on decaying wood – in turn providing food for the birds. As much as 40% of woodland wildlife depends on decaying wood for survival, supporting studies that suggest it may have formerly comprised around 30% of Britain's ancient wildwood. The high density of decaying wood and associated species at Sherwood – some of them endangered through national habitat loss – supports this, and is part of the reasoning behind Sherwood's SSSI and NNR status.

ABOVE: The Parliament Oak, Clipstone, 1856
BELOW: Wood pasture at Birklands, 2016

King John's Palace – a royal hunting lodge and residence at Clipstone, in the heart of Sherwood – was first mentioned in the reign of Henry II who contracted building works and initiated a deer park in the late 12th century.

The Parliament Oak – a shadow of its former self but quite likely Sherwood's oldest surviving oak – is said to be the venue for a parliament hastily assembled by King John in 1212 to deal with a Welsh uprising. This he did in no uncertain terms by hanging 28 Welsh hostages, none of whom were over 14 years old.

Kings continued to reside at Clipstone until the late 15th century, when the royal passion for hunting diminished, and by 1525 the kings' houses had fallen into decay. Ruins of the palace are still visible today. Charles I was the last king to use Sherwood as a hunting forest.

Sherwood's trees suffered the usual fate and were felled for timber, to be used in the building of substantial structures including Nottingham Castle and the roof timbers of St Paul's Cathedral. A gail in 1222 caused devastation at Sherwood, prompting Henry III to instruct verderers, foresters and the keeper of the hays on how to manage the fallen timber. And of course large parts were managed in a sustainable way through coppicing and shredding.

In 1609, a survey by Royal Commissioners declared over half of Sherwood's 50,000 oaks unsuitable for Navy ship-building. That proportion rose to around 95% of 37,000 oaks in 1686, suggesting that a great many oaks were felled in the interim, with unsuitable oaks – the hollow ancients and veterans – persisting in abundance. By 1790 only 10,000 or so oaks remained.

Rich seams of coal saw Sherwood suffer the impact of heavy mining in the 19th century along with the associated pollutions and lowering of the water table. The coal industry declined following the two world wars due to competition from cheaper imports. The threat of fracking beneath Sherwood is a real cause for concern in the 21st century.

SHERWOOD FOREST

It was a fragment of one of those vast sylvan tracts wherein Norman kings once hunted and Saxon outlaws plundered; and although the plough had for centuries successfully invaded brake and bower, the relics retain all their original character of wildness and seclusion.

From *The New Generation* by Benjamin Disraeli, 1844

Above, Below, Right: Sherwood oaks, c1905, 2018 and 2016

In the 1920s the Forestry Commission started managing large areas of Sherwood Forest, dedicating around 6,000ha (14,826 acres) to coniferous plantation. Today, their remit includes protecting historic species and habitat.

The two world wars levied their own effect on the forest as the military requisitioned the great manor houses, felled large areas of woodland, drilled for oil and stored munitions.

Most of Sherwood's ancient oaks survive at Birklands (from the old Norse term *birch lunds*), near the village of Edwinstowe, where earthworks at Thynghowe were discovered by amateur historians and have recently been confirmed as a Viking meeting place.

Dead, ancient and veterans account for over 43% of Birkland's oaks, way above the national average. Since 1969, 182ha (450 acres) of the forest have been managed by Nottinghamshire County Council, who lease the land from the Thoresby Estate. A new consortium led by the RSPB opened a visitor centre in Edwinstowe in 2018 to cater for the 360,000 annual visitors.

SHERWOOD FOREST

The Major Oak

Edwinstowe, Nottinghamshire

Robin Hood walks the forest free,
Under the fresh green leaf;
And the proud sheriff of Nottingham
He knew it to his grief.

From *The Lytell Geste of Robin Hood*, c1450

If Sherwood Forest is the best known forest in Britain, then the Major Oak at Birklands must be the most famous oak in the country, if not the world.

Inextricably linked to England's favourite folk hero, Robin Hood, whether he existed or not, tales of the outlaw and his merry men are responsible for many of the tree's visitors, and since Victorian times have probably secured its survival since its previous life as a working pollard had lapsed.

Standing in ancient wood pasture, the tree is the centrepiece of the Sherwood tourist experience. It was fenced off in 1974 to protect it from damaging root compaction caused by the sheer volume of visitors. Later, mulch was spread around the roots to add nutrients, but some was removed in 2017 as too much had been applied and was only adding to the problem. The top layer of soil is as compact as it was 40 years ago, depriving the upper roots of air and nutrients.

Formerly known as the Cockpen Tree, it was renamed after Major Hayman Rooke who featured a drawing of the tree in his 1790 book *Remarkable Oaks*.

Estimates of the 10.66m (35ft) girthed oak's age range from 600 to 1,000 years, a large margin for error, impossible to verify due to its cavernous hollow. However, comparing archive and contemporary photographs reveals no perceivable change in over a century, lending credence to the idea that the old beast could lean towards the upper end of the age bracket.

OPPOSITE: The Major Oak, 1915
ABOVE AND BELOW: The Major Oak, 2016

SHERWOOD FOREST

There is a very old oak in Clipston park, about five miles south-east of Welbeck, and in the same county, which the common people call the Parliament-oak, from an idea that a parliament was once held under it.

From *Remarkable Oaks* by Hayman Rooke, 1790

ABOVE: The Shambles Oak in 1886 at Birklands – part of the Thoresby Estate – is said to have been used to store Robin Hood's venison. Damaged by fire in 1913, it collapsed in a storm in 1961.

The Dukeries

Sherwood Forest, Nottinghamshire

During the peak years of the Royal Forest in the 12th and 13th centuries, large tracts of land were gifted to the Church, resulting in eight religious and monastic estates which held rights and influence over Sherwood Forest.

Following the Dissolution of the Monasteries in 1536, Henry VIII sold the confiscated lands to his friends and acquaintances, creating in part what became known in the 18th century as the Dukeries – five manorial estates which aimed to profit from Sherwood by planting oak for timber, leasing grazing rights and land for agriculture.

Thoresby Hall was granted to George Pierrepont; Welbeck Abbey, Rufford Abbey, Worksop Priory and Clumber Park to the Talbot family. Other manors were also granted such as Newstead Abbey, which was given to the Byron family (and was later home to the famous poet Lord Byron), and Woollaton Park in Nottingham.

While dominion under the Dukeries certainly changed the face of Sherwood, over time they helped preserve some of the forest's ancient trees. At Welbeck, which came into the hands of the Duke of Portland, stood a fine assembly of old oaks, including the Duke's Walkingstick – only 4.26m (14ft) in circumference, rising 21.3m (70ft) before its crown, which stood taller than Westminster Abbey's roof at 33.8m (111ft), until the end of the 19th century when it was cut down. The Two Porters, so named as they flanked the gateway at the entrance to the estate, measured 7.6m (25ft) and 7m (23ft) in circumference in 1903. The smaller of the pair still stands.

SHERWOOD FOREST

Surprisingly, the Greendale Oak soldiered on, its 10.7m (35ft 3in) trunk surviving until the 1970s, when it was described as 'a tumbled heap of seasoned timber, festooned still with old chains and monstrous supports.' Today, nothing remains of the tree, except perhaps some furniture carved from its branches for the Countess of Oxford in the late 19th century.

LEFT: The Greendale Oak, 1775
ABOVE: Welbeck Abbey, 1818
BELOW: The longest lime avenue in Europe, planted around 1840 at Clumber Park, 2018

The Duke of Portland is perhaps best remembered in a story concerning Welbeck's prize tree; the Greendale Oak. During a dinner party in 1724, the duke claimed one of his trees so large that a coach and four horses could pass through it, if a tunnel were cut. The challenge proved irresistible to his guests, so the duke had a hole cut 1.9m (6ft 3in) wide by 3.1m (10ft 3in) high through the tree's hollowing trunk. A specially made narrow coach led by his four thinnest horses was duly driven through the tree, and the duke won the wager. A tradition followed whereby, after their wedding, all subsequent dukes and their new brides would return to the estate through the tunnel.

Wollaton Hall
Nottingham

Once a village at the southern reaches of Sherwood Forest, Wollaton is now fully absorbed into the western suburbs of the city of Nottingham.

Already a Saxon manor known as Olafston belonging to Ulfi before the Conquest, by 1176 Adam de Morteyn was described as Lord of Wollaton.

In the 14th century the manor came into the hands of the Willoughby family, who expanded the estate, carving a large tract of land from the forest which included the parishes of Cossall and Trowell, and resulted in the destruction of an entire village called Sutton Passeys.

Two herds of around 80 red and 120 fallow deer that roam the estate are a legacy of the deer park that was enclosed with a wooden pale between 1492 and 1510.

The current manor house, built between 1580 and 1588 for Sir Francis Willoughby, was probably designed by Robert Smythson following the completion of Longleat House. Willoughby, one of England's richest men, had amassed a fortune from his family's Nottinghamshire coal mines – established in the 13th century – and is said to have paid for the building stone and labour with coal.

In the early 19th century, the park was enclosed within an 11km (seven mile) red brick wall to retain the deer and maintain privacy, distinguishing it as one of only three deer parks remaining in Sherwood Forest, along with Thoresby and Welbeck. Beeston Lodge – a fortified gatehouse – was added following an attack on Wollaton by rioters angry with the proposed reform bill of 1831.

In 1881 the Willoughbys declared Wollaton to be 'too near the smoke and busy activity of a large manufacturing town' and had vacated the property.

Nottinghamshire County Council bought the park in 1924 for the benefit of the public, marking the end of the Willoughbys 500-year tenure. While part of the estate was developed for housing, and around half of the 202ha (500 acre) park was used for the creation of a golf course,

ABOVE: Wollaton Hall, 1818
BELOW: Ancient hollow pollard lime, 2017
OPPOSITE: Red deer hinds at Wollaton Park, 2017

the house and deer park were retained: the former houses the city's Natural History Museum while the latter accommodates the wild deer which roam freely around the park.

In 2011, Woolaton Hall was used in the film *Dark Knight Rises* as the location for Wayne Manor, the fictitious residence of Batman's secret identity – Bruce Wayne. Beneath the hall, sandstone caves accessed through the wine cellar hold a water reservoir known as the Admiral's Bath (where Admiral Sir Nesbit Josiah Willoughby bathed during the 18th century). The caves provided the perfect setting for the Batcave in the film. And, just 10km (6 miles) to the south, the real village of Gotham provided Bob Kane with the name of his city in the Batman stories.

Above ground, Wollaton retains a wealth of veteran and ancient trees, planted throughout its long history. A double avenue of sweet chestnut *(Castanea sativa)* and oak *(Quercus robur)* planted in the 17th century leads north from the house, with a double lime tree avenue planted around 1700, leading to the east, and ancient lime and beech trees, including the county's champion copper beech *(Fagus sylvatica purperea)*, scattered across the parkland. Beside the house, a cedar of Lebanon grove *(Cedrus lebani)* remains from the late 18th century.

Wollaton's most magnificent tree, however, must be its giant oak *(Quercus robur)*, standing at the peak of Arbour Hill, which has survived successive plantings of Scots pine *(Pinus sylvestris)* and non-native stands of larch *(Larix decidua)*, giant sequoia *(Sequoia giganteum)* and rhododendron *(Rhododendron)*.

The oak's large girth of 7.1m (23.3ft), spreading buttress roots and massive canopy of medusa-like branches likely dates it back – along with several other hollow pollard specimens scattered across the park – to the creation of Woolaton Park by Sir Francis Willoughby almost 500 years ago.

ABOVE: Lime avenue leading to Wollaton Park, c1915
BELOW: 6m sweet chestnut in an avenue leading to the house, 2017
OPPOSITE: The Wollaton Oak, 2017

Forest of Kesteven Lincolnshire

Lincolnshire, a mix of rolling hills, fen and coastal marshland, and one of England's least-wooded counties managed to escape the clutches of Royal Forest Law. The exception to the rule was the Forest of Kesteven, from *Ceostefne*, of Celtic/Norse origin meaning a 'meeting place in the wood'.

Situated in southern Lincolnshire, across rolling limestone hills in the west to the fens in the east, Kesteven illustrates well how ancient forests were not necessarily densely wooded throughout, and here included large wetland areas in the fens. That is not to say Kesteven was without trees, as wood pasture featured prominently, with several ancient, millennial trees attesting to the fact, and ancient woods such as Bourne – listed in the Domesday Survey of 1086 – still extant but today largely laid out to coniferous plantation. Hereward the Wake – Kesteven's outlaw hero – based himself there while building forces for his powerful resistance against the Normans in 1067.

The Bowthorpe Oak at Bowthorpe Park Farm in Manthorpe, near Bourne, is England's fattest example of the species *(Quercus robur)* – a massive, ancient hollow pollard measuring 12.66m (41.5ft) around its giant bole. A veritable cavern – once said to have held 39 people – the tree is a living relic dating back to Kesteven's beginnings, perhaps even predating the Conquest; it has witnessed the demise of both the ancient Priory and subsequent Manor House that formerly graced the grounds.

In 2016, the tree was nominated for 'England's Tree of the Year' competition. It finished in a disappointing fifth place, but not before a Channel 4 crew filming the tree for the accompanying TV show managed to cram 30 people inside.

Just 21km (13 miles) to the north west of Bowthorpe, in an orchard at Woolsthorpe Manor, stands what it probably England's most famous apple tree *(Malus domestica)*. It lays claim to being the tree from which Sir Isaac Newton watched an apple fall, hence formulating the law of gravity. Ironically, the tree itself succumbed to those very forces, and fell to the ground around 200 years ago, but has since righted itself, and once again grows strong, still providing a good crop of apples.

Hereward split up the war-arrow, and sent it through Kesteven, and south into the Cambridge fens, calling on all men to arm and come to him at Bourne, in the name of the earls.
From *Hereward, the Last of the English* by Charles Kingsley, 1866

ABOVE AND OPPOSITE: The Bowthorpe Oak, c1915 and 2015

BELOW: Woolsthorpe Manor, c1850

Grimsthorpe Park Linconlshire

Lincolnshire's best-preserved remnant oak wood pasture can be found at Grimsthorpe Park, on the western edge of Kesteven Forest, first mentioned in the Domesday Survey. It takes its name from the Norse *Grim* (Odin, father of all Nordic gods), and *thorpe* (village), and was described as wooded in 1147 when a Cistercian order of monks from Fountain's Abbey arrived. They named it Vallis Dei – the valley of God – and established Vaudey Abbey.

Nearby, King John's Tower is all that remains of a castle granted to Ranulph de Blondeville in 1217; the current house was commissioned in 1716. Henry VIII granted the land to William, Baron Willoughby de Eresby in 1516 and, 500 years later, it still belongs to the family.

The park covers almost 1,200ha (3,000 acres), and in 1536 held two deer parks of red and fallow deer, thought to have originated in the 12th century. By the 18th century, almost the entire park was enclosed with a wooden pale creating one huge deer park.

An ancient right of way leading north from the village of Creeton – with its Bronze Age round barrow and Saxon churchyard crosses – follows field boundaries lined with living and fallen ancient hollow pollard ash trees, remnants of a working past when the trees were systematically harvested for firewood.

Grimsthorpe's oak wood pastures feature veteran field maple, ash and the now scarce wild service tree. It has gained SSSI status for its rich habitat, hosting 250 species of beetle and several species of bat which roost in the hollows of its veteran and ancient trees.

Oaks dating back to Domesday persisted until the last century, today it is probable that several date from the Tudor era; the largest, with a girth of 9.32m (30.5ft), has probably survived in part due to its secluded location in a medieval ditch.

At High Wood, the oak wood pasture mostly appears younger, interspersed with veteran and ancient specimens, some of it planted following the visit in 1771 of Lancelot 'Capability Brown', who was also responsible for horse chestnut and lime tree avenues – the latter now resplendent in abundant halos of mistletoe.

One fallen oak displaying 170 growth rings – dating its origin to around 1847 – demonstrates a continuity of planting which continues to the present. Current parkland management includes grazing by longhorn cattle, coppicing, tree regeneration and leaving decaying wood in situ as habitat, to preserve biodiversity.

Out of Ymir's flesh was fashioned the earth,
And the ocean out of his blood;
Of his bones the hills, of his hair the trees,
Of his skull the heavens high.
From *Grimnisol, The Ballad of Grimnir*
c10th century

ABOVE: Grimsthorpe Castle, 1818
BELOW: Ancient hollow pollard ash, 2018
OPPOSITE: Oak wood pasture 'the Brackens', 2018

Needwood Forest Staffordshire

Historically, the Midlands played host to several Royal Forests, and the region retains a wealth of ancient oaks, especially in the area of Needwood Forest. It was described in Elizabeth's reign as 'thinly sett with old oakes and timber trees', reflecting a legacy born from a long history of open-grown, wood pasture trees.

A golden Celtic torque – raised from its earthly grave by a fox digging its lair – attests to Iron Age settlement; and a Saxon manor is recorded as being in the possession of Earl Algar – son of Lady Godiva – before the Norman Conquest saw William lay claim.

Needwood's distance from London was repeatedly cited as justification for disafforestation (which means exempt from forest law as opposed to cutting down trees), as it was infrequently visited by monarchs; added to that, its fertile soils were ripe for conversion to agriculture. At the end of the Civil War, during which Needwood had suffered heavy tree losses, the forest was offered for sale in 1651 to help pay off the army. A petition sent to Cromwell, signed by gentry and commoners alike, highlighted the importance of forest rights as an everyday necessity for the local community. As a result, only half the forest was taken by the state; the rest was reserved for common rights, which along with the usual right to collect fuel wood included a right to 'hoar lynt' – the white timber of lime trees left after they had been stripped of bark used for making rope and matting.

With the restoration of the monarchy in 1660, Charles II reinstated Needwood as a Royal Forest, described in a survey of 1684 as containing over 38,000 good timber trees in open forest, worth an estimated £30,699, with an additional 9,000 in parkland. 'Many of the trees are of soe large dimensions and length, that there may be picked out such great quantities of excellent plank and other timber, fitt for shipping, as is not to be found in any of your majestie's other forests in England'.

Needwood was finally disafforested through an Act of Parliament in 1803, once more in the face of strong opposition, notably from the poet Francis Mundy, who first composed a poem 'Needwood Forest' in 1776, complemented by the lament 'Fall of Needwood' written during its enclosure. This time protests were to no avail, as Needwood was divided among various claimants by 1811, described as 'highly cultivated' by 1851.

Ah, Needwood! I, whose early voice
Taught thy shrill echoes to rejoice;
I, who first pour'd the sylvan song
Thy glades, thy banks, thy lawns along;
I, who with artless pencil drew
Thy Forest charms of varied hue,
Approach thee now with different strain,
That mourns thy wrongs, yet mourns in vain.

From *The Fall of Needwood* by Francis Mundy, 1808

ABOVE: The Turley Chestnut BELOW: The Tutbury Elm – two former giants of Needwood Forest from *The Natural History of Stafford* by Robert Garner, 1844
OPPOSITE: Longhorn cattle graze beneath ancient Needwood oak wood pasture, 2017

NEEDWOOD FOREST

The Swilcar Oak

Yoxall, Staffordshire

A majestic tree, which is only in moderate proportion, as an ornament to nature in the country, is really an enormous mass, and would show as a large and glorious structure among the dwellings and palaces of man in town.
Mr Burgess quoted in *Sylva Britannica* by Jacob George Strutt, 1830

The Swilcar Lawn Oak was one of the great open-grown parkland oaks of Needwood, gracing a grazed wood pasture 'lawn' at the southern edge of King's Wood, later known as Forest Banks. It grew on lands that fell into government possession following the enclosure of 1803 at Agardsley Park, Yoxall.

In 1771, the tree, measured by a labourer, was found to be 5.79m (19ft) in circumference. Jacob G Strutt recorded it at 6.5m (21.3ft) in 1830, indicating an increase in growth of 71cm (2.3ft) in 61 years. In his book, *Sylva Britannica,* Strutt declared historic records confirmed it to be 600 years old, and included an engraving of the tree.

When Francis Mundy composed *The Fall of Needwood* following the enclosure of Needwood Forest, he included a heartfelt lament for the tree – a tree he knew well, having lived nearby at Holly Bush House, an easy walk to the old oak. And while he feared the worst for the tree, as doubtless many others were lost following enclosure, old Swilcar continued to thrive for another century, outliving Mundy by at least 70 years.

High in the midst with many a frown
Huge Swilcar shakes his tresses brown,
Out-spreads his bare arms to the skies,
The ruins of six centuries.
Deep groans pervade his rifted rind
– He speaks his bitterness of mind.
"Your impious hands, barbarians, hold!"
From *Needwood Forest,* and *The Fall of Needwood* by Francis Noel Clarke Mundy, 1776

ABOVE: Swilcar Oak from *Natural History of Stafford* by Robert Garner, 1844
OPPOSITE: The Swilcar Oak by John Smith after H Moore, c1810

Hail, stately Oak! whose wrinkled trunk hath stood,
Age after age, the sov'reign of the wood;
You, who have seen a thousand springs unfold
Their ravell'd buds, and dip their flowers in gold;
Ten thousand times yon moon re-light her horn,
And that bright eye of evening gild the morn!
From *Needwood Forest,* and *The Fall of Needwood* by Dr Darwin to Francis Noel Clarke Mundy, 1776

NEEDWOOD FOREST

The Gospel Oak
Hoar Cross, Staffordshire

The circumference of the oak at the base is about 32 feet. It is only recently it has been enclosed from the roadside.

Gospel oaks were once found widely across Britain. They are remembered in the names of pubs, schools, community centres, even an entire inner urban area of north west London. Gospel oaks were historic landmark trees that acted as local meeting places and boundary markers.

While many have been lost – either crowded out of expanding urban environments or deemed 'unsafe' and cut down in their senescence – some remarkable gospel oaks remain.

One such tree survives at Hoar Cross, near Yoxall. Now residing in a private garden, the 5.6m (18.37ft) hollow oak *(Quercus robur)* is sited on the corner of Thorny and Dark Lanes; it provided a convenient stopping point for funerals en route to Yoxall, before a church was erected at Hoar Cross in 1872. It is most likely a natural pollard, but today the tree is in its final stages of life, pocketed with holes and fissures, providing habitat for myriad creatures. At one point the tree evidently provided target practice for one resident – the bole stippled with air-gun pellets directed from an upstairs window of the adjacent house.

The custom of communities marking parish boundaries by walking them annually, performing ceremonies at certain spots, and reciting gospels at 'gospel oaks', was still recorded as commonplace by Jacob George Strutt in 1840.

My view is that British oaks were sacred to earlier religions, demonstrated so clearly during a visit to Japan, where Shinto worshippers performed Norito – ritual prayer – to sacred trees. To them, the *kami*, or spirit, is within the tree – a shrine itself – the very reason many of Japan's ancient trees remain.

Amongst objects in Nature, associated probably with Celtic times, is a remarkably antique oak known as "The Gospel Oak," at Hoar Cross, by the roadside, midway of Hoar Cross village and Yoxall, at which, until Hoar Cross Church was recently built, funerals halted and set down the deceased, on their being conveyed to Yoxall Church for interment. With respect to a similar oak and custom near Penallt Church, Monmouth, Roscoe states. "Here is an evident continuation of the oak of Druidic and Celtic custom altered into Christian forms." This oak at Hoar Cross seems also to have been one of the Copt Oaks with the top cut off to admit of a cross piece of wood being fastened at the apex to render the tree an object of Celtic worship.

From *History & Antiquities of Uttoxeter* by Francis Redfern, 1886

ABOVE: The Gospel Oak at Stoneleigh, Warwickshire 1834 – now lost
OPPOSITE: The Gospel Oak at Hoar Cross, 2017

NEEDWOOD FOREST

NEEDWOOD FOREST

ABOVE: 6.25m (20.5ft) girthed ancient oak at St George's Park, 2017

On the morn he arrives at an immense forest, wondrously wild, surrounded by high hills on every side, where he found hoary oaks full huge, a hundred together... He perceived a dwelling in the wood set upon a hill. It was the loveliest castle he had ever beheld...pitched on a prairie, with a park all about it, enclosing many a tree for more than two miles. It shone as the sun through the bright oaks.
From *Sir Gawayne and the Green Knight*, c1360

St George's Park

Burton-on-Trent, Staffordshire

When visiting St George's Park in August 2017, I arrived with mixed feelings of excitement and trepidation. Two of my passions – ancient trees and football – had become unlikely bedfellows following purchase of the site in 2001 by the Football Association, who planned to develop a state-of-the-art centre for England's national football teams.

Located on Needwood Forest's plateau along with nearby Yoxall, the estate was formerly known as Byrkley Park, after the family of the same name who hailed from Berkeley Castle in Gloucestershire, and who claimed ancient, noble Saxon heritage.

By the 13th century the family had a hunting lodge at Byrkley, a centre from which to hunt their private Needwood Chase, plentifully stocked at the time with deer, wild boar and wolf. The family's support for Simon de Montfort's rebellion against Henry III in the 1260s ultimately saw them forfeit their lands to the Crown, and Byrkley Park became part of the Royal Forest of Needwood. A keeper was employed at the lodge to run forest affairs.

In 1337 the Chief Forester fined a man from Tatenhill two shillings for stealing three fallen oak tree tops near the fishpond; Robert Dicon sixpence for felling lime trees; Richard Merriot sixpence for trespassing two colts; and the Rector of Tatenhill Church 12 pence for trespassing 140 sheep – all at Byrkley. As well as keeping 'order' in the forest, the 'Woodmote Court' was a good fund-raiser.

Edward IV and James I were known to have frequently engaged in the royal hunt from Byrkley Lodge in the 14th and 15th centuries, a period when Needwood Forest became associated with the Arthurian legend of *Sir Gawain and the Green Knight*, reflected in local dialect, topography and tradition.

Over the centuries, Byrkley Lodge saw several reincarnations, the last of which being the construction of Byrkley Lodge in 1775, when it was one of only three buildings to stand on the Needwood Forest plateau. It remained until 1952, when the heirless Billy Bass died, and the estate was sold; the lodge was demolished the following year.

Famed as it is for its ancient and veteran wood pasture oaks, Byrkley Park seems also to have had an abundance of small-leaved lime trees *(Tilia cordata)*, including a 6m (21ft) girthed pollard behind the lodge, which had a 1.8m (6ft) circumferenced mature holly *(Ilex aquifolium)* growing from its hollow. The tree fell in a storm in 1840, as noted by Sir Oswald Mosely – forefather of the infamous fascist of the same name – in his *Natural History of Tutbury* in 1863.

Despite the construction of all-weather football pitches, facilities and a car park at St George's Park, an unusually high number of ancient and veteran oaks survive in the 198ha (490 acres) of remaining wood pasture and woodland. The largest of these oaks – a squat, hollow pollard that I dubbed 'St George's Oak' – measures 7.35m (20ft) in circumference and may well hark back to the origins of Byrkley Park.

Referring to first edition Ordnance survey maps, it is clear to see that many more trees once graced the grounds in an open wood pasture landscape, and while some may have been lost during the park's transformation to football centre, its use as a training base and airfield during the Second World War had previously also had an impact.

St George's Park illustrates in a nutshell Britain's continually changing private forest landscape – from Chase to Royal Forest, to manorial estate, through military use to centre of national football.

The fact that St George's Park currently operates under a Natural England Higher Level Stewardship Agreement, which involves managing the land for environmental benefits, bodes well for its remaining ancient trees which once more provide wood pasture for grazing old breed longhorn cattle.

Thrice-venerable Druid, hail!
O may thy sacred words prevail,
May NEEDWOOD'S oaks successive stand
The lasting wonder of the land!
From *Needwood Forest* by Francis N C Mundy, 1776

ABOVE: St George Oak at 7.35m – largest oak in the park, 2017
BELOW: Needwood oaks, 1893

Beggars Oak

Bagots Park, Staffordshire

Bagot's Park takes its name from the Bagot family who have lived at the 260ha (650 acre) estate of Blithfield Manor since the late 14th century.

Surrounded by ancient woodland, Bagot's Park appears to host a great remnant of Needwood Forest, notably Bagot's Wood, which lines the hills to the north of the park. The park itself was once notable for its ancient oaks and scrubby grazing – typical wood pasture landscape – until the mid-1960s when the area was converted into arable land, destroying obstacles to the plough – including ancient trees – with bulldozer and explosives.

Several celebrated oaks were recorded for posterity by various sources including Rake's Wood Oak, Long Coppice Oak, Bett's Poll Oak, Lodge Yard Oak, Squitch Bank Oak and Beggar's Oak.

The last of these, Beggars Oak, was measured at 6m (20ft) around its bole and 20.7m (68ft) around its roots in 1830 by J G Strutt, growing to 7.3m (24ft) and 22.8m (75ft) when measured in 1904 by Henry John Elwes who described the tree as 'One of the best Oaks of its kind that I know.'

Situated near a right of way through the park, its large buttressed roots provided a natural seat, and the tree became a meeting place, providing shelter for the itinerants after whom it was named. Strutt declared the oak secure from the axe, falling under protection of Lord Bagot, a prolific tree planter who established around two million oaks on his Welsh and Stafford estates. The tree was removed in the 1940s.

The park spawned the Bagot goat – Britain's oldest documented breed of goat. The small black and white horned animal has run feral there since 1389. Thought to have been introduced as a gift from the Crusades by King Richard II, the rare breed also survives at Levens Hall in Cumbria – another Bagot estate.

The roots rise above the ground in a very extraordinary manner, so as to furnish a natural seat for the beggars chancing to pass along the pathway near it.

From *Arboretum et Fruticetum Britannicum* by John Claudius Loudon, 1838.

ABOVE: Squitch Oak from *Natural History of Stafford* by Robert Garner, 1844

BELOW: Beggars Oak, c1925

The Horn Dance
Abbots Bromley, Staffordshire

At dawn every Wakes Monday – the first Monday following each 4th September – villagers from Abbots Bromley perform a Horn Dance, as they appear to have done for hundreds, if not thousands of years.

Six Deer-men carrying ancient reindeer antlers on wooden skulls, a Hobby Horse, a Fool, Maid Marian (a man dressed as a woman), and a Bowman perform a traditional dance to music played on a melodion.

Starting at the village green, dancers are welcomed as bearers of good luck, stopping at locations throughout the village, and at surrounding pubs and farms in Needwood Forest. Over the course of the day they cover a distance of around 16km (10 miles).

The origins of the Horn Dance remain unclear, with the first written account appearing in 1686, yet clues hint at its greater antiquity. In 1976 a sample of one of the ancient reindeer antlers was radiocarbon dated to around 1065, placing it in the Saxon period. It is likely that they were brought over from Scandinavia, and could reflect an ancient Saxon ritual, but they may have been replacing an older pair of antlers, used to assert rights over Needwood Forest.

Cave paintings in Lascaux, France, reveal Stone Age images of people dressed in animal skins adorned with antlers, being chased by bowmen – as reflected in the Abbots Bromley Horn Dance – and suggest the memory of an ancient ceremony enacted to ensure success in the hunt. Dance and mime are still employed by tribes in Africa and South America for that purpose, and it is possible that the Abbots Bromley dance had similar roots. The old Druidic religion, gradually replaced by Saxon and then Christian religions, tended to survive at least in part in Britain's forest groves. The old religion soon became demonised and disparagingly referred to as 'witchcraft'.

At Abbots... a sort of sport... called the Hobby-horse dance, from a person that carried the image of a horse between his legs... and in his hand a bow and arrow... keeping time with the Music: with this Man danced six others, carrying on their shoulders as many reindeer heads, 3 of them painted white, and three red... with which they danced the Hays and other country dances.
From *The Natural History of Staffordshire* by Robert Plot, 1686

ABOVE: Abbots Bromley Horn Dance, c1900
OPPOSITE: Abbots Bromley Horn Dance, Blithfield, 2006

Seahenge Holme-next-the-Sea, Norfolk

Norfolk provided evidence of Britain's earliest human occupation, when footprints and stone tools were uncovered on the beech at Happisburgh in 2013. At around 900,000 years old, they are the oldest known hominid footprints outside of Africa.

In comparison, Seahenge – an early Bronze Age timber circle uncovered by shifting sands due west on the Norfolk coast in 1998 – is recent history. Nevertheless, it confirms that Norfolk people were making use of oak to construct large timber structures over 4,000 years ago.

Dendrochronology showed that around 15-20 oak trees were felled for the purpose and dragged by honeysuckle rope from nearby mixed oak woodland in the spring of 2049BC. Some timbers were shaped on arrival – revealing marks made by up to 50 bronze hand axes. A large upturned oak stump sat centre circle. It is thought to have been used for excarnation, the ceremonious decomposition following the death of an important person. The body would have been left to the elements, picked clean by birds and animals, the bones later removed for burial.

The timbers were shaped into posts set in an enclosed circle standing 3-4m (10-13ft) high. Bark was left on the outside of the posts, the finished structure resembling a giant hollow oak trunk over 20m (65.6ft) in circumference.

Originally built inland on saltmarsh, over time this would have given way to freshwater reed swamp, which in turn created the peat that enveloped and preserved Seahenge. In due course the sea reclaimed the land, gradually eroding the preserving peat until the monument was once again revealed at Holme Beach, illustrating the changing nature of the coastline, and the landscape in general.

Before the monument was removed for study and preservation – amidst much local protest by those who thought it should be left in place – it was captured by local artist Wendy George in her definitive photograph (right).

The preserved remains of Seahenge are now housed in a special exhibit at Lynn Museum.

I feel the rope against my bark,
  And the weight of him in my grain,
I feel in the throe of his final woe
  The touch of my own last pain.

And never more shall leaves come forth
  On the bough that bears the ban;
I am burned with dread, I am dried and dead,
  From the curse of a guiltless man.

From *The Haunted Oak* by Paul Laurence Dunbar, 1901

ABOVE: Carved detail of the Seahenge oak stump centrepiece, resembling a raven head, 2019

BELOW: Peering through the silhouette of the entrance to Seahenge, 2019

OPPOSITE: Seahenge at Holme-next-the-sea, by Wendy George, 1998

Thetford Forest Norfolk

The enclosures are, in general, small, and the hedges high, and full of trees. This has a singular effect in travelling through the country: the eye seems ever on the verge of a forest, which is, as it were by enchantment, continually changing into enclosures and hedgerows.

From *Rural Economy of Norfolk* by William Marshall, 1787

At 19,000ha (48,000 acres), Thetford contains Britain's largest lowland pine wood, yet interestingly, the county of Norfolk appears to have never had a forest in the traditional sense at all.

Thetford Forest is a man-made plantation, laid out in the 1920s at Breckland as one of the Forestry Commissions's first major projects. It is a heath-like landscape of gorse, sandy ridge and open-grown trees.

Breckland had been exploited for flint since the Neolithic, as evidenced at Grimes Graves, a flint-mining complex worked between about 2600 and 2300BC. But by the 14th century, much of Breckland was turned to rabbit warren.

Now a patchwork of pine, broadleaf and heathland, the forest is an SSSI, home to woodlark and nightjar, roe, red and fallow deer. It was was once abundant with red squirrels. A 1,700ha (4,200 acre) reserve designated in the 1990s was estimated to contain between only ten and 20 red squirrels and, despite efforts to increase their numbers, they appear to be as good as gone.

Outside of Thetford, oak and ash are dominant in the hedgerows between the arable fields, and echoes of the forest hunt survive at places like Lynford Stag, where a hall has stood since 1500. Part of a lime avenue leading to Lynford Hall remains beside the pine plantation.

Despite Norfolk's open aspect, it has many trees, and has hosted some fine ancient specimens.

ABOVE: Open-grown veteran pine, 2019
BELOW: Veteran oaks line the A134 at Lynford, 2019

The Winfarthing Oak
Winfarthing, Norfolk

Ye who this venerable oak survey,
Which still survives through many a stormy day,
Deposit here your mite with willing hands,
To spread in foreign climes, through foreign lands
Inscription on a plaque hung over the oak's hollow, c1850

The Winfarthing Oak was probably Norfolk's largest ever recorded oak. It stood in Winfarthing Great Park near the Duke of Albemarle's Quiddenham Hall Estate, and measured a colossal 12m (40ft) in circumference at shoulder height in 1820. Two waggon loads of timber were recovered from a limb that fell in 1811.

The tree was capable of holding 30 people within its hollow trunk, which was once set with a table and chairs. A brass plaque hung over the entrance hollow by the then tenant farmer Mr Doggett, invited donations to the bible society. Said to have been known as 'The Old Oak' at the time of the Conquest, the tree finally collapsed in 1953.

The Bale Oak
Bale, Norfolk

Close to All Saints Church at Bale in north Norfolk stood another giant hollow oak, which measured 11m (36ft) in girth.

By 1850 it was dead, and for a time became the abode of a cobbler, who cut a door through the church side of the trunk, and practised his trade there throughout the summer. The hollow shell was apparently large enough for the job, and was said to have held 20 people standing comfortably inside.

Records reveal the removal, around 1790, of a large branch which had come within a metre (3ft) of the church tower, which stood 22m (72ft) from the tree trunk. The engraving above reveals that by 1853 all of the tree's branches had been removed, and in 1860, the Lord of the Manor, Sir Willoughby Jones ordered that the tree be removed. Amid much local mourning, the remains were carted off to Cranmer Hall at Fakenham.

ABOVE: The Bale Oak, 1853
LEFT: The Winfarthing Oak, 1853

Babes in the Wood

Waylands Wood, Norfolk

Norfolk's best known ancient wood is probably Waylands in the south of the county, near Watton, to the north of Thetford Forest.

Its ancient credentials date at least to the Saxon period – it was named after the Norse god of smiths – since when it has probably been worked for coppice and standards, a custom still practiced under the auspices of the Norfolk Wildlife Trust, who look after the 31.7ha (78 acre) SSSI.

Primarily ash, hazel and maple coppice with oak standards, hornbeam and bird cherry, the wood is rich in native wild flowers, with 125 species recorded, including bluebells, yellow archangel, wood anemone, early purple orchid, bugle, and Norfolk's only known colony of yellow star of Bethlehem. It is also home to the nuthatch, a bird rarely seen elsewhere in Norfolk.

The wood's notoriety stems from its connection with the *Babes in the Wood* legend, as it has long been held as the location for the story. It tells of two young children put into the care of their uncle by their parents, who both lay on their death beds at nearby Griston Manor. The children would gain their inheritance, so long as they both survived to adulthood. The wicked uncle was next in line, so hired two villains to murder the poor children. They were taken to Wayland's Wood, where in a fit of conscience, one of the ruffians killed the other as he could not bear to see the children murdered. Even so, he left them in the wood, where after a time, cold and hungry, they died in each others arms, leaving the uncle to claim their inheritance after all.

A huge oak, said to be the very tree beneath which the babes died, was struck by lightning and fell in 1879, prompting a surge of souvenir hunters eager to own a piece of Norfolk legend.

Wayland's Wood is also known locally as Wailing Wood, reflecting the cries of the unfortunate children who died there, and are said to have haunted it forever more.

He bargaind with two Ruffians rude,
Which were of furious mood,
That they should take the children young
and slay them in the Wood.
No burial these prettye babes
Of any man receives,
Till Robin-redbreast painfully
Did cover them with leaves.

From *The Norfolk Gentleman* by T Millington, 1595

ABOVE: Waylands Wood, 2008

BELOW: *Babes in the Wood* by Randolph Caldecott, 1879

Hethel Old Thorn

Hethel, Norfolk

In a field behind Hethel church, otherwise surrounded by woodland, sits Britain's smallest nature reserve. At only 0.025ha (0.06 acre), it may strike the casual observer as curious, until the realisation dawns that it hosts Norfolk's and possibly Britain's oldest hawthorn tree *(Crataegus mongyna)*. Known as the Hethel Thorn or Witch of Hethel, the tree itself is the nature reserve.

Age estimates range from 700–1,000 years, and it carries an array of stories and folklore as one might expect for such an historic tree.

In 1755 its waist measurement was recorded at 2.75m (9ft), in 1841 4.34m (14.25ft), described at the time as presenting a full crown, 'a thick grotesque mass, 31 yards around, covered in lichen and crowned with mistletoe, the trunk a mere shell – just a ruin', by James Grigor in his *Eastern Arboretum*.

Stories linger of the tree being used as a meeting place for a peasants' revolt against King John. The neighbouring church has Saxon origins, and may have appropriated an earlier pagan site.

Over the years, churchgoers used the thorn for maypole dancing and large sprays of the tree and pieces of the trunk were removed for souvenirs. This took its toll on the tree until almost nothing was left of the original trunk. Yet Grigor's lament for the thorn's former splendour appears unfounded 170 years later. The tree has layered – regrown into twisted fragmented trunks the crown gloriously lush in foliage, flower and haw, devoid of the parasitic (yet anciently sacred) mistletoe it once bore.

Given to the Norfolk Wildlife Trust in 1960 by F W Myhill, it was fenced to protect it from grazing cattle and, it seems, souvenir hunters.

The first Sir Thomas Beevor said, that he was in possession of a deed bearing date early in the thirteenth century, in which, referring to it as a boundary tree, it is mentioned as 'the old thorn'.

From *The Eastern Arboretum* by James Grigor, 1841

ABOVE: The Thorn, Hethel, by Henry Ninham, 1841
BELOW: Hethel Old Thorn, 2019

NORFOLK

Kett's Oak Hethersett, Norfolk

Kett's Oak stands on a busy roadside verge near Hethersett. It is the best known and most easily accessible of three oaks to have been named after Robert Kett, a 16th-century tanner and landowner. Having received a mob of angry commoners intent on liberating his enclosed land in July 1549, Kett listened to their concerns and, agreeing with them, became leader of Kett's Rebellion, or the Norfolk Commotion.

After a rousing speech beneath Kett's Oak, he led a march to Norfolk, which gathered momentum as it went, reflecting a sense of injustice felt by local people who saw common lands disappear through enclosure, where they had previously grazed their animals.

They set up camp on Mousehold Heath, overlooking Norwich, beneath another tree which became known as the Reformation Oak. By now they had attracted 12,000 followers. From there they sent 29 grievances to the Protector Somerset. In response they were asked to disperse, but refusing to do so were declared traitors by Edward VI, who sent troops to quell the rebellion. A pitched battle ensued at Dussindale, where around 3,000 rebels were killed.

Kett was captured the following day at Swannington, tried and hanged at Norwich Castle. The same fate befell his brother William, strung up from the tower at Wymondham Abbey. Other rebels were hanged from the Hethersett oak, where Kett's uprising had begun.

At only 4.5m (14.7ft) in circumference, it may appear doubtful that Kett's Oak existed in 1549, and perhaps the tree was named long after the event. Yet iron bands still evident today were attached to the hollow trunk around 1884, and evidence a slow-growing tree. It certainly exhibits veteran characteristics, and upholds Kett's name and story, so long held as traitorous through historic propaganda, and stands in contrast to the farmed fields of rape that surround it, on the common land lost long ago.

That Arch Rebel Kett, who in the reign of Edward VI (becoming leader of the fanatic insurrection in Norfolk) made an Oak (under the specious name of Reformation Oak) council house, and place of convention where he sent forth his traitorous edicts.

From *Sylva or a Discourse on Forest Trees* by John Evelyn, 1664

ABOVE: Kett beneath the Oak of Reformation, engraved 1781
OPPOSITE: Kett's Oak, Hethersett, 2019

Charnwood Forest Leicestershire

The name Charnwood is thought to derive from either *Cerne wudu* (cairn wood) or *Quern wudu* – a reference to the plentiful supply of stone plainly visible in rocky outcrops across the region.

Charnwood may never have been a Royal Forest under Norman rule, but it was likely so in Saxon times – a swainmote assembled three times a year at Copt Oak to pass judgement on offenders breaking Forest Law in the open air under a large hollow oak.

The Domesday Survey of 1086 mentions just one settlement, that of Charley, 'ley' denoting a clearance in the forest. New settlements and agriculture continued encroachment over the next 200 years.

John Leland, antiquary to Henry VIII who visited around 1540, described it thus: 'First, I came out of Brodegate Park into the forest of Charnwood, commonly called the Waste. This great forest is a twenty miles or more in compass, having pleanty of wood', a fact clearly remembered in the surviving place names of Woodhouse, Woodthorpe and The Oaks, and reflected in documents mentioning pannage – the right to feed pigs on acorns. A document from 1673 describes the sale of; '6090 oak and ash trees, within Beaumanor liberty, on the Forest of Charnwood... for the sum of £1,178'.

Large tracts of trees were lost to the Industrial Revolution's appetite for timber and charcoal, and mining and quarrying, occupations evident since the Neolithic. By 1812 the forest was enclosed, despite strong opposition from local people concerned about their common rights.

John Spanton's map of 1858 depicts the forest stretching from Coalville in the west to Barrow in the east, Loughborough in the north to Ansty in the south.

Today, Charnwood provides valuable wildlife habitat. Since 1990, The National Forest project has aimed to merge ancient woodland with newly planted areas to link the ancient forests of Needwood and Charnwood.

O Charnwood, be thou called the choicest of thy kind,
The like in any place what flood hath happed to find?
No tract in all this isle, the proudest let her be,
Can show a sylvan nymph for beauty like to thee:
The satyrs and the fawns, by Dian set to keep,
Rough hills and forest holts were sadly seen to weep,
When thy high-palmed harts, the sport of bows and hounds,
By gripple borderers' hands were banished thy grounds.
From *Polybion* by Michael Drayton, 1613-22

ABOVE: The Copt Oak 1842 – under whose branches the local swainmote or council was held three times a year. 7.30m in girth when it fell in a storm in 1855, the tree was subsequently fashioned into a representation of the Druidic God Jupiter, an order named after the Greek word for oak – *drys* – their sacred tree.

OPPOSITE: Ancient oaks at Bradgate Park, 2017

Bradgate Park Leicestershire

Bradgate Park, nestled in the south east of Charnwood Forest in undulating, rocky terrain, cradles some of Britain's oldest fossil remains.

Evidence of human occupation dates to the Bronze Age. Formerly part of the Waste of Charnwood, by the Norman era Bradgate was reserved for the hunt, as it was rich in wild boar, red deer and wolf.

Tenure passed from the Crown to the Earl of Winchester, Lord of the Manor of Groby, who by 1241 created a deer park, enclosed by a ditch and bank topped with a wooden palisade. In 1278, the Earl paid 'a pair of gilt spurs' annually to the King for the privilege.

By 1445, the Grey family owned the estate and had built one of the first unfortified brick manor houses in England, styled to circumvent the King's right to occupy fortified buildings. Henry II had forcibly demonstrated his right in 1176 by demolishing Leicester and Groby castles to deter aspiring rivals.

In April 1841, a golden eagle – the last to be seen at the park – was killed and taken into the possession of the Earl of Stamford at Dunham Massey.

In 1921, the park, along with nearby Swithland Wood – an important ancient woodland to the north east of Bradgate – was purchased from the Greys by Charles Bennion, who presented it for 'the benefit of the people of Leicestershire and visitors to the county' in 1928. The Bradgate Trust has managed the SSSI ever since.

The slow-growing nature of the many veteran and ancient oaks at Bradgate clinging to rocky outcrops in the poor, thin soil, offers strong support to claims of their longevity, evidenced by the two photographs taken a century apart (right).

To this day, around 450 red and fallow deer roam the 336ha (830 acres) of the park – Leicestershire's only remaining enclosed deer park – with some of the reds shown to share the same DNA as their earliest Bradgate ancestors, introduced some 800 years ago.

Yon oaks, of a thousand shapes and hues–(and under them, in all her beauty and innocence, the Lady Jane has wandered)–this fragrance from the decaying year–this babbling stream, that collects the brooding mist–yon old crumbling gables and turrets that pierce the dull distance–these are your November glooms. And look at the deer–not the smooth, sleek gentlemen of the undulating paddock, misnamed a Park–but wild, and bold, and stately as they move among the bright fern or under the ancient oaks.
From *History of Charnwood Forest* by T R Potter, 1842

ABOVE AND BELOW: Imperceivable change in over a century between photographs – all five trees remain – easily recognisable from their unique shape, 1905 and 2017

OPPOSITE: Red and fallow deer roam wild amongst the ancient oaks.

CHARNWOOD FOREST

The Bradgate Oak
Bradgate Park, Leicestershire

Following the death of her cousin Edward VI in 1553, Bradgate Park's most famous resident, Lady Jane Grey, great-granddaughter of Henry VII – was proclaimed Queen, but was then overthrown by Mary I just nine days later. Held prisoner at the Tower of London, Jane was convicted of high treason and beheaded the following year. The 'nine-day queen', just 16 years old at the time, was held in high esteem as learned and altruistic, a victim of medieval politics and often remembered as a martyr.

Around 70 veteran and ancient oaks remain scattered in the park, many of them pollards, believed to be those of local legend that recall the 'beheading' of the trees on the morning of Jane's execution; the trees too lost their crowns in honour of the untimely death of Lady Jane Grey.

The story doubtless reflects the working practice of pollarding for sustainable wood undertaken at regular periods on the Bradgate oaks. The large number of extant ancient and veteran oaks of varying ages at the park demonstrates the continuity of species and the relevance of Bradgate Park as Leicestershire's most important site for ancient oaks.

Bradgate's oldest oak, an ancient hollow, pollard propped at every turn, measures 8.57m (28ft) in circumference, and stands in Bowling Green Spinney, one of several small stone-walled woodlands planted in the 19th century as a covert for game birds.

Remaining tree rings from the trunk underwent dendrochronological testing and the oak's age was estimated at around 820 years, taking the planting of the tree back to the very inception of the deer park.

Queen Adelaide's Oak

Bradgate Park, Leicestershire

One fine morning in July... a message came to say that the Queen Dowager... would wish to have a picnic in Bradgate Park. The venison was good, so were the trout, and last not least the crayfish.

On Queen Adelaide's Picnic, July 1842, from a plaque at Bradgate Park

In July 1842, Queen Adelaide (1792-1849), Queen Consort to William IV until his death in 1830 and aunt to Queen Victoria, decided to picnic at Bradgate Park, where she was a frequent visitor. Pitching under a large veteran oak standing near the ruins of Bradgate House, Adelaide was said to have enjoyed the venison, trout and crayfish – all of which were available in abundance at the park.

The hollowing tree stands in proud health, fenced and propped for its protection, and named after the Queen along with several pubs, a hotel, a street and, more distantly, the capital city of Australia.

ABOVE: Queen Adelaide's Oak, 2017
LEFT: The Bradgate Oak and ruins of Bradgate House, 2017

Shakespeare's Oak

Stoneleigh Abbey, Warwickshire

LEFT: Bust of William Shakespeare

OPPOSITE: Shakespeare's Oak, 2017

BELOW: Shakespeare's Crab Apple Tree, 1857

The Forest of Arden arguably ranks alongside Sherwood and Windsor as one of Britain's most famous, due largely to its being the setting for Shakespeare's play *As You Like It*.

While never a Royal Forest as such, Arden covered an area stretching from Tamworth to Stratford-upon-Avon, west and north of the River Avon. Predominantly wooded with oak and lime, it may have had a significant impact on the surrounding Roman roads, which tended to avoid the forest.

The source of Shakespeare's play was an earlier romance by Thomas Lodge, which was set in the Forest of Ardennes, in France; however, it is likely that the play's backdrop is largely drawn from the Bard's experiences in Arden, where he spent much of his childhood.

Shakespeare's association with and partiality for waxing lyrical about trees and forests runs deep. A crab apple in Arden – under which he is said to have fallen asleep when drunk – was named after him, and had all but disappeared at the hands of souvenir hunters by the early 19th century. A mulberry in his garden in Stratford-upon-Avon, said to have been planted by the man himself, was cut down by subsequent owner the Reverand Francis Gastrell in the 1850s when he grew tired of requests to view it. The last oak of Birnam Wood, as described in *Macbeth*, is still celebrated in the Birnam Oak, Perthshire, an ancient, 7m (23ft) hollow tree on the banks of the Tay, which would most likely have been mature during the Bard's lifetime.

At Stoneleigh Abbey, on the eastern fringes of Arden, stands the forest's largest oak *(Quercus robur)*, a giant hollow maiden measuring 9.28m (30.4ft) around its bole, recently fenced for protection and named after Shakespeare. The abbey, founded in 1134 on the edge of a deer park – which now hosts a golf course and business park – passed into private hands following the dissolution of the monasteries. Some wood pasture oaks were retained in 1809 when Humphry Repton was invited to landscape the grounds, and many other historic Arden oaks survive in the area's half-timbered buildings.

They say he is already in the forest of Arden, and a many merry men with him; and there they live like the old Robin Hood of England: they say many young gentlemen flock to him every day, and fleet the time carelessly, as they did in the golden world.

*To-day my Lord of Amiens and myself
Did steal behind him as he lay along
Under an oak whose antique root peeps out
Upon the brook that brawls along this wood*

*Lo, what befell! he threw his eye aside,
And mark what object did present itself:
Under an oak, whose boughs were moss'd with age
And high top bald with dry antiquity.*

From *As You Like It* by William Shakespeare, 1599

Salcey Forest

Northamptonshire

Salcey Forest from the viewing platform, 2017

Medieval Northamptonshire hosted a great band of forest stretching over 80km (50 miles) from Stamford in the north to Milton Keynes in the south.

To the north lay Rockingham Forest, to the south Whittlewood, with Salcey Forest sandwiched between them. It was named for its sallow (sallowey) wood, an historically important tree, exploited industrially for charcoal-burning, tanning, and wattle and daub, and provider of early spring nectar for pollinators.

Royal hunting grounds for the Saxon nobility, the Northamptonshire forests were subsequently reserved under Forest Law by their Norman conquerors. The area was by then well populated, incorporating entire towns and villages and was a good example of the mosaic, patchwork nature of a medieval forest. Early forest records referencing trees are scarce, but those relating to poaching abound, indicating a bountiful supply of deer, therefore suggesting an open-wooded treescape.

'Fox-trees' are mentioned, however in reference to timber trees granted to foresters in return for controlling foxes. 'Derefal wood' (deer-fall) – another Northamptonshire colloquialism – alluded to the practice of twig-cutting for winter deer feed, often referred to elsewhere in the country as 'tree-hay'.

Common rights in Salcey Forest were restricted in the late 18th century, and lost entirely in 1826 when Salcey was disafforested by Act of Parliament, and subsequently enclosed to bolster large estates for the landed gentry. It was this period that saw the forests of Northamptonshire suffer large-scale tree felling.

During the Second World War, elephants employed from redundant circuses to haul felled timber used to bathe in the 'Elephant Pool' in the forest to cool down.

Salcey Forest remains Northamptonshire's largest ancient woodland at 159.6ha (394 acres), an SSSI replete with visitor centre, treetop walk and an abundance of wildlife.

The Salcey Forest Oak

Salcey Forest, Northamptonshire

Upon the whole, this bears every mark of having been a short-stemmed branchy tree, of the first magnitude; spreading its arms in all directions round it.
From *Letter on Growth of Oaks* by Thomas South, 1783

The Salcey Forest Oak, one of the most picturesque sylvan ruins that can be met with anywhere.
Sir Thomas Dick Lauder, 1784-1848

ABOVE: The Salcey Forest Oak by J G Strutt, 1840
BELOW: An ancient Salcey oak, 2017

Salcey remains in the care of the Forestry Commission and, while still exploiting timber, aims to actively promote education, recreation and biodiversity in the forest.

Scattered among ancient woodbanks, coppices and Iron Age camps stand reminders of Salcey's sylvan past in its 'Druid oaks', great veterans of the forest.

The largest and most celebrated of these was the Salcey Forest Oak, a hollow giant which in 1830 measured 12.14m (39.9ft) around its waist, the same in height, with a complete arch 4.47m (14.7ft) tall that lead to a 8.83m (29ft) space within – large enough to sit ten people comfortably. Earlier that century Major Hayman Rooke declared the tree to be 'no less than fifteen hundred years old'. Around this time it became known as Tom Keeper's Stable. Its cavernous bole formed a natural manger, so it was used to house Tom's horse.

Nothing remains of the tree besides some illustrations, including Jacob George Strutt's sublime 19th-century engraving. A clue to its former location marked on an early OS map places it near the south western edge of Salcey Lawn – a large lawn in private ownership, surrounded on all sides by the forest – open wood pasture, much as a large part of overgrown Salcey Forest would once have appeared.

The Milking Oak

Salcey Forest, Northamptonshire

ABOVE: The Milking Oak, 2017

Other ancient Salcey 'Druid oaks' are included on a walk map produced by the Forestry Commission, although several lie prostrate.

The Church Path Oak, sited on a trackway crossroads between Crab Tree Thick and Hazel Copse, is said to have been favoured by William Henry, Sixth Duke of Grafton – father to the Warden of the Forest – who would stop, sit and contemplate beneath its boughs on his way to and from Piddington church. It fell in 1995, its decaying hulk now habitat to myriad creatures, its story remembered on a commemorative plaque.

The Milking Oak – so called after a local habit of milking cattle in its shade – stands in the overgrown fringes of woodland bordering the south eastern edge of Salcey Lawn. Its 6.41m (21ft) hollowing trunk once supported a branch that extended 7.62m (25ft), and provided ideal shade for milking. I suspect Salcey Lawn previously extended beyond the Milking Oak, an open wood pasture ideal for cattle and veteran oaks alike.

The largest and most likely oldest surviving oak in Salcey Forest is the King Charles Oak on Salcey Lawn. Named after Charles II who is said to have sheltered in its 10.62m (34.84ft) hollow trunk while on the run from Parliamentarian forces following the execution of his father in 1649. It would appear Charles had a penchant for oaks, as he supposedly hid in several of them, including the Meavy Oak in Dartmoor and most famously the Boscobel Oak in Shropshire, en route to the south coast for his self-imposed exile to France. It is true, however, that Oak Apple Day – a public holiday honouring the tree that saved his life and the monarchy – was established to commemorate Charles' restoration to the throne in 1660.

Cowper's Oak

Yardley Chase, Northamptonshire

History, not wanted yet,
Leaned on her elbow, watching Time, whose course
Eventful, should supply her with a theme.
From *Yardley Oak* by William Cowper, 1791-92

At the edge of Salcey Forest stood Yardley Chase, preserved as a 357ha (883 acre) site, historically chased for the hunt by the Normans, and serving the lords of medieval Castle Ashby to the north.

Commanded partly by the estate heir Earl Compton and partly by the military since the Second World War, a classic wood pasture treescape saw Yardley Chase granted SSSI status in 1984. This was in recognition of its habitat value, which includes invertebrates that depend on the presence of both live and decaying wood to maintain their life cycle. The long absence of agriculture in the MOD section has helped maintain an important biodiverse landscape.

William Cowper – a godfather to romantic poetry – lived in the area between 1767 and 1795. Cowper frequently walked the chase. A favourite tree – the Yardley Oak – was immortalised in his unfinished poem 'Yardley Chase'. Written in 1791, the poem lay undiscovered until his friend and biographer William Hayley unearthed it after his death, along with letters describing in detail the size and form of several ancient Yardley oaks. Cowper has the Yardley Oak at 6.8m (22.5ft) in circumference, hollow and ruinous. Early photographs display it in rude health, when it became known as Cowper's Oak, in deference to the poet. Souvenir hunters, including Hayley himself, carried much of it away. The poem, drawings and photographs are all that remain of the tree.

Yardley Oak by William Harvey, 1823

BELOW: Cowper's Oak, 1898
Described in 1805 by artist James Andrews as a 'traditional and melancholy reflection on history and the mutability of fortune.'

SALCEY FOREST

Gog and Magog

Yardley Chase, Northamptonshire

Just a mile to the north of the tree named in his honour, Cowper recorded another venerable pair of open-grown oaks. These two were celebrated under the pseudonyms Gog and Magog, after the last survivors of an ancient race of British giants, held by legend to have been slain by Brutus' refugee army on arrival from Troy.

Standing 50 yards apart, Cowper found Gog – the larger of the pair – to measure 8.68m (28.5ft) in circumference. By 1892 the tree had grown to 9.75m (32ft) – expanding over a metre in girth through a century. With Magog standing at 8.84m (29ft), both trees were considerably larger than Cowper's Oak. A pair of giant oaks sharing the giants' names can also be found at Glastonbury – the 'Oaks of Avalon' – while effigies of Gog and Magog are kept at the Guildhall in London to protect the city, paraded at the Lord Mayor's show each November.

Previously, Gog was known as Judith's Oak, after a local belief that the tree was planted by William the Conqueror's niece, from Castle Ashby, ascribing almost 1,000 years to its age. By the late 1800s both trees were dead hulks. Forty years on and only Gog remained, as it does today, dead, yet full of life, home to Yardley's invertebrate populations, upright in a field of corn, statuesque with stag-headed branches like flailing arms.

Where agriculture supplants wood pasture, and a farmhouse succeeds the medieval hunting lodge, Gog endures, a hundred years dead, still a giant at 8m (26.25ft) around its bolling even without bark; a great illustration of oak's longevity not only in life, but also in slow decay.

ABOVE: Gog, 2017.
BELOW: Jeremiah Whitney at Gog collecting faggots (bundles of firewood sticks) to fuel Castle Ashby, c1900

Staverton Park

Woodbridge, Suffolk

Suffolk is blessed with a multitude of ancient, giant oaks. Remnants in hedgerows and of old wood pasture pepper the largely flat landscape.

At Staverton Park and Staverton Thicks, near Woodbridge, the county's greatest collection is found, often held as one of Europe's prime examples of ancient oak wood pasture.

Around 4,000 veteran and ancient oak pollards grace the 80.8ha (200 acre) site, a more magnificent and grotesque grouping of Tolkienesque Ents you are never likely to meet.

The estate was seized by the Crown under Henry III from the Earl of Norfolk in the 1260s, and was subsequently turned into a deer park – a function it still retains some 750 years later. This continuity of purpose, coupled with the fact that Staverton Park is still in private ownership (the owners turned down the offer of a grant to grub out the old oaks in the 1960s), has helped preserve a treescape that may date back to the wildwood.

Staverton's current character, however – a Site of Special Scientific Interest, Nature Conservation Review site and Special Area of Conservation in Suffolk's Area of Outstanding Natural Beauty – owes much to its long history of management as a deer park.

Pollarding of the oaks – a practice which appears to have lapsed around 200 years ago – has helped lend the ancient oaks their distinct gnarly appearance, the space between the trees historically kept open by the grazing habits of pigs, deer and cattle.

The deer herds are now contained by a moveable fence, although small numbers of wild deer persist, joined by the reintroduction of some cattle and sheep. A previous lack of grazing allowed bluebells and Bracken to bedeck the sandy soil in spring

ABOVE: Munkjack deer skull, 2017
BELOW: 200-year-old ancient birch, 2017

and summer respectively, with holly, birch, rowan and hawthorn making strong inroads, although marvellous ancient specimens of all species are widespread throughout the park.

The sandy soil combined with Britain's area of lowest rainfall has bestowed a diminutive stature on the oaks, and while an estimate of 400 years is often assigned to their age (local tradition suggests some may have been planted by monks from nearby Butley Abbey in the 16th century) it is quite possible that some of these slow-growing oaks date back to the park's 13th-century inception. They make a stark contrast to nearby Rendlesham Forest – a dense plantation of mostly non-native coniferous trees under the care of the Forestry Commission.

King George VI Oak
Staverton Park

Staverton Park's largest ancient oak measures 7m (23ft) around its gnarled and hollowing trunk, and stands at the edge of the park, close to the public footpath that runs alongside it.

The tree acquired its name following a visit by King George VI who very nearly ended the tree's life. Whilst hunting at Staverton in 1946, the King's Land Rover backed into the oak, an act for which he was apologetic, concerned that he had damaged the old veteran, which mercifully, was made of sterner stuff and still stands.

A keen hunter, the King's hunting-log asserts that he 'bagged' 1,055 woodcocks over his 43 year hunting career.

On his final hunt, 90 pheasants, two pigeons, three mallards, 17 rabbits and a hare were taken. The latter was shot by the king.

King George VI Oak, 2017

Staverton Thicks

Woodbridge, Suffolk

To the south of Staverton Park is Staverton Thicks, formerly known as Butley Thicks from a time when it belonged to Butley Abbey. While presently fenced from the park it was formerly very much part of it.

Early OS maps clearly show the former deer park was once almost twice its current size, and extant ancient woodbanks are still traceable on the ground. Transformation to heath and then clearance for agriculture took place.

Today, the character of the Thicks is quite different to that of the park. While many veteran pollard oaks are present, the Thicks are best known for presenting some of the oldest, and certainly tallest hollies in Britain. Some reach 20m (70ft) in height, dwarfing the slower-growing senior oaks beneath them, depriving them of light and sending them into slow decay.

Both species had surely cohabited blithely together for eons, but the decline of oak pollarding and cutting of tree-hay from holly for winter animal fodder some two centuries ago saw a marked change towards a denser closed-canopy treescape when compared to the park.

The relationship between oak and holly was previously mutually beneficial: oaks grew up under the thorny protection of holly; birds, eating holly berries, then dropped seeds to the ground replete with fertiliser from their perches in the branches of the oaks, thereby completing the regenerative cycle.

What can be noted from Staverton – at both the Park and the Thicks – is a succession across age ranges, which has been interpreted as compelling evidence suggesting the oaks naturally regenerated, as opposed to being planted by human hand. Natural regeneration no doubt aided by red squirrels and jays, who by burying great numbers of acorns each autumn, inevitably forgot some the following spring.

ABOVE: A phoenix tree – fallen and regrown where it fell, 2017
BELOW: Ancient holly, the Thicks – among Britain's tallest, 2017
OPPOSITE: Staverton Park oak wood pasture, 2017

FOREST OF SNOWDONIA

The Nannau Oak

Nannau, Dolgellau, Gwynedd

One of Wales' most revered oaks both in stature and folklore stood in the medieval deer park on the Nannau Estate in Gwynedd until the night of the 27th July 1813, when it blew down in a storm after being struck by lightning. It was the same day that Sir Richard Colt Hoare had made a painting of it for posterity, which still hangs in his family home at Stourhead.

Known variously as Derwen Ceubren yr Ellyll (Hollow Oak of the Demon), Nannau Oak, Spirit's Blasted Tree and Hobgoblin's Hollow Tree, the oak has good reason for attaining its notoriety.

Nannau was the seat of Howel Sele, cousin to Owain Glyndwr, Welsh freedom fighter and the last of his countrymen to hold the title Prince of Wales. There was bad blood between them, due in part to Howel's sympathies towards the English, but they were brought together and apparently reconciled by the abbot of nearby Cymmen Abbey in 1402.

Presently, together with Owain's friend Maddoc, the cousins set out for the hunt in Nannau Woods. Howel, a keen marksman, raised his bow towards a grazing doe spotted by Owain. Then, turning at the last, released his arrow at his cousin's chest, glancing from armour hidden beneath his tunic, the arrow left him unscathed.

After that, Howel's house was burnt down and his whereabouts were unknown. And that is how it remained for 40 years until the skeleton of a large man, still grasping a rusty sword, was discovered inside the Nannau Oak's hollow trunk.

All Nations have their omens drear,
Their legends wild of woe and fear;
To Cambria look – the peasant see,
Bethink him of Glendowerdy,
And shun the spirit's blasted tree.
From *Marmion* by Sir Walter Scott, 1808

ABOVE: The Nannau Oak, drawn in 1853
OPPOSITE: Oaks in 'Coed-y-Moch' (Pig Wood), Nannau, 2019

It seems that Owain, furious at his cousin's treachery, had, along with Maddoc, either killed or mortally wounded Howel and entombed him within the void of the tree's bole.

Some large veteran oaks still stand at Nannau. The largest measures 7.8m (25.5ft) around its hollowing, mossy trunk, just 0.6m (2ft) short of its infamous relative, and perfectly reflecting its form.

The Brimmon Oak Newtown, Powys

My favourite character was Mervyn Jones, who got very emotional describing his fight for the 500-year old Brimmon Oak.
Ardal O'Hanlon, *Tree of the Year*, 2016

In 2009, the Welsh Government proposed the construction of a bypass to the south of Newtown in Powys. The town had long suffered from heavy traffic congestion – a plan to ease congestion was first suggested in 1949 – and it was hoped the bypass would improve traffic flow and encourage industrial growth in the area.

The road was to be carved through fields and hedgerows to the south of the town, including the family farm of Mervyn Lloyd Jones. While not opposed to the bypass in principle, Mervyn was dismayed that the route necessitated the removal of an ancient oak *(Quercus robur)*, 6.8m (28.8ft) in circumference, and of a pond with crested newts.

Mervyn's family have farmed the land at Lower Brimmon for 400 years. Throughout that time, the Brimmon Oak has been a constant, a backdrop for family gatherings and photographs over generations, including setting the scene for the wedding of Mervyn's great aunt Polly in 1901 (right).

Mervyn understood perfectly the ecological value and historic significance of the great Welsh oak and, fired by a strong personal attachment, set about trying to save it. His protest was met with a proposal to uproot and move the tree, which can prove catastrophic to veteran and ancient specimens. Further pressure ensured the bypass would be diverted, but subsequent plans revealed it would pass within 3m (9.85ft) of the tree trunk, resulting in serious root damage which would also threaten the tree's existence.

Mervyn left a public enquiry in 2105 in despondent mood. He was then put in touch with Rob McBride, a self-styled 'tree hunter', who had added the Brimmon Oak to the Woodland Trust's Ancient Tree Inventory in 2009. Rob suggested they promote a petition to save the tree on social media, which had the effect of procuring over 5,000 signatures of support. In 2016, the Brimmon Oak won both Welsh and UK Tree of the Year awards, appearing on a TV programme of the same name, in which I appeared as judge, and it finished runner-up later that year in the European competition.

This new-found fame helped persuade planners to divert the road, avoiding the trunk by 15m (49.2ft) in accordance with British Standards. The bypass was completed in 2019 and the oak remains steadfast, dubbed 'the tree that moved a bypass,' thanks to the sustained efforts of Mervyn, Rob and friends.

ABOVE: Great aunt Polly's wedding party under the Brimmon Oak, 1901

BELOW: The Brimmon Oak, 2015

The Old Oak Clun, Shropshire

Clunton and Clunbury, Chungunford and Clun
Are the quietest places, Under the sun.

From *A Shropshire Lad* by AE Housman, 1896

AE Housman's poetic description of Clun may seem apt today but, straddling the Welsh border, Clun's ancient forest bore witness to violent Welsh struggles against both Saxon and Norman advances. Locally, Housman's poem is held to derive from an older source, where 'wickedest' substitutes 'quietest'.

The old pollard oak at Clun (right), which housed a postbox within its hollow cavernous trunk, may be long gone, but an ancient yew, measuring 10.74m (35.2ft) around its bole – one of two surviving veterans that stand in the churchyard – is very likely to have stood through both invasions.

ABOVE: The Old Oak with letter-box inside, Clun, by P B Abery, 1901
BELOW: Wild Edric meets Godda, Churchman's Card, 1936

Wild Edric Clun, Shropshire

Following the Norman Conquest, when land was divvied up amongst new lords and knights in return for their services in battle, pockets of resistance surfaced, particularly at the new kingdom's extremities. These were often led by former Saxon nobles whose lands had been confiscated.

One such resistance fighter was Wild Edric, who held manors across Shropshire and Herefordshire. From his hideout in Clun Forest, Edric raided the counties between 1067 and 1069, including the sacking of Shrewsbury and Hereford towns. In 1070 Edric appears to have made peace with William, bringing his rebellion to an end.

The historic Edric is hard to define through a misty veil of legend that has attached itself to him. One story tells how, lost in Clun Forest, Eadric chanced upon a house of seven beautiful dancing maidens. One in particular, Godda, took Edric's eye, and he proposed marriage. Godda agreed, on condition that Edric must never reproach her sisters, which of course many years later he did, blaming them one day for her lateness back from the forest. Godda disappeared, never to be seen again. Depending on the version, Edric either died of grief, rides the sky in a 'wild hunt', or was condemned with his men to forever haunt Shropshire's lead mines. Miners knew them as 'The Old Men', and thought that to hear their 'knocking' in the mines was a portent of an imminent good load.

The Gregynog Oak
Gregynog, Powys

A National Nature Reserve and SSSI, the Gregynog Estate is one of Wales' most significant ancient parkland and wood-pasture sites, providing rich habitat for a wide spectrum of wildlife. This includes the wood warbler, pied flycatcher, redstart, brown hare, great-crested newt, dragonflies, invertebrates and bats.

In the 18ha (45 acre) Great Wood to the north of the manor house, around 250 ancient and veteran oaks – 15 of which measure over 5m (16.4ft) in circumference – support nationally important strains of fungi and 140 species of lichen, including the rare *Enterographa sorediata*. Meaning 'floury granular internal writing lichen', its granular flour-like appearance reveals black, scribble-like fruits when scratched.

Found only in old-growth woodlands in the British Isles, Gregynog's example of the lichen was discovered on the Gregynog Oak – at 6.65m (21.8ft) the estate's largest and probably oldest oak – in wood pasture at the old rabbit warren to the south of the house.

Lichen demands clean air but, despite Gregynog's proximity to the Midlands – birthplace of the 18th century Industrial Revolution and its incumbent pollution – it thrives in the mild, damp, Welsh climate.

Gregynog's rich parkland heritage is no accident. A continuous history spanning at least 800 years – eulogised by the 12th-century poet Cynddelw – it was the seat of the Blayneys for almost 250 years from the mid-16th century, and became the area's leading working landed estate.

In 1913 the property was split into lots and sold off. The hall and woodlands were bought by the philanthropic Davies sisters in 1920, reducing its former 17,284ha (18,000 acres) to just 750ha (303 acres), effectively saving it.

In 2016, the Gregynog Oak was nominated Welsh Tree of the Year and, although judging of the competition (in which I participated) took place at at Gregynog Hall, the tree narrowly missed out to its neighbour, the Brimmon Oak.

O! Care, when with thy train I've toil'd all day,
Give me at eve thro' these lov'd haunts to stray,–
Woo peace and contemplation to my breast,
While ev'ry jarring thought is charm'd to rest.
From *Walking in the woods of Gregynog* by Mrs Darwall, 1794

ABOVE Gregynog Hall and the Great Wood, 1874
BELOW AND OPPOSITE: The Gregynog Oak, 2016

ANCIENT SUNKEN FOREST

ANCIENT SUNKEN FOREST

The Sunken Hundred Borth, Ceredigion

In May 2019, Storm Hannah battered the coast of Borth in Mid Wales, uncovering a proliferation of weathered tree stumps along the Ceredigion coastline.

I visited the quiet fishing village and resort in June of that year and, at low tide one misty afternoon, tree stumps were clearly visible for 3-5 km (2-3 miles) along the shoreline, albeit for less than an hour, before the sea reclaimed them into its murky depths.

Yet this was not a new event. Sightings of a 'sunken forest' have been recorded intermittently for at least a century. Pollen analysis published in 1938 was reinforced by subsequent studies of sediment, crustacea and marine organisms as well as by carbon dating and dendrochronology of the tree stumps themselves.

They were found to be the petrified remains of an ancient fenland forest. Oak, pine, birch, willow and hazel stumps, roots and branches, still soft and wood-like to the touch, had lain preserved beneath the sand in acidic peat for between 4,500 and 5,000 years, their growth rings and root systems clearly visible.

A 17th-century legend, probably derived from the 13th-century *Black Book of Carmarthen*, tells of the loss of 'Cantre'r Gwaelod' (the Sunken Hundred), a low-lying kingdom that stretched for 32km (20 miles) west of Borth into Cardigan Bay. The kingdom – protected from the encroaching sea by dykes and floodgates – was under the care of Seithenyn. Described as a notorious drunk, through his negligence, the sea swept through open floodgates, submerging the land forever with it.

In the 1960s, a local butcher fittingly discovered the skeleton of an auroch, the extinct ancestor of domestic cattle. Archaeology revealed Mesolithic tools, fossilized human and animal footprints, scattered burnt stones and fragments of a wattle walkway – indicating the presence of people in an environment of rising water levels.

The legend of Cantre'r Gwaelod could recall distant memories of the submergence of wooded lands by rising sea levels, which occurred following the last ice age. In 2012, large-scale coastal defences at Borth were constructed to withstand rising sea levels caused by 21st-century climate change.

Cwm Byddog

Radnorshire, Powys

At Cwm Byddog near Hay-on-Wye in Mid Wales stands a small ancient wood spanning a deep ravine, and hosting some of Radnorshire's oldest oaks. Lapsed pollards – have been left unworked for decades – the largest measures 6.5m (21.3ft) around its bole, and is estimated to be around 450 years old.

A huge lapsed coppice alder – with a reputation for providing the best charcoal for gunpowder – grows by the stream on the valley floor.

The quiet, tranquil setting displays a broad range of wild flowers including bluebell, yellow archangel, cuckoo-pint, wood anemone, ransom, golden saxifrage, dog's mercury and early purple orchid. There are also over 100 species of tree epiphyte, moss and lichen and the rare wood decay specialist beetle *(Dorcatoma substriata)* – each of these individually provide a good indicator of ancient woodland; but when found together in such abundance they provide a certainty.

The valley may not always have appeared so peaceful as it does today, however. A motte and bailey castle was built at its highest point and was thought to have been constructed by Cadwallon ap Madog in the 12th century. Prince of Maelienydd, founder of Cwmhir Abbey in 1176, Cadwallon was ally to Owain Gwynedd – first Prince of Wales – and had rallied with him against Henry II at the Battle of Crogen in the Ceiriog Valley in 1165, marked by the monumental 'Oak at the Gate of the Dead'. Cadwallon certainly built other castles in the area and, living by the sword, died by it: he was killed by the men of Roger Mortimer, his nemesis, in 1179, while returning under protection from Henry II's court, and having signed a peace treaty. Mortimer was imprisoned for the murder, but nevertheless managed to gain control of Maelienydd and Cwmhir Abbey by 1195.

The 3.4ha (8.4 acre) site at Cwm Byydog – a nature reserve – has been managed by the Radnorshire Wildlife Trust since 1998, to protect its rare flora and fauna, and prolong the life its ancient oak pollards.

In the year 1174, Melyenith was in the possession of Cadwallon ap Madawc, cousin german to prince Rhys; Elvel was held by Eineon Clyd, and Gwyrthrynion by Eineon ap Rhys, both sons-in-law to that illustrious prince.

From *The itinerary through Wales* by Giraldus Cambrensis (c1146-c1223)

ABOVE: Largest of the oak pollards at Cwm Byydog, 2018
OPPOSITE: Ancient oak pollards at Cwm Byydog, 2018

Moccas Park Wye Valley, Herefordshire

I fear those grey old men of Moccas, those misshapen old men that stand waiting and watching century after century, biding god's time with both feet in the grave and yet tiring down and seeing out generation after generation… No human hand set those oaks. They are 'the trees which the Lord hath planted'. They look as if they had been at the beginning and making of the world, and they will probably see its end.
Diary entry, Reverend Francis Kilvert, Saturday 22 April 1876

Tracing the origin of Moccas Deer Park prior to the early 17th century is difficult. Links to Arthurian legend, Arthur's Stone, a Neolithic burial chamber, a Norman motte and bailey castle and the presence of a 13th-century deer park at Dorstone Parish attest to a long history of human occupation in the area. Yet the rich bounty of ancient trees in the 137ha (338 acre) NNR (National Nature Reserve – the first of its kind) and SSSI (Site of Special Scientific Interest) reveal a heritage treescape that could have been carved from Britain's early wildwood. A rare beetle *Hypebaeus flavipes*, has been found in just four individual British oak trees – all of them at Moccas Park.

The estate escaped excessive landscaping, although in the 18th century both Humphry Repton and Lancelot 'Capability' Brown submitted plans to the then owner of Moccas Court, Sir George Cornewall who, while implementing some landscaping, largely ignored them.

Sweet chestnuts measuring over 10m (33ft) in girth and thought to date to 1661, veteran ash, field maple, beech and hawthorn speckle the landscape, but it is the ancient, hollow, pollard oaks that mark Moccas as one of the country's most important wood pasture sites.

In 1830, the celebrated Moccas Oak *(Quercus robur)* was measured at a staggering 11m (36ft) in circumference. By 1890 it was dead, no trace by 1930, but saved for posterity in Jacob George Strutt's fine engraving.

ABOVE: The Moccas Oak by J G Strutt, 1840
OPPOSITE: Ancient 8m Moccas Oak, 2017
BELOW: Fallow deer graze among the ancient oaks, 2017

While Sir George may not have implemented Brown and Repton's plans to the letter, a huge quantity of timber amounting to some £20–30,000 was removed from the site during his tenure. This was at least partially offset by the efforts of his forester, J Webster, who claimed to have planted 300,000 oaks and other trees in the park. While he was criticised by some for planting the trees too densely – crowding out established veterans – many of his plantings survive to this day, mature specimens of over 200 years contributing to succession.

Today Moccas remains in private ownership, having passed through only four families since the 13th century. The park's current owners, the Chester-Masters, keep it private, due to its ecological importance for biodiversity, and have commissioned Natural England to manage it under a Higher Level Stewardship Agreement.

The wood pasture supports a diverse range of fungi and lichen, habitat for an impressive population of invertebrates, bats and birds. I spotted ravens, herons, buzzards, bees nesting in a hollow ash and a large hare on my visit. Hares were said to have been abundant in 1814 – a long-term Moccas resident.

Around 300 fallow deer graze the park (a process supplemented by cattle and sheep), which is enclosed by drystone wall and wooden park pale, as it has been for centuries.

Since 1985, over 1,000 trees have been planted as part of a restoration project, using early OS maps (which mark the location of mature individual trees very accurately) as a guide for planting density. Coniferous plantations are being systematically removed, to release veteran trees from overshading. The veterans are also being haloed to release them from younger, light-depriving trees. In addition, since 1990, five to ten young oaks a year are being pollarded in traditional fashion, and decaying wood is left in situ to ensure continued and future habitats for the rare biodiversity that Moccas Park hosts, and has probably hosted for millennia.

As we came down the wooded slopes of the lower hillside into the glades of the park the herds of deer were moving under the brown oaks and the brilliant green hawthorns, and we came upon the tallest largest stateliest ash I ever saw.

Diary entry, Reverend Francis Kilvert, 22 April 1876

ABOVE: 8m (26ft) girthed giant ash, as mentioned by Reverend Francis Kilvert in 1876. 2017

OPPOSITE: Ancient oaks in the deer park, 2017

Kentchurch Court
Herefordshire

But she to none of them her love did cast,
 Save to the noble knight Sir Scudamore,
 To whom her loving hart she linked fast
 In faithfull love, t'abide for ever more.
From *The Faerie Qveene* by Edmund Spenser, 1590

ABOVE: Kentchurch Court, c1910

BELOW: Ancient sweet chestnuts in the old deer park, 2018

OPPOSITE: Ancient yew in the old deer park, sweet chestnut felled a century ago, and yet never collected by the purchaser, 2018

Straddling the English/Welsh border near Hereford, the ancient manor of Kentchurch Court covers an area of some 2,000ha (5,000 acres) across the Monnow Valley.

The estate's origins can be traced back to 1042 when Edward the Confessor (1003-1066) commissioned Ralph Scudamore – a stonemason from Normandy – to build a motte and bailey castle in the Norman style at Ewyas Harold, to defend against attacks from Wales. The castle was sleighted in 1052, possibly when Gruffydd ap Llywelyn – the last King of Wales – ravaged Herefordshire, sacking Leominster in the process.

The Scudamores built a manor house on the present site in the 14th century; an early tower survives and is said to have harboured the Welsh freedom fighter Owain Glyndwr following his defeat by the English and subsequent disappearance in 1412.

In 1547, one John Scudamore enlarged the estate by purchasing 44ha (110 acres) of the adjacent deer park from the Knights Hospitaller. The land, originally a gift from Richard I, had previously been reserved for the royal hunt. It is in the old deer park – where a herd of 250 fallow deer still roam – that some of Hereford's finest ancient trees survive, dating back to the estate's foundation and including a champion hazel, a possible champion field maple, some colossal yews, oaks, small-leaved limes and sweet chestnuts, many of which have their roots in the medieval period. The yews in particular are living links to the county's early forest. Kentchurch tradition still holds it bad luck to fell a yew.

A thousand years later, Kentchurch remains with the Scudamore family, as a private residence which occasionally opens its gardens to the public. It is that luxury of time and space, of being (partially) left alone, that is in part responsible for the longevity of Kentchurch's trees.

Jack O'Kent's Oak Herefordshire

The presence of great geological features, huge boulders and standing stones is often explained in mythology as the result of titanic struggles between adversaries – devils and giants, heroes and villains.

One such character, Jack or John O'Kent, features strongly in the folklore of the Welsh marches and Herefordshire, and is remembered not only in the landscape but also in one of the largest oaks in Britain, which bears his name.

Standing on high ground in the old deer park at Kentchurch Court, Jack O'Kent's Oak *(Quercus robur)* measures a hefty 11.37m (37.3ft) around its burred and gnarled trunk, a survivor of ancient wood pasture which probably dates back to the arrival of the Scudamore family 1,000 years ago. On my visit, a colony of honey bees had recently made the hollow trunk their home – their preferred natural habitat. Once there were many more hollow trees in the landscape; thankfully bee populations are now underpinned by the nation's bee keepers. The oak is in good company: its nearest neighbour, a 9.2m (30ft) yew *(Taxus baccata)*, topiarised by grazing deer – a process which could have inspired the fashion of yew topiaries in the 17th and 18th centuries – is in all probability older still.

Jack is said to have outwitted the Devil on several occasions, colluding with him to build a weir on Orcop Hill and create a fishpond. The requisite rocks were dropped on Galway Hill, 4.8km (3 miles) away, visible today at 'White Rocks'. Another tale tells of Jack asking the Devil to help him build a bridge across the River Monmow from Grosmont to Kentchurch, promising the first soul to cross it as payment. Spying a dog, Jack threw a bone across the completed bridge. The dog followed, thus denying the Devil a human soul. Fearing for his own soul, Jack stabled horses in the cellar at Kentchurch in readiness for a hasty retreat should the need arise. On his deathbed he is said to have requested that his 'liver and lights' (offal) be impaled on the church steeple, for a dove and raven to fight over. His soul would only be saved if the dove triumphed. Nobody seems to know the outcome of the duel…

There is an aged oak in Kentchurch Park, belonging to Colonel Scudamore, called John O'Kent's oak, to which he is said to have fastened his dogs.
From an introduction (1851) to *John a Kent and John a Cumber* by Anthony Munday, 1590

ABOVE: Bees nesting in the hollow of Jack O'Kent's Oak
BELOW AND OPPOSITE: Jack O'Kent's Oak, 2018

KENTCHURCH COURT

The Forest of Dean Gloucestershire

One of Britain's best known forests, Dean lies between the great rivers Severn and Wye. A Saxon Royal Forest prior to the Norman invasion, William I continued to hold it under Forest Law, and it was from there, in 1069 that he issued an order to 'exterminate the people of Northumbria' in retaliation for a Norman defeat at York. More than 100,000 perished in the reprisal, and 'Fire, slaughter and desolation made a wilderness there,' according to William of Malmesbury.

Dean's long history has seen many changes. Rich in iron ore and coal, the forest floor was extensively mined by ancient Britons and Romans, and by the 13th century held 72 forges. A royal charter states that 'any man born of a free father in the Hundred of St Briavels, who had worked for a year and a day in a mine, might become a free miner'. A mark of the forest's long-term industrial exploitation.

A great hurricane of 1662 was said to have torn down 'no less than three thousand oaks'. In 1638 Charles I sold the forest wholesale to Sir John Wintour, who proceeded to exploit its remaining trees, partly to supply oak timber for navy ships. Following protestations from commoners almost to the point of rioting, a commission was set up to investigate Wintour's activities. Of 30,000 timber trees recorded, Wintour's tenure of decimation left only 200 standing. An Act of Parliament in 1688 enclosed 4450ha (11,000 acres) to ensure timber supplies to the royal dockyards.

A thousand years ago, wolves, wild boar, red, roe and fallow deer were common, documented in the hunts of King John and Henry III – 100 boar were ordered for a Christmas feast in 1254. By 1300 the wolves were extinguished, the boar were hunted out within a century, and the deer were removed in 1850. Small numbers of roe have returned, yet surprisingly around 60 boar – either escaped or released in 1999 – have made a resounding comeback, and number around 1,000 feral animals.

The queen of forests all, that west of severn lie;
Her broad and bushy top Dean holdeth up so high,
The lesser are not seen, she is so tall and large.
Micheal Drayton, 1563-1631

ABOVE: Wye Valley from Symonds Yat, c1910
OPPOSITE: Wye Valley from Symonds Yat, 2015
BELOW: The Newland Oak, Dean's largest recorded oak at 13.72m (45ft) in circumference in 1950. Collapsed under snowfall in 1955, died after being set fire to in 1970. Photo, 1898

Happy is the eye, betwixt the Severn and the Wye.
Old Dean proverb

FOREST OF DEAN

Irregular tracks and horrid shade so dark and dreary as to render its inhabitants more fierce and audacious in robberies.
William Camden, 1607

Raglan Castle Oak

Raglan, Monmouthshire

Raglan Castle is sometimes described as one of the most impressive castles in Wales. Of late construction, the current building was begun in 1435 by Sir William ap Thomas, the 'blue knight of Gwent', probably on the site of an earlier Norman motte and bailey. It was extended by his son, William Herbert, who was knighted for military service under Henry VI. He was also loyal to Edward IV during the Wars of the Roses, an allegiance that cost him his head after defeat at the battle of Edgecote Moor in 1469.

The castle passed to Sir Charles Somerset, Earl of Worcester, and it was under his tenure that the gardens were developed, linking it to the parkland and deer park.

During the Civil War, Raglan Castle, still in the hands of the Royalist Herberts, came under siege by Cromwellian forces. The castle garrison, amounting to 800 soldiers, felled an avenue of trees leading to the castle gates to prevent them from being used by Parliamentary forces. The siege lasted for two months, one of the longest in the Civil War. The castle was built so well, however, that orders to sleight it were only partially accomplished.

In the 1950s, a piece of Tudor oak-wood panelling originally sacked from the castle was discovered in a cow shed. It was restored and displayed in the visitor centre.

By the 19th century, the castle parkland was turned over to agriculture. Surprisingly, after such a turbulent history, a hollow 5.26m (17.25ft) girthed sessile oak *(Quercus petraea)*, stands forlorn, within sling-shot of the castle walls. A lone veteran survivor of a medieval wood pasture landscape, pollarding suggests a previous life as a worked tree.

Above: Raglan Castle 1900
Below: Raglan Castle Oak 2016

The Broadstone Oaks

Staunton, Monmouthshire

On a high wooded ridge offering spectacular views to the Black Mountains between Staunton (stone town) and Coleford, stands the Buck Stone, one of only a few 'rocking stones' in Britain.

Apparently named after the once-numerous bucks that took rest in its shade, at a certain angle it was said to take on the appearance of a buck.

In 1885, a party of actors set off from the Agincourt Inn at Monmouth, with the landlord, to see if the Buck Stone actually rocked. Arriving in high spirits, they cajoled the 40-ton stone into action and, dislodging it, saw it crash downhill and break into several pieces. The Commissioners of Woods and Forests, at a cost of £500, hauled the broken stones back up the hill, and cemented them into place. The Buck Stone rocks no more.

In the valley below at Broadstones Farm stand a further clutch of natural stone boulders, the largest known as the Broadstone after which the farm is named. Overlooked not just by the Buck Stone but by most of the visiting population, an avenue of veteran sessile pollard oaks appear to grow from the very stones themselves. They line either side of the English/Welsh border, and were likely planted to mark the purpose, growing under protection of the stones from grazing animals.

A placard at the farm, now a campsite and fishery, declares: 'In 1775, nothing happened here.' It may be true, although throughout history the border has been hotly contested. Now the hollowing, gnarled ancient markers stand as roosts for owls and bats.

Nearby, Staunton Woods are reputed to have inspired John Walter Bratton to write lyrics for 'The Teddy Bear's Picnic' in 1932. He met with his girlfriend Maud there, who told him; 'Every teddy bear who's been good, is sure of a treat today'.

If you go down to the woods today, you're sure of a big suprise.
ABOVE: The Buck Stone, 1910 BELOW: A Broadstone oak, 2014

Tintern Abbey Monmouthshire

*...the lambs on the tree-nooked hillside this day bleating
heard in Blake's old ear,
& the silent thought of Wordsworth in eld Stillness
clouds passing through skeleton arches of Tintern Abbey –
Bard Nameless as the Vast, babble to Vastness!*
From *Wales Visitation* by Allen Ginsberg, 1967

ABOVE: Tintern Abbey, c1910
BELOW: Ancient yew growing from rocks at the Devil's Pulpit, 2018
OPPOSITE: Tintern Abbey seen from the Devil's Pulpit, 2018

The sprawling ruins of Tintern Abbey paint an evocative scene, nestled amongst ancient upland woodlands on the Welsh bank of the River Wye.

From at least the 18th century, poets and artists have been drawn to the region, inspired by the picturesque scene, bestowing diverse literature ranging from the romantic writings of William Wordsworth to the LSD-fuelled musings of Alan Ginsberg.

When Wordsworth visited, the abbey had been in ruin for over 260 years, falling to Henry VIII's dissolution in 1536, when he granted land rights to the Lord of Chepstow, Henry Somerset.

Founded by Walter of Clare in 1131, Tintern was the first Cistercian Abbey in Wales, lucky to have survived intact through the medieval Welsh uprisings.

Exempted from Forest Law in a charter of 1223, Tintern profited from its agricultural granges, pasture and coppice with standard hillside woodlands, which it used to fuel its quarries, forges and tannery. The woods remain well stocked with a broad range of native trees, rising steeply to Devil's Pulpit at Offa's Dyke – a natural rock formation from where the Devil is said to have tried tempting the monks of Tintern away from their spiritual calling without success.

Some staggering, ancient, twisted yews grow near the crest of the hill, although several are dying from overshading caused by beech trees. But one yew in particular survives in fine fettle, perched beside the Devil's Pulpit, its serpentine roots inexplicably clinging to bare rock.

The day is come when I again repose
Here, under this dark sycamore, and view
These plots of cottage-ground, these orchard-tufts,
Which at this season, with their unripe fruits,
Are clad in one green hue, and lose themselves
'Mid groves and copses. Once again I see
These hedge-rows, hardly hedge-rows, little lines
Of sportive wood run wild: these pastoral farms,
Green to the very door; and wreaths of smoke
Sent up, in silence, from among the trees!
With some uncertain notice, as might seem
Of vagrant dwellers in the houseless woods,
Or of some Hermit's cave, where by his fire
The Hermit sits alone.

From *Lines Composed a Few Miles above Tintern Abbey*
by William Wordsworth, 1798

Wychwood Forest

Oxfordshire

Wychwood is a classic example of Britain's changing landscape. Now largely agricultural, it retains some of the largest areas of ancient semi-natural broadleaved woodland in Oxfordshire.

Neolithic barrows and Bronze Age earthworks confirm prehistoric human occupation, suggesting a more open landscape around those developed areas – open vistas of surrounding countryside were a prerequisite at defensive and sacred sites. Grim's Ditch, an Iron Age linear earthwork enclosing 3,400ha (8,400 acres), contains gaps which may have been plugged by areas of woodland now lost.

By Roman times, the area was crossed by Akeman Street – a major Roman road linking Watling Street with the Fosse Way. It was an era that saw vast clearance of woodland to fuel the Roman occupation and prepare the land for agricultural use. Following the fall of the Empire and the Roman retreat from Britain, some areas returned to greenwood; today, 1,500 years later, they are classified as ancient woodland.

Wychwood acquired its name in the Saxon period: *Hwiccewudu* meaning wood of the Hwicce tribe. It was hunted by the Saxon elite: King Ethelred (The Unready) had a hunting lodge built at Woodstock and held a council there in the late 10th century, issuing a decree of peace for the nation.

By 1086, Wychwood was a Norman Royal Forest, covering an area around 32,400ha (80,000 acres) according to the Domesday Survey of that year. The perambulation in 1300 asserted forest bounds encompassing lands from Chadleigh in the north and Witney in the south, Taynton in the west and Woodstock in the east, by which time it had reduced in size to 20,000ha (50,000 acres).

A late 18th-century report by Crown Commissioners declared only 173 oaks fit for ship-building, where previously the Navy had taken 500. Common rights then offered grazing only; the removal of deadwood was punishable by heavy fine, ensuring Oxford's gaol received a steady flow of poachers.

By 1792 only 1,500ha (3,700 acres) of the forest remained, finally disafforested in 1857, opening the way for enclosures to follow.

WYCHWOOD FOREST

Blenheim Park Oxfordshire

The Wychwood Project – a charity that aims to restore and conserve the Royal Forest – and the Woodland Trust who have re-wooded previously agricultural land, have revived interest in Wychwood Forest. Remnant ancient woodland can be found near Bruern Abbey, and living links in the form of ancient trees survive at Cornbury, and most notably at Blenheim Park.

Formerly known as Woodstock – a stockaded settlement in the woods – Blenheim was the site of Ethelred's Saxon hunting lodge, and may have already been a royal residence in the days of King Alfred.

In 1110, Henry I – youngest son of the Conqueror – set about creating a Royal Palace of stone on high ground to the west of the River Glyme (later turned into a lake by 'Capability' Brown) and opposite the current Blenheim Palace. He also had the park enclosed by a stone wall 11.25km (seven miles) in circumference – the first of its kind – to contain not only the King's deer and wild boar, but also a menagerie of exotic wild animals. There were lions, leopards, camels, lynx and a porcupine – reported at the time to have shot its sharp quills at dogs which tried to attack it.

As well as revising Forest Laws with the Assize of Woodstock in 1184, Henry II found time to woo his love Rosamund in the park, which was also the scene of his first major disagreement with Thomas à Becket.

Later, King John was a frequent visitor to Blenheim, staying there shortly after sealing the Magna Carta in 1215. Henry VIII hunted and shot there too. Records from the time detail 'browsers to cut winter fodder for deer' (most likely holly – 'tree-hay'), for which they received a 'billet of wood as long as the handle of his axe, as thick as he could carry'. Henry's daughter Elizabeth had a less pleasant stay, imprisoned under order of her sister Mary, before her eventual ascension to the throne. Charles I sought refuge from the plague at the palace, and hunted two bucks there in 1644, before the Parliamentarians took Woodstock by siege in 1646, five years before Charles's execution.

ABOVE: Blenheim Palace, 1818
BELOW: Ancient Blenheim oak, 2016

The Beast of Blenheim

High Park, Blenheim Park, Oxfordshire

Where the oaks and bracken exist was meant to remain as an example to all time of the imposing effect of a medieval forest.

Charles Spencer-Churchill, ninth Duke of Marlborough, 1871-1934

Although little of the original Wychwood Royal Forest remains in Oxfordshire – with most woodland laid out to non-native plantation forestry – a rich bevy of ancient oaks survives in High Park at Blenheim. This fine remnant of ancient oak wood pasture was formerly the site of Woodstock's medieval deer park, with trees that could date back to Henry I's walled enclosure of 1110 or beyond.

Almost 1,000 veteran and ancient oaks are scattered across High Park, with many more dead and decaying left to lie as they fall – key components of Blenheim Park's SSSI status, designated in 1956. Unlike most of Blenheim Park, High Park is a private area unaccessible to the general public, and it retains an air of wildness about it. Deer were kept here until the First World War, and some wild fallow, roe and muntjac still roam the oak pasture.

The largest girthed oak *(Quercus robur)* at High Park, and for that matter the whole of Oxfordshire, measures 10.37m (34ft) in circumference, a giant millennial pollard and living link to the ancient Royal Forest. Unnamed – unusual for such an iconic tree – it seemed fitting to call the hollow, mossed sentinel The Blenheim Beast. Perhaps Ethelred's Oak would be more apt, as the tree may have been a sapling in those distant Saxon days.

On one visit I spied insect traps set within the hollow trunk, by former Kew scientist Aljos Farjon to discover just what creatures the tree still supports. Three 'Red Data Book' – documenting rare and endangered species – beetles are already known there.

Blenheim's 2017 Management Plan endeavours to maintain minimum intervention into deadwood habitats; halo young growth from around veteran trees; monitor the impact of Acute Oak Decline found on some oaks; and plant acorns collected from ancient High Park oaks in preference to natural regeneration.

ABOVE AND BELOW: The Blenheim Beast, 2016

The King Oak

High Park, Blenheim Park, Oxfordshire

They paused in an open space of meadow-land, beautifully skirted by large oaks and sycamores, one of which, as king of the forest, stood a little detached from the rest, as if scorning the vicinity of any rival. It was scathed and knarled in the branches, but the immense trunk still showed to what gigantic size the monarch of the forest can attain in the groves of merry England. 'That is called the King's Oak,' said Joseline; 'The oldest men of Woodstock know not how old it is: they say Henry used to sit under it with fair Rosamund, and see the lasses dance, and the lads of the village run races, and wrestle for belts or bonnets.'

From *Woodstock* or *The Cavalier a tale of 1651* by Walter Scott, 1826

ABOVE: Ancient Blenheim oak, 1903
OPPOSITE: The King Oak, 2016

Of the many fine oaks at High Park, perhaps the most impressive is the King Oak *(Quercus robur)*, an ancient pollard that, at 9.1m (29.85ft) in circumference, ranks as one of its oldest, with estimates suggesting the tree could date back to the reign of Henry I.

Historic as the oak is, the name may have been transferred from an even older specimen, described in *The Just Devil of Woodstock,* by Thomas Widdows in 1666. In 1649, Commonwealth Commissioners arrived to commandeer the estate, and took to staying in the run-down palace buildings. According to the story, they were driven from the estate by the Devil, who threw glass, stones, bones and stinking water at them, and lit faggots of wood from the King Oak – felled by the commissioners for representing the monarchy. After the Restoration, the poltergeist was revealed to have been Joe Collins, a royalist.

Winston Churchill – arguably Blenheim's most famous resident – was born at the palace in 1874 and, following his death 90 years later, was buried at St Martin's Churchyard in Bladon, within sight of High Park. It was likely Blenheim's giant oaks that inspired his quote: 'Solitary trees, if they grow at all, grow strong'.

WYCHWOOD FOREST

The Harry Potter Tree
Blenheim Park, Oxfordshire

ABOVE AND BELOW: The Harry Potter Tree, 2019 and 2016

The current Blenheim Palace, built between 1705 and 1722, was gifted to John Churchill, First Duke of Marlborough, for his contribution to the War of the Spanish Succession. Originally Woodstock Park, the estate was renamed after the defining Battle of Blenheim in 1704, fought against a Franco/Bulgarian alliance in Blindheim, Bavaria.

Between 1768 and 1771, Lancelot 'Capability' Brown embarked on a ten-year landscape project, damming the River Glyme to create Blenheim's lake in 1763, and in the process flooding the lower rooms of Sir John Vanbrugh's Grand Bridge, constructed in 1710.

As part of his vision, Brown planted thousands of trees, retaining some established in the park and adding others where appropriate to enhance the vistas. Either side of the Grand Bridge, Brown planted four stands of native beech *(Fagus sylvatica)*, many of which remain as mature specimens to this day.

On the cascades, to the west of the bridge on the north bank of the lake, Brown introduced stands of cedar of Lebanon *(Cedrus lebani)* – a celebrated Middle Eastern tree – which have grown into sizeable examples. The largest of the stand was described in 1965 by the late Alan Mitchell – esteemed forester, dendrologist and botanist – as the most remarkable of its species in the country, measuring 26m (85ft) high, 8m (27ft) broad, with a 6m (20ft) bole.

The hollow tree has since been named the Harry Potter Tree, as it appears in a scene from the fifth Harry Potter film, *Order of the Phoenix*, where a young Severus Snape – wizard and potion master – can be seen dangling by his feet from the canopy, the butt end of a mischievous spell cast by Harry's father, James.

In 2016, concerned about decay, heritage tree specialists supported the canopy of the ageing tree with tension cables, which were connected to other trees in the grove.

ABOVE LEFT: Veteran lakeside oak photographed in 1906 and 2016

ABOVE RIGHT: Ancient oak in High Park

LEFT: Lost grindstone in High Park – a relic of the wood's working past, 2015

RIGHT: Swan glides across the lake, 2015

Before the hill stands the cedar, abundant and tall, Her good shadow is full of rejoicing, It covers the thorn bush, covers the dark-hued sloe...
From *The Epic of Gilgamesh*, c2100BC

Kingswood Forest Gloucestershire

Visiting Kingswood, a busy suburb east of Bristol, you could be forgiven for being unaware that it was once central to Kingswood Forest, a Saxon royal hunting ground that extended from the River Severn to the Sodbury Hills, running south almost as far as Bath.

Administered from Bristol Castle, the first recorded Chief Ranger of Kingswood (the King's Wood) was Ella, who died in 920. A Saxon Royal Palace or hunting lodge was established at Pucklechurch, and it was there that King Edmund I, grandson of Alfred the Great, was killed in 946. During a feast on St Augustine's Day, Edmund spotted an uninvited guest, Leofa – a previously exiled thief – who he approached, took by the hair and threw to the ground. Leofa leapt to his feet and stabbed the king in the chest. For his trouble, Leofa was killed on the spot by the King's men, but too late, Edmund had been assassinated.

After the Conquest, Kingswood continued as a Royal Forest until 1228 when Henry III committed large tracts of it to common land.

In the 15th-century, a church was dedicated to St Giles, patron saint of woods (due to his hermitic isolation in a wood near Nimes), at Stapleton.

Following the Dissolution of the Monasteries, further lands were disafforested, until 1631, when Charles I separated Bristol Castle from the forest and opened the forest to mining, quarrying, pasture and timber cutting, initiating the enclosure of land by lords of adjacent manors and other local landowners. Kingswood subsequently became notorious as a haunt of thieves and outlaws.

In the 17th century, coal was exploited to supply the increasing demand from industrial Bristol. The miners were described by city merchants as 'a barbarous and ungovernable people'. Another viewpoint might be that they were not afraid to stand up for their rights, which were commonly abused. John Wesley felt sufficiently motivated to give his first open-air sermon in Kingswood at Hanham Mount in 1739.

Common rights were withdrawn by the Stapleton Enclosure Act in 1779, after which development increased rapidly, expanding into the densely populated suburb seen today.

Evidence of the ancient forest is revealed in the unlikeliest of places: the Staple Hill Oak, marked on a map of Kingswood from 1610 (around which the village of Staple Hill developed), is remembered by a pub of the same name. Remnant open-grown oaks survive on a roundabout near Siston Common; and place names such as Cock Road (after the Woodcocks that once frequented Kingswood), Woodstock and King's Chase abound.

Red deer rut amongst oak wood pasture at Ashton Court 2017

Near Bristol, lieth Kingswood-forest. formerly of a much larger extent, but now drawn within the bounds of five thousand acres. It consists chiefly of Coal-mines; several Gentry being possessors of it by Patent from the Crown.
From *Britannia* by William Camden, 1586

Here King Edmund died on St Augustine's Day. It was widely known how he ended his days, that Liofa stabbed him at Pucklechurch. And Æthelflæd of Damerham, daughter of Ealdorman Ælfgar, was then his queen.
From *Anglo-Saxon Chronicle*, MS tr. Michael Swanton, 2005.

KINGSWOOD FOREST

The beautiful vale of Ashton, the place of all others which I remember with most feeling.
Robert Southey (1774-1843)

ABOVE: Ashton Court, c1915
BELOW: Red deer stag, 2017
OPPOSITE: The Fattest Oak – 8.72m, 2017

Ashton Court Bristol

Deriving from Saxon 'Ash Town', Ashton Court contained a sixth-century log-and-thatch hunting lodge before the estate was gifted to Geoffrey, Bishop of Coutances, builder of Bristol Castle and provider of war horses to William I.

William de Lyons, once thought to have come to Britain with the Conqueror in 1066, in fact purchased Ashton Court c1290 and built a manor house. In 1392, his descendent Thomas was granted licence by Richard II to enclose a deer park and rabbit warren, providing a perfect setting and continuity of habitat for the many ancient oaks, small-leaved limes and sweet chestnuts that still thrive.

Another constant was the presence of the Smyth family, commencing with John, a successful Bristol merchant who purchased the manor from Richard Choke in 1545 and extended the park, but never lived there.

Later Smyths did make Ashton Court their home. John Hugh commissioned Humphry Repton to remodel the east front of the house, plant avenues of trees and wooded enclosures in the late 18th century. The renovation was never realised, but around 10,000 parkland trees were planted for Repton, and many still remain, including some veteran sweet chestnuts. Sir John Hugh Smyth also had an 11km (seven-mile) wall, not less than 3.6m (12ft) high at any point, built around the estate to contain the deer and cattle and probably exclude unwanted guests, according to his misanthropic reputation.

The estate provided steady employment to foresters, gamekeepers and carpenters who worked the woods, copses and grazing as sustainable resources. A Victorian photograph shows an avenue of elm trees leading to the house, all lost before 1900, an all too familiar fate of the elm.

Grenville Smyth, a keen fox hunter, had cedars of Lebanon and giant sequoias planted near the house in the 1880s, several of which survive.

The estate remained in possession of the Smyths, not without struggles, trials and tribulations, until 1946 when Dame Esme died. The house and grounds remained empty and fell into decline until 1959 when purchased by Bristol City Council, who have restored it over the years. Two golf courses and deer enclosures, one for red and one for fallow, were added in 1976, and a management program was introduced to preserve SSSI status for wood pasture habitat hosting rare invertebrates.

Ashton Court's future is unclear, as the council struggles to make it pay. Events such as the annual Balloon Festival and music concerts may help.

KINGSWOOD FOREST

The Domesday Oak
Ashton Court, Bristol

Ashton Court's sylvan legacy, owed mainly to its long, continous parkland history, has left Bristol with its finest collection of ancient and veteran trees.

The 350ha (865 acre) site ranks among the finest in the west country, hosting 444 recorded veteran trees including oak, small-leaved lime, ash, hawthorn, sweet chestnut, field maple and crack willow – many of them pollards.

At the head of a ridge above a field named The Goram, a row of six giant sweet chestnuts, thought to have been planted in the 15th-century, leads to Ashton Court's best known and probably oldest tree, an ancient sentinel named The Domesday Oak *(Quercus robur)*. As with other trees in Britain that share the name, the oak's 9.19m (30ft) circumference proffers an assumed millennial status. Official estimates offer an age of 700 years, suggesting a planting commensurate with the establishment of the 14th-century deer park.

Concerns were raised over the tree's future when a large crack appeared in its trunk in 2011 causing a supporting cable to break. Five A-frame beams made from green oak were specially constructed to prop the fragile beast. They were expected to last a century but, unfortunately, nature had other ideas, and in 2014 a sizeable part of the tree collapsed, substantially reducing its size.

The large amount of decaying wood was left where it fell, to encourage to Ashton Court's rare habitat species, supporting brown tree ants *(Lasius brunneus)* jewel beetles *(Agrilus sinuatus)* and other saproxilic beetles.

Thankfully, the tree lives on, providing a luxuriant crown which still produces acorns, from which I have grown several saplings, with a view to replanting near their parent tree and hopefully prolong the gene pool and heritage of the Domesday Oak.

ABOVE: Ancient sweet chestnut, 2014
OPPOSITE: The collossal wreck of the Domesday Oak, 2014
BELOW: Veteran oak, 2014

Leigh Woods Bristol

When a boy, he was almost a resident amongst St Vincent's Rocks and Leigh Woods. The view, from the Coronation Road, of the Hotwells, with Clifton, and its triple crescents, he thought surpassed any of its kind in Europe.

From *Reminiscences of Samuel Taylor Coleridge and Robert Southey* by Joseph Cottle, 1847

ABOVE: Nightingale Valley, Leigh Woods, 1906
BELOW: Veteran 3.85m (12.6ft) pollard oak, 2017
OPPOSITE: Leigh Woods in autumn seen from Clifton – Nightingale Valley rising to Stokeleigh Camp, 2017

Nineteenth-century Poet Laureate Robert Southey's fondness for the panorama looking north across the River Avon to Bristol is perfectly tenable. He surely appreciated the vista due west across the Avon Gorge as well, at a time before Brunel's iconic suspension bridge had been constructed. Equally attractive, Clifton Down offers a spectacular view towards Leigh Woods, rising from Nightingale Valley up to its Stokeleigh Iron Age Hillfort, a key vantage point overlooking the gorge. Southey spent much time there, and lies buried in Long Ashton churchyard.

An ancient woodland covering 200ha (500 acres), long connected with Ashton Court, Leigh Woods was in danger of development following completion of the Suspension Bridge in 1864, built to provide easy access to Bristol. Previously, river crossings had been restricted to Rownham Ferry or Bedminster Bridge.

Following housing development, the Leigh Woods Land Company was formed to preserve the area's natural beauty. By 1909 a large part of the woods were gifted to the National Trust, in whose care it remains today, the remainder controlled by the Forestry Commission.

The southern part of Leigh Woods was historically grazed oak wood pasture until the end of the 19th century, the northern part was semi-natural ancient woodland consisting mainly of coppiced hazel and ash with oak standards, surrounded by a wood bank to exclude deer and other grazing animals. An extension of Ashton Court Estate, Leigh Woods was a busy, working woodland.

A record from 1386 accounts for 16 boat loads of coppice wood for delivery to St Augustine's Priory, and the cutting of timber to construct the south-west wing extension at Ashton Court in the 17th-century.

Lead and copper smelting, coal mining and quarrying – including quartz crystals known as Bristol diamonds and celestine – all took place between the 17th and early 20th centuries, leaving their mark on the landscape. During the Second World War a large area of the wood was felled for the war effort, with further losses to veteran oaks recorded in the 1950s.

Leigh still retains around 200 oak pollards, several visible as the wood is entererd from its southern entrance on North Road. Restoration pollarding has been carried out on some of the oaks since the 1990s, including the clearance of around 700 ash and sycamore trees, which were shading out the oaks, along with the reintroduction of cattle grazing to restore and maintain the wood pasture features.

Veteran yews *(Taxus bacatta)* are common on the thinner soils, with one specimen dividing the parish wall, built in 1813, which it predates by a good couple of centuries. An even larger specimen stands further into the wood, beside a large recently monolithed beech. Ancient coppard small-leaved limes *(Tilia cordata)*, and lapsed coppiced specimens of the rare wild service tree *(Sorbus torminalis)* also grow in the wood.

Leigh Woods naturally harbours a broad diversity of wildlife, including bats that roost in the veteran hollowing trees and in caves, rare invertebrates, including white letter hairstreak butterflies, false darkling and soldier beetles, a large variety of birds including the threatened bullfinch and breeding pairs of ravens and peregrine falcons.

Nationally rare plants, including Bristol rock-cress, western spiked speedwell, fly orchid, bee orchid and others have also been recorded, and an abundance of bluebells and wood anemones flower in springtime.

Each year Leigh Woods attracts thousands of visitors from Bristol and beyond to walk, experience nature, run and mountain bike.

ABOVE: Oak pollard in Leigh Woods, c1900
BELOW: 4.73m (15.5ft) veteran yew, 2016

Bristol Whitebeam

Avon Gorge, Bristol

Science tells us that the Avon Gorge was formed during the last ice age, when the river was diverted and forced its way through the rock. Bristolian legend, however, tells another story...

Two giants – Goram and Ghyston – both sought the hand of Avona, a beautiful Wiltshire maiden. Avona promised her hand to the first who could drain a great lake to the south of Bristol. The giants set to work, but Goram tired and soon stopped to rest, while Ghyston forged on, dug the Avon Gorge to drain the lake in Avona's honour, and was duly married to her. Goram, inconsolable in his loss, threw himself into the Severn and was drowned. You can still see his head and shoulders in the estuary rocks of Flat Holm and Steep Holm. Ghyston's cave on St Vincent's rocks on the east side of the gorge is named after the victor.

Studies in the 16th century revealed the gorge to harbour some rare plants with some 30 species thriving there, including Bristol rock cress, Bristol onion, autumn squill and spiked speedwell. The steep rock faces have kept the gorge largely tree-free and have provided a sanctuary for the plants, cementing its place as a top UK botanical site.

Twenty-one species of whitebeam – the widest diversity of the species found anywhere – favour the steepness of the gorge, away from other competing trees. Three of these species are endemic to the Avon Gorge and Leigh Woods: Bristol whitebeam *(Sorbus bristoliensis)*, Leigh Woods whitebeam *(Sorbus leighensis)* and Wilmot's whitebeam *(Sorbus wilmottiana)* are found wild nowhere else on earth. There are probably only around 100 living specimens of Wilmot's whitebeam growing in the gorge.

Other endemic variants of whitebeam occur 24km (15 miles) to the south in Cheddar Gorge – the location offering a similar environment – and in the Wye Valley 32km (20 miles) away.

The story makes these to have been mighty gyants, and they contended which way the Rivers Avon and Frome should vent themselves into the Severn.
From *The Ancient and Present State of Glocestershire* by Sir Robert Atkyns, 1712

ABOVE: Clifton Suspension Bridge and Avon Gorge, c1910
BELOW: Bristol whitebeam at Leigh Woods, 2017

The Forest of Essex

*I loved the forest walks and beechen woods
Where pleasant Stockdale showed me far away
Wild Enfield Chase and pleasant Edmonton.
While giant London, known to all the world,
Was nothing but a guess among the trees,
Though only half a day from where we stood.*

From *A Walk in the Forest* by John Clare, 1840-41

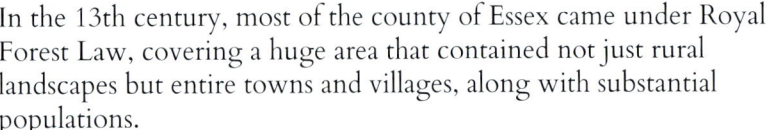

In the 13th century, most of the county of Essex came under Royal Forest Law, covering a huge area that contained not just rural landscapes but entire towns and villages, along with substantial populations.

England's last Saxon king, Harold, established a school of learning at Waltham (meaning town in the forest), building on an earlier religious house founded by Canute. Edward the Confessor also frequented the forest, building a hunting lodge at Havering, just 32km (20 miles) from his palace at Westminster. It was said to be his favourite palace, save one annoyance: the continual warbling of nightingales, who 'disturbed his meditations and drew his mind from God'. In the Civil War, Cromwell's troops destroyed the palace and stabled horses in its chapel.

The Charter of the Forest, granted by Henry III in 1217 under direct pressure to re-establish rights of access for free men, released much of the Forest of Essex from Forest Law. But the King reneged on the deal just three years later, claiming that surveyors were mistaken in their judgement of its bounds, and the forest was restored to him.

Edward I, finding himself short of funds, disafforested Essex in return for a large sum of money. The forest bounds were reduced to a smaller area nearer to the capital, and named Waltham Forest after its nearest town. In 1301 it covered an area of 24,280ha (60,000 acres) and had changed little in size 300 years later.

As Waltham grew, by the 17th century the forest borders became truncated, and smaller areas took the names of neighbouring towns Epping and Hainault, by which they are still known.

ABOVE AND OPPOSITE: Old Knobbley, 2017
BELOW: Veteran wood pasture oak at Mistley, 2017

Old Knobbley Mistley, Essex

At Furze Hill in Mistley near Manningtree, stands one of Essex's largest old oaks. Measuring 9.6m (31.5ft) near the base of its squat, hollow bole, it is thought to be in the region of 800 years old.

Bordering Mistley Common to the east, close to the Stour Estuary, Furze Hill (named after gorse – common in overgrazed areas) was part of Mistley Manor, bought in the early 18th century by Richard Rigby, who built Mistley Hall there. The village, known as Mistleythorn at that time, appears to have been just outside the bounds of Essex Forest.

Densley wooded today, a host of younger veteran pollard oaks at Furze Hill and the plotting of open-grown trees on first edition OS maps, attest to its previous life as wood pasture hosting open-grown trees harvested for firewood over centuries.

In the 17th century, the common may have been the setting for local women trying to escape the clutches of Matthew Hopkins from Manningtree, self-proclaimed Witch Finder General. Hopkins was responsible for the death of around 300 women accused of 'making covenants with the Devil'.

Despite Old Knobbley's status as one of Essex's most enduring oaks, the tree was little known outside the local area, until the turn of the last millennium when a website was created in its honour. In 2016, Old Knobbley was nominated for the Tree of the Year Competition, narrowly missing out on the title to the Major Oak, but gaining celebrity status along the way.

In January 2018, not for the first time, the tree was set fire to, and a near calamity was avoided due to the efforts of the local fire brigade. Children from Mistley Primary School were so upset by the news, that some of them wrote to the local newspaper to share their feelings for the tree.

Owned by Mistley Parish Council, Old Knobbley and friends (now retired) stand as community assets.

Epping Forest Essex

Epping, situated between East London and Essex, is the 'Cockney Forest'. While it may be renowned for its amenity as a recreational and leisure destination, the 2400ha (5930 acres) ancient woodland has supplied the city and its local commoners with firewood for centuries.

Unlike Hainault, which largely lost its ancient trees in the early 19th century to steam ploughs in the drive for more agricultural land, Epping retains good remnants of the former Essex Forest. Noted in the Domesday Survey as Essex's largest concentration of woodland, it still hosts large numbers of veteran trees. Hornbeam dominates the low ground, beech the high, with oak in between.

An immense forest extends itself, beautified with woods and groves, and full of the lairs and coverts of beasts and game, stags, bucks, boars, and wild bulls.
From *A Description of the most noble city of London* by William Fitz-Stephen, 11th century.

Grazing rights for commoners necessitated the pollarding of trees as opposed to coppicing, to protect regrowth from browsing – a working practice which providing a sustainable source of wood before the term sustainable was ever coined.

Historically, the forest was well stocked with large, browsing mammals. Its last wild boar was reputedly hunted down by the Earl of Essex in the 16th century. Epping's last red deer herd was removed

ABOVE: Beech pollards at Monk Wood, Loughton, 1909
LEFT: Beech pollards, 2017

to Windsor in 1827, pine marten was last seen in 1883, and the last polecat was killed in the 1890s.

Deer parks were established for the hunt in the 13th century at Fairmead, Monkhams and Copped Hall, and Queen Elizabeth's Hunting Lodge (built by Henry VIII in 1543) still stands near Chingford.

Dick Turpin, while famed for his notorious exploits as a highwayman, supplemented his living by selling poached venison, or 'black mutton' as it was known. Fallow deer are still plentiful, but after concerns over their numbers being reduced in road accidents, a large herd was contained in 1959.

Above: Hornbeam pollards, 2017
Left: Hornbeam pollards, 1909
Below: Oak pollards, 2017

Enclosure started early in Epping Forest, but accelerated in earnest in the 19th century, driven largely by Lord Monington who, as Lord Warden, sought to turn it into farmland. A task that he more or less accomplished at nearby Hainault Forest. In the face of conviction, Thomas Willingdale, a woodman from Loughton, defended his right to lop wood for winter fuel. Thomas' stand against enclosure was a catalyst that led to the Epping Forest Act in 1878, which secured the future of Epping under the stewardship of the Corporation of London, in whose care it remains. A precedent was set across the country.

Amesbury Banks

Epping Forest, Essex

*While I roved about the forest, long and bitterly meditating,
There I heard them in darkness, at the mystical ceremony,
Loosely robed in flying raiment,
   sang the terrible prophetesses.
"Fear not, isle of blowing woodland, isle of silvery parapets!"*
From *Boadicea* by Alfred Lord Tennyson, 1864

ABOVE AND BELOW: Amesbury Banks, 1909 and 2017

As elsewhere, Epping Forest was inhabited from prehistory. The British freedom fighter Casivellaunus watched Julius Caesar and his Roman army advance across the River Lea, from a vantage point at Amesbury Banks, an Iron Age hill-fort in the north of the forest. Casivellaunus was defeated, and for good measure Caesar laid waste to a large tract of forest. Its legacy lives on in the name of Brentwood (meaning burnt wood).

However, it is perhaps Britain's foremost Celtic heroine whose story is most fondly associated with Amesbury Banks. Over a century after Caesar's initial foray into Britain, Boudicca, queen of the Iceni, found herself on the receiving end of a public whipping at the hands of the Romans after the death of her husband, Prasutagus. This humiliation, along with the rape of her two daughters and the loss of her throne, stirred Boudicca to revenge.

In AD61 a fierce revolt followed and saw the violent sacking of Colchester and London. Boosted by victory, Bouddica's huge army, now numbering some 230,000 men, women and children, marched on to Veralamium (St Albans).

She was utterly defeated by Suetonius, who, having just annihilated the Druids at Anglessey, inflicted a massacre on the Celts. The Queen, along with her daughters, took her own life rather than be captive to the Romans.

While historians favour the West Midlands, on the great Roman road of Watling Street as Boudicca's final resting place, the exact location remains unknown. An Epping Forest legend, however, connects her with Amesbury Banks, asserting that her last stand was there, in the forest, and that she lies buried beneath the trees, along with her slaughtered warriors and their families.

The Fairmead Oak

Epping Forest, Essex

At Fairmead Bottom, on a mound of the lower slope of Hill Wood, once stood the Fairmead Oak, a grand old open-grown pollard. Thought to have been 800 years old, the tree last bore leaves in the early years of the 20th century, yet its huge form persisted in slow decay until the 1950s when it was destroyed by fire.

Legend has Henry VIII eating his breakfast under the shade of the Fairmead Oak on the morning of 19th January 1536, in anticipation of the sounding of cannons from London, to signal the execution of his second wife, Anne Boleyn. Sure enough, the cannons rolled their thunder, confirming to Henry that the deed was done. He promptly set off for a days' hunting, 'returned gaily', and the very next morning married Anne's maid of honour, Jane Seymour.

Henry had a hunting lodge and deer park at Fairmead, which became the venue of the annual 'Epping Hunt', where every Easter Monday, the people of London were granted the right to hunt for a day in the forest. A long-held belief that it was accorded by Henry III in the 13th century cannot be substantiated, but it seems to have been entertained by Edward IV two centuries later.

By the 19th century the hunt had become 'a holiday to all the idle, dissolute, vagabondish people of London', with a solitary fallow deer carted from pub to pub; it was all but discontinued by the 1860s.

Now grazed by longhorn cattle, Fairmead Bottom retains an open aspect, and contains two oaks thought to have descended from the Fairmead Oak.

The stag was roused from his lair, and hunted according to the old style known as hunting "at force." He broke from the cover of the forest, led into the open country towards Hainault, and gave a final and exciting chase. After a good run he was killed at West Ham, and the chase of the wild red deer in Epping Forest was over for ever.

From *London's Forest* by P J S Perceval, 1909

ABOVE: *The mighty dead - Fairmead Oak, Chingford*, print from a painting by Louis Burleigh Bruhl, 1909

Huntsmen and hounds with difficulty reached their appointed place, while the pollard oaks and beeches swarmed with men and boys eager to view the release of the stag.

From *London's Forest* by P J S Perceval, 1909

The Tottenham Oak

Bruce Castle Park, Tottenham, London

Veteran trees can be found in the most unlikely of places. Tottenham, hardly known as a green oasis, nurtures Harringey's largest and probably oldest oak at Bruce Castle Park.

The 6.22m (20.4ft) hollowing, veteran sessile oak *(Quercus petraea)* is the centrepiece of Tottenham's first public park, opened in 1892, and it may have stood in the grounds for up to 500 years.

The current manor house dates to the 16th century, and stands as one of England's oldest red-brick buildings. A 15th-century round tower is thought to be Britain's last surviving 'hawk mews' – a relic of hawking, a popular pastime of the age.

Bruce Castle is the last of Tottenham's four recorded manors, and could date to the 11th century, when a building is said to have been erected by Earl Waltheof, husband of William the Conqueror's niece, Judith. The estate passed to Robert the Bruce, who stayed at the manor when he made the 'king's peace' to Edward I in 1302. The Crown took possession from Robert after he asserted his claim to Scotland's throne in 1306.

Over the following four centuries, Bruce Castle witnessed a succession of resident lords and barons, and entertained visits from both Henry VIII in 1516 (when he met up with his sister, Margaret, Queen of Scots there), and his daughter Elizabeth I in 1593.

By 1827 the Hill family had bought the estate and turned it into a private boarding school for boys, which remained open until 1892 when Tottenham Council took ownership and made it a public park, and turned the house into a museum and archive.

Public access has seen the Tottenham Oak become dear to many, and in 2018 the tree was nominated for Woodland Trust's Tree of the Year competition. It finished as a runner up, securing an arboricultural survey and monetary grant to ensure its continued care.

Robert Bruce retired to England, and, settling on his grandfather's estate at Tottenham, repaired the castle, and acquiring an adjacent manor, named it and the castle Bruce.
From Old And New London by Walter Thornbury, 1876

ABOVE: Bruce Castle, c1876
BELOW: The Tottenham Oak, 2018

Britain's Oldest Door Westminster Abbey, London

The middle (door), which is very thick, lined with skins like parchment, and driven full of nails. These skins, they by tradition tell us, were some skins of the Danes, tann'd and given here as a memorial of our delivery from them.
From *History of the Abbey Church of St Peter's, Westminster* by John Dart, 1723

Little remains of Edward the Confessor's 11th-century Westminster Abbey, constructed on a religious site that may have its origins in the seventh century. Today's abbey is largely the legacy of a complete rebuild ordered by Henry III in the mid-13th century, and dedicated to Edward, who had by then been canonized.

In the outer vestibule which leads to Henry's Chapter House – where monks met for prayer and the king held early parliaments – stands the only remaining Saxon timber relic of Edward's abbey. The Pyx Door, an inauspicious portal, leads from the vaulted Vestibule to a small room. It once continued to the Pyx Chamber, the passageway blocked following a burglary in 1303, when it was used as a treasury.

The robbery appeared to be an inside job, and the abbot along with 38 monks were summoned to the Tower of London for questioning. Two were found guilty, but all monastic suspects were exonerated. Richard Pudlicote from Oxfordshire, however, found in possession of some of the stolen treasure, was sentenced to death and taken from the Tower to Tothill Lane in a wheelbarrow, where he was hung. Following his death, folklore relates how Pudlicote's skin was flayed, and attached to the door to deter would-be thieves.

In 2005, dendrochronology on the 1.27m (4ft) x 2m (6.5ft) Pyx Door revealed its five panels to be made of seasoned local oak, and that it was reduced in size by about 100mm (4in) on all sides prior to relocation in its current setting. A construction date of around 1050 conferred an age of almost 1,000 years on the still-functioning door – Britain's oldest – fitting perfectly with Edward's construction period.

Further analysis discovered that the traces of skin were in fact cow hide, thus dispelling the human skin myth, which probably developed from tales of pillaging Danish pirates being flayed alive and pinned to doors. A macabre Georgian fascination saw pieces of skin removed from church doors across the south east as souvenirs. It seems likely that monastic doors were covered with cow hide for painting, a tradition lost over the centuries.

ABOVE: Entrance to Vestible and Chapter House – man seated is just to the right of Britain's oldest door, 1881
BELOW: Britain's oldest door, 2019

GREATER LONDON

The Old Oaks

Tooting, Greater London

A region of villas and nursery gardens, very pleasant.
From *Handbook to the Environs of London* by James Thorne, 1876

Between Balham, Tooting and Streatham lie Tooting Bec and Tooting Gravely Commons, which once stretched from Battersea to Mitcham.

The name Tooting derives from its Saxon dweller Totas, and by the time of Domesday in 1086 was known as Totinges. By then there were two manors: one given by William the Conqueror to Richard of Tonbridge, who bequeathed it to the Norman abbey of Notre Dame du Bec; the other belonging to Chertsey Abbey, which passed into the hands of the De Gravenell family.

Like Wandsworth to the north, Mitcham to the south and Wimbledon to the west, Tooting's commons gave rights to commoners to graze livestock, gather heather and turf and cut firewood by pollarding trees out of the reach of grazing animals.

In 1600 Elizabeth I visited, and it is thought that the avenue of veteran oaks that line Dr Johnson Avenue – the road that divides the two commons – were planted.

At the time the area was still largely rural, and it remained so until the mid-19th century as London's population expanded into the suburbs. Dissected by road and railway lines, the threat of development loomed. Following community protests, the Metropolitan Board of Works acquired Tooting Bec Common in 1873 and Tooting Graveney Common in 1875, and was entrusted with their preservation. Responsibility passed to Wandsworth Borough Council, who came under severe critisism in 2017 for felling a 150-year-old avenue of horse chestnut trees. Dubbed the 'Tooting Chainsaw Massacre', 72 trees were removed despite strong local opposition supported by the Mayor of London, Sadiq Khan.

Led only by an archive photograph showing 'The Old Oaks' (right), I was surprised to find a large number of remnant oaks on the commons, the largest of which – a 4.8m (15.7ft) girthed ancient hollow pollard – recalls age-old rural practices in a modern urban recreational environment.

ABOVE: The Old Oaks, c1910

BELOW: Oak avenue at the division of the two commons, thought to have been planted in 1600 following the visit of Elizabeth I, 2018

OPPOSITE: The common's fattest, oldest, hollow pollard oak, 2018

The felling of trees, barking of timber, making fagots, repairing roads, cost £581... and to collect acorns for the deer incurs an expense of £45... Against this has to be placed, £450, sale of livestock, £642 sale of timber, £352 for grazing rents, and £240 for venison-fees.
From *Revenue and Expenditure of the Forests*, 1851

Richmond Park Greater London

Given its proximity to the capital and the effect of 4,500,000 million visitors a year, it is a minor miracle that Richmond Park survives as a National Nature Reserve at all. Yet the park finds itself ranked among the country's top ten locations for veteran and ancient oaks and their associated rare invertebrates and fungi, hosting 347 strains of beetle and ten of Britain's 18 species of bat.

Fires deliberately started in the Second World War diverted 600 Luftwaffe bombs away from the city, and the loss of 1,000 trees (few were veterans) during the Great Storm of 1987 are evidence of a fortuitous history against all odds.

In terms of medieval deer parks, Richmond's founding was relatively late. Charles I emparked the 1,000ha (2,500 acre) site with a brick wall between 1634 and 1637 and stocked it with red and fallow deer for the hunt. It was another nail in the coffin for his tenure as king, representing a penchant for extravagance over the interests of the country.

Deer parks had existed at Richmond and Sheen since 1292 – Henry VIII hunted at Sheen Chase – and, while their precise boundaries remain unclear, their long standing as treed landscapes is evident.

Before Charles' intervention, Richmond Park was a mixture of wood pasture and common land. It wasn't until 1751 that, after a long battle, limited access was granted to the public. Full access was granted a century later with the Crown Parks Act.

The oldest oaks in the park, such as the hollow Royal Oak *(Quercus robur)* – 6.11m (20ft) in girth and estimated to be around 750 years old – survive from ancient wood pasture and pre-date the deer park. Richmond's ancient oaks are mostly lapsed pollards; the practice has recently been reintroduced with the planting of 200 open-grown oaks sourced from Richmond acorns, which are pollarded in January every three years.

ABOVE: The Royal Oak, 2019

BELOW: Ancient border oaks near Pembroke Lodge, over a century apart, 1910 and 2019

OPPOSITE: Game in Richmond Park, 1840

King and Queen Oak

Chenies, Buckinghamshire

There has been a manor house at Chenies since at least 1180, when it was owned by the Cheyne family after who the village, formerly Isenhampstead, became known. A deer park had been established by 1335, although its boundaries are difficult to define today. Surviving features from that period include a dungeon, a well and a priest hole. But perhaps most remarkable of all is an ancient oak *(Quercus robur)* named after Queen Elizabeth, that stands on the lawn just south of the 15th-century manor house, seat of Sir John Russell, the First Earl of Bedford.

Elizabeth stayed at Chenies, and is said to have lost a piece of jewellery whilst sitting beneath the tree, hence the oak's name. Several stories depict Elizabeth's penchant for resting under oaks, with the trees concerned all receiving her epithet. She apparently heard of her imminent rise to sovereignty whilst reading her bible beneath Elizabeth's Oak at Hatfield House; shot a deer under cover of Elizabeth's Oak at Midhurst Park; and 'hung her slippers' (a polite medieval term for spending a penny) from Elizabeth's Oak at Ninfield, en route to Brighton.

Elizabeth's father Henry VIII visited in 1534 and 1542 as a friend of John Russell, and it seems an earlier name for the tree – King's Oak – was probably thanks to him (as evidenced by the early 20th-century postcard, right).

While a relatively small 6.5m (21.3ft) trunk circumference may not appear to uphold a local belief bestowing 1,000 years on the tree, the archive photograph and clear evidence on the ground of it once having a much larger footprint (I estimated it to have previously measured around 9m (29.5ft), could rank Queen Elizabeth's Oak alongside the 120 or so other 9m plus champions of the British oak world.

The olde House of the Cheyneis is so translated by my Lorde Russel that litle or nothing of it yn a maner remaynith untranslated: and a great deale of the House in ben newly set up made of Bricke and Timber: and fair logginges be new erected in the gardein. The House is within diverse Places richely painted with antique Workes of White and Blak. And there be about the House 2 Parkes, as I remember.

From *Itinerary of John Leland,* 1535-43

ABOVE: Postcard marked as King's Oak, 1905

OPPOSITE: Known as Queen Elizabeth Oak, 2018 Still producing acorns – the current owner Charles having planted several for succession – the oak, in its decline, provides habitat for moss, lichen, invertebrates, hornets and little owls.

Burnham Beeches
Buckinghamshire

Julius Caesar declared in his account of the 'Gallic Wars' that although Britain shared most of Gaul's species of tree, beech was nowhere to be seen, leading some to claim it non-native, and subsequently introduced. However, pollen records and anciently submerged coastal forests have confirmed that beech is indeed native, at least in south east England and southern Wales.

Perhaps England's most famous beech woods are found in the Chilterns. These tall and magnificent trees are associated with bodgers (chair makers) who lived and worked amongst them, pole-lathing beech wood into legs for Windsor chairs, an industry that boomed around High Wycombe from the early 1800s up until the 1950s.

Buckinghamshire's greatest collection of ancient beech trees, however, lie further east at Burnham Beeches. Situated between historic Bernwood Forest to the north and Windsor Great Forest to the south, Burnham Beeches was never part of a Royal Forest. It was almost lost to development in the late 19th century until the Corporation of London stepped in and purchased the 374.6ha (925.6 acre) site for the 'recreation and enjoyment of the people' in 1880. Today, around 420 mostly beech and some oak pollards remain.

Consisting of wood pasture, ancient woodland, coppice woods, ponds, streams and grassland, Burnham Beeches is an historic 'wooded common', and it abuts common heathland and woodland. It is a remnant working landscape – worked mainly for firewood – with human

RIGHT: Burnham Beeches – commoner collecting a fuel faggot amongst ancient pollards, cattle graze in the background, by A Wilmore, c1890

occupation dating to at least the Iron Age (an earthwork enclosure from the eighth century BC is still visible).

Already a Saxon manor held by Elmar in the time of Edward the Confessor, the Domesday Survey records Walter Fitz Otho as Lord of Burnham in 1086, with 'woodland enough to feed 600 swine'. Pannage – the practice where pigs fed on mast and acorns amongst the pollards each autumn – was an important medieval commons resource, along with livestock grazing and firewood pollarded in cycles above grazing height every 12 to 20 years.

In 1226 Burnham came under the auspices of Burnham Abbey, which continued to harvest its woodland resources until the Dissolution of the Monasteries, when Henry VIII appointed himself as overlord.

Local tradition cites Burnham Beeches as the source for Oliver Cromwell's musket stocks during the Civil War between 1642 and 1651.

It is difficult to say how long Burnham Beeches has been continually pollarded, but with the age of some beech trees estimated at between 400 and 500 years (the process of pollarding appears to prolong their natural life), and the oldest tree on site – Druid's Oak – thought to be around 800 years, Burnham Beeches may have been operating in that way for a thousand years or more.

Burnham Beeches' decline coincided with the rise of the coal industry around 200 years ago. Coal was cheaper, and largely replaced firewood as the go-to fuel source (although Queen Victoria is said to have insisted on having charcoal from Burnham Beeches delivered all the way to Balmoral for the Royal fire). As a result, the pollards were neglected, left to grow where they stood.

Surprisingly, two world wars seem to have had little effect on the ancient trees, despite a large area of Burnham being requisitioned for military transport in the Second World War, when only

ABOVE AND BELOW: Ancient beech pollards, Burnham Beeches, c1900 and 2013

ten pollards were reported to have been lost.

By the late 20th century, coupled with a decline in grazing, many of the trees had become top heavy, were unstable, and overshaded by new growth. It was suggested the trees should be left to their own devices, but a team led by Helen Read started to experiment by clearing dense regrowth around the ancient trees and re-pollarding them.

Some casualties were expected, and some trees suffered, but all the pollards now have individual management plans aimed at prolonging their lives. New pollards are also being created from young trees along with the reintroduction of grazing, with cattle, ponies, pigs and sheep employed to maintain an open wooded landscape.

Burnham Beeches is an internationally important nature reserve hosting over 60 rare or endangered species, and receives around 500,000 annual visitors.

ABOVE & BELOW: Burnham Beeches a century apart, 1910 and 2013

The Cage Pollard

Burnham Beeches, Buckinghamshire

ABOVE: Gray's Beech, immortalised in his poem, c1930
BELOW: The Jenny Lind Tree, c1915

BELOW: Pollards at Burnham Beeches, 1910
OPPOSITE: The Cage Pollard, 2013

The Victorian fascination with Burnham's ancient trees, coupled with its close proximity to London, ensured that Burnham Beeches became a popular destination for artists, poets, singers, composers, musicians and tourists alike.

The poet Thomas Gray (1716-1771) is believed to have written a verse of his poem *Elegy Written in a Country Churchyard* after visiting a favourite spot beside the stream near Burnham's southern edge, where a 'nodding beech' was named after him.

Similarly, Felix Mendelssohn (1809-1847) is said to have been sufficiently inspired to compose his music for *A Midsummer Night's Dream* on one of his frequent visits and had a beech named after him.

Jenny Lind (1820-1887), a Swedish opera singer known as the 'Swedish Nightingale' and close friend of Mendelssohn, is believed to have practised arias beneath a giant beech that was subsequently named after her.

Along with the composer Frederic Chopin and actress Fanny Kemble, Mendelssohn and Lind were drawn to Burnham Beeches to be entertained by the historian George Grote and his socialite wife who moved to East Burnham from London in 1838.

All the above-named trees were lost either to storms or decay, but images of them were captured for posterity in archive photographs (see right). The stump of Mendelssohn's Beech, which fell in the storm of 1990, was removed and relocated at the Barbican as a memorial. Young replacement trees have been re-planted and stand in their place.

Today's centrepiece beech, named The Cage Pollard by Helen Read after its hollow, fragmented, cage-like trunk 5.21m (17ft), is one of Burnham's oldest pollards, twisted and decaying, propped for support, fenced for protection. The tree featured in the 1991 film *Robin Hood Prince of Thieves* as the backdrop in a burial scene.

*There at the foot of yonder nodding beech,
That wreathes its old fantastic roots so high,
His listless length at noontide he would stretch,
and pore upon the brook that babbled by.*
From *Elegy Written in a Country Churchyard* by
Thomas Gray, 1745

BERKSHIRE FOREST

The Aldworth Yew Aldworth, Berkshire

At only 3.53m (11.5ft) in circumference, the Aldworth Yew's diminutive size belies its ancient status – estimated at between 1,000 and 2,000 years. Ring-counts made by Allen Meredith in 2015 suggest the higher age, with 530 rings counted in 22.8cm (9in) of decaying wood. Dendrochronology confirmed 51 growth rings in just one centimetre of wood, so it is likely the tree predates the early 13th-century church, connecting it with earlier pagan worship.

The Ridgeway, an ancient trackway running from the Berkshire Downs to Wiltshire and often described as Britain's oldest road, passes close by, and a complete Roman pottery kiln was found just a mile to the south west.

By the 13th century, Aldworth Manor was in the hands of the Norman de la Beche family, remembered by nine over-sized stone effigies known as the Aldworth Giants, reflecting a folkloric tradition of ancient giants residing in the village. Elizabeth I visited the church with the Earl of Leicester to see the giants in the 16th century, when four of them were known as John Long, John Strong, John Never Afraid and John Ever Afraid.

According to tradition Aldworth yew was used to make long bows for both Alfred the Great in the ninth century and for English archers at the Battle of Agincourt in 1415. The area is certainly rich in yew – four other veterans stand in the churchyard, and many others line the surrounding hedgerows.

Alfred, Lord Tennyson (1809-1892) lived at Aldworth Manor for a time, and was so taken with the place that as poet laureate he made his title 'Baron Tennyson of Aldworth'. His 1849 poem *In Memoriam* is thought to be an ode to the Aldworth Yew.

In 1644 the tree measured 8.2m (27ft) in circumference, the same in 1760, 1799 and 1896 when it was described by Reverend W L Newman as a ruin, a description that still fits its present condition.

A shadow of its former self, the tree remains, having survived lightning strikes and storm damage in January 1976. Encouragingly, the tree has grown two new stems from its rootstock – thus confirming yew's propensity to regenerate.

Old Yew, which graspest at the stones
  That name the under-lying dead,
  Thy fibres net the dreamless head,
Thy roots are wrapt about the bones.
From *In Memoriam* by Alfred, Lord Tennyson, 1849

ABOVE: The Aldworth Yew, 1921
BELOW: The Aldworth Yew, 2018

The Old Oaks Basildon Park, Berkshire

BELOW: The Old Oaks, c1930

Each year, as the snowdrops flower, I make an annual pilgrimage to my local postcard fair in Somerset. I usually leave with a few gems, some familiar, others not so. In 2017 I left with an image of the Basildon Oaks. Until then I was unaware of their existence, so I set off to visit the National Trust property in Berkshire.

Basildon Park has seen plenty of activity during its 800-year history. First granted to Elias de Colleshull by Edward II in 1311, it passed to the Yonges in the 16th century, and was purchased by the Fanes in 1654.

Sir Francis Sykes, who made his fortune in Bengal with the East India Company, bought the estate in 1771 and built the Georgian manor house as a base from which to realise his political ambitions. Allegations of corruption dogged Sykes, damaging his finances and political career. Basildon was inherited by his son of the same name, who went down in history as the inspiration for Charles Dickens' cruel villain Bill Sykes in *Oliver Twist* in 1838. In that same year Sykes sold the property for £97,000 to Hampshire-born millionaire James Morrison.

The estate's fortunes continued to decline, and in 1924 Basildon House was offered for sale to America – to be taken apart and rebuilt brick by brick – for the sum of £1,000,000. The proposal never came to fruition.

Through the two world wars, Basildon was commandeered for military training, and held German and Italian prisoners of war. It is no small miracle so many veteran trees on the 162ha (400 acres) of parkland survived this period, including a late 17th-century horse chestnut, hawthorn and black mulberry, and limes and oaks planted during the Sykes era. Imagine my surprise and joy when I discovered that one of the Basildon Oaks featured on the postcard (above) was still standing – its 6.43m (21ft) hollow, gnarled trunk probably dating to the Tudor era when the Yonges ruled the roost.

'What a beautiful oak!' exclaimed Miss Temple... 'It has the reputation of being planted by Sir Francis Walsingham,' said Ferdinand. 'An ancestor of mine married his daughter. He was the father of Sir Walsingham, the portrait in the gallery with the white stick. You remember it?' 'Perfectly: that beautiful portrait! It must be, at all events, a very old tree.'

From *Henrietta Temple: A Love Story* by Benjamin Disraeli, 1859

Aldermaston Court

Aldermaston, Berkshire

The village of Aldermaston (named after the Saxon Ealdorman associated with the area) is best known for its atomic weapons centre, but was historically a manor of King Harold – England's ultimate Saxon King – from where he could hunt the western reaches of Windsor Forest. Following Harold's death at Hastings in 1066, William seized Aldermaston along with his other estates.

In the early 12th century, Henry I granted the manor to Robert Achard, who founded the church there, and a deer park has featured since at least 1202. The 15th-16th-century manor house burnt down in 1843, and the current house dates to 1848. In 1938 the estate was auctioned and bought by Associated Electrical Industries, so ending family ownership.

The grounds remain largely open wood pasture, with some landscaping, and include around 20 ancient pollard oaks, the same number of sweet chestnuts, and many more veteran and notable trees. The parkland was much reduced firstly by the RAF stationed in its southern part during the Second World War, then more severely in 1950 by the Atomic Weapons Research Establishment which remains active and is a source of much controversy.

Previously many more ancient trees would have stood in the grounds – including the giant Domesday Oak, now lost – with survivors mostly shaded out by regrowth from competitors, and little or no management to support them.

Since the 1930s, Aldermaston has been an important centre for the production of cricket bats, using the locally grown cricket bat willow *(Salix vitellina)*. For this, around 70 trees are cut each year from sustainable stock numbering around 1,000.

In 2014, property developers Praxis bought Aldermarston Court and submitted plans to build 227 houses, with the loss of around 180 trees. Praxis argued that their destruction was necessary in order to secure the survival of the remaining trees, a point hotly contested by the Woodland Trust and other environmental bodies. In 2018, West Berkshire Council declined the planning application.

This is an unprecedented planning application in terms of the devastating impact on an historic wood pasture and parkland, which is an incredibly valuable wildlife habitat. And to say that the remaining fraction of deer park can only be managed properly by first building houses on it is a complete contradiction.

Jill Butler, ancient tree specialist, 2016

ABOVE: Aldermaston Court, c1910
BELOW AND OPPOSITE: Ancient Aldermaston oaks, 2018

BERKSHIRE FOREST

Windsor Great Forest

Berkshire, Surrey

Thy forests, Windsor! and thy green retreats,
At once the Monarch's and the Muse's seats,
Invite my lays. Be present, sylvan maids!
Unlock your springs, and open all your shades.
From *Windsor Forest* by Alexander Pope, 1713

Human occupation at Windsor dates back to at least the Bronze Age, with archaeological evidence revealing a well-established 9th-century Saxon community on the south bank of the Thames. It was the site of a former Roman settlement and a vantage point for travel and hunting forays into the forest.

The name Windsor derives from 'windlass (lifting equipment) by the river', and refers to the original settlement at Old Windsor. New Windsor grew up around Windsor Castle to the north west of the old town. It was built by William I shortly after the Norman Conquest – then a wooden motte and bailey fortress designed to protect London and subjugate the Saxons.

Windsor was prime hunting land, not densely wooded, but open wood pasture on the London clay soil in the north, changing to scattered birch on the Bagshot sands in the south.

William was quick to establish Forest Law at Windsor to quench his thirst for the hunt. Forest borders were further extended by his son Henry I, who was the first to take up residence at the castle around 1105. Since then it has been the principal residence of the monarchy, and the world's longest continually inhabited castle.

By 1132 Windsor Great Park held the largest royal deer park in England, with the forest reputed to be 120 miles in circumference, the great Crouch Oak at Addlestone marking its south eastern boundary.

Wood cutting in Windsor Forest, engraved by T A Prior from a painting by J Linnell, c1860

In 1215, due north of Windsor at Runnymede, King John was forced by his Barons to seal Magna Carta – binding English rulers to 'refuse justice to none'. The event is likely to have taken place in the shadow of the ancient Ankerwyke Yew – a tree estimated to be a thousand years old at the time, and remaining in good health today.

Two years later, John's ten-year-old son and successor Henry III sealed the Charter of the Forest, which for the first time provided a degree of protection for the common man who worked in the forest.

The year 1222 saw a great storm wreak devastation in Windsor's woodlands, and Henry ordered that the timber be recorded and sold – a right usually reserved for foresters. By then, Windsor was notorious for outlaws, and in 1234 Henry, whilst on his way to Reading, narrowly evaded the charms of one Richard Siward – who terrorised the area with a band of 40 men.

Between 1275 and 1278 numerous trees were felled to provide fencing to enclose the park, and deer numbers were in decline. Red deer were transported from Wiltshire's Chute Forest to re-stock.

'Wild bulls' – escaped cattle rather than aurochs (their extinct wild ancestors) – were captured and sold to pay the expenses of the king's children. Old breed longhorn cattle have more recently been introduced to naturally graze and maintain the historic oak wood pasture, much as their extinct ancestors shaped the wider treescape in the prehistoric era.

Henry VIII was so keen on the hunt that he extended the forest all the way to his palaces at Hampton Court and Nonsuch near Epsom. Ten years after his death it reverted to its previous footprint.

Efforts by Charles I to re-enforce Forest Law played a part in his downfall – its harsh rules popularly resented – and by the coming of the Civil War upkeep of the forest had deteriorated; oaks were felled, deer were killed and destruction of the park pale was extensive.

With the restoration of the monarchy in 1660,

ABOVE: The Watch Oak, where hunters waited for their prey, 1850
BELOW: The Watch Oak, hollow, 7.2m in circumference, 2018

Charles II took back control of the forest and re-stocked the park with deer for the hunt. In 1680 he established the Long Walk with a 4.25km (2.64 mile) double avenue of elms, which mostly survived until Dutch elm disease claimed them in the 1920s.

James II took to hunting fox around 1685, a pursuit previously considered unsuitable for a king, founding a tradition that would continue with the gentry even after it was outlawed in 2004.

History remembers the Waltham Blacks – a band of poachers who blackened their faces to avoid detection. Driven by a sense of injustice foisted on them by Forest Law and land enclosures, from 1722 a gang of seven targeted Windsor, to poach its deer and fish. They were confronted by keepers and shot one of them dead. The 'Black Act', passed in 1723 to combat poaching, saw to the execution of four of the men, whose bodies afterwards hung in chains in the forest.

Later that century in 1789, Virginia Water – the largest man-made lake of its time in Britain – was dug by troops overseen by William Augustus, Duke of Cumberland, Ranger of Windsor Great Park. Although the park continued to provide deer for the table for subsequent monarchs, Windsor was finally disafforested in 1817 by Act of Parliament.

After an absence of some 30 years, a herd of red deer was re-established by The Duke of Edinburgh – Ranger of Windsor Great Park – in 1979. Around 500 deer roam the fenced enclosure, descended from two stags and 40 hinds relocated from the Royal Estate at Balmoral.

An SAC and SSSI, Windsor Great Park and Forest remains the de facto hotspot for ancient oaks and their associated invertabrates and fungi, hosting several thousand veteran trees and over 100 ancient pollards.

William's obsession for the hunt almost a millennia ago has effectively bestowed a legacy of ancient oak wood pasture, the like of which is unrivalled in Britain or Europe, however unwittingly that may have been.

A woodcutter who went to sleep in the forest of Bruelle (Brill in Bucks) was horrified, on waking, to find that he had been stricken blind. He suffered long in his affliction, until in a dream he was directed to offer prayer in eighty-seven churches. This he did and, at the end of his pilgrimage, he went to Windsor, where he sat in the King's porch. King Edward the Confessor, hearing of the man's trouble and of his dream, sent for him and placed his hand, dipped in holy water, upon the blind man's eyes. Immediately the woodcutter's sight was restored.
From *Legends of Britain*, Churchman, 1936

ABOVE: Longhorn cattle grazing in the Cranborne area of the park amongst ancient oak pollards thought to have grown from acorns planted in 1580 – a 5.26ha (13 acre) plot representing England's first known large-scale plantation.

LEFT: Edward the Confessor restoring the woodman's sight.

The Legend of Herne the Hunter

Why, yet there want not many that do fear
In deep of night to walk by this Herne's oak.
From *The Merry Wives of Windsor* by William Shakespeare, 1597

Herne was a huntsman in the service of King Richard II around the end of the 14th century. According to legend, he saved the King's life by standing between him and a charging stag, receiving severe injuries in the process.

Philip Urwick, a powerful wizard, arrived on a black horse and tied the antlers and skull from the dead stag to Herne's head and had him carried to his hut on Bagshot Heath to recuperate. Herne recovered, but in the meantime Urwick had colluded with two keepers who were jealous of Herne's relationship with the King, and magically took his hunting skills away. No longer able to shoot or ride straight, Herne was relieved of his duties and, wielding a chain, rode off into the park with the antlers still on his head. In a fit of madness, he hung himself from a large oak tree in Home Park close to Windsor Castle.

A pedlar discovered Herne hanging from the tree and, returning later with help, found that the body had disappeared. That night the tree was struck by lightning in a thunderstorm, and thereafter nothing went the way of the two keepers. Urwick told them to meet at Herne's Oak at midnight, where the ghost of Herne appeared and ordered them to hunt with him nightly in the forest. This they continued to do until the deer stocks of the park were depleted almost to extinction. The King, determined to discover the cause of his royal herd's decline, joined the midnight meet where Herne's ghost revealed the whole story. The two keepers were hung from Herne's Oak, their ghosts said to ride with Herne's phantom at midnight to this day, searching for damned souls.

The earliest written record of Herne comes from Shakespeare, and it is likely that the Bard drew on Celtic and Saxon folklore recalling the horned deities Cernunnos and Woden (who hanged himself on the World Tree Yggdrasil), possibly weaving in the story of a Windsor poacher called Horne.

ABOVE: Herne's Oak from *A Picturesque Tour of the River Thames in its Western Course* by John Murray, 1862
The original Herne's Oak was cut down in 1796, and its name was transferred to a nearby tree. In 1863, that tree came down in a storm and was replaced by its current namesake planted by Queen Victoria in 1866.

BELOW: Herne the Hunter from *Windsor Castle* by Harrison Ainsworth, c1843.

OPPOSITE: Ancient 10m (33ft) girthed hollow oak at Cranbourne, Windsor Great Park, 2015

The Signing Oak
Windsor Great Park

One of the largest living oaks at Windsor Great Park survives in the deer park close to the Gallop – a ride with sweeping views towards the castle. An ancient hollow pollard, with a 9.72m (30ft) girth, the tree is thought to date back to the park's inception when William the Conqueror initiated construction of the castle.

It was named the Signing Oak after a Statement of Intent was signed beneath its branches in 1972 recognising the park's importance as a special conservation area by the Crown Estate Commissioners and the Nature Conservancy Council (now Natural England). This paved the way for the park's designation as an SSSI and SAC in the year 2000.

The oak sits in very open pasture, protected by a low fence. It harbours the rare oak polypore fungus *(Buglossoporus Piptorus quercinus)*, thought to occupy only around 300 trees nationwide, 100 of which reside in the park at Windsor, its British stronghold. Beside it lies one of its own large limbs that fell in 2009.

Few know the ancient oaks at Windsor better than Ted Green, conservation consultant for Windsor Great Park and founder member of the Ancient Tree Forum, who has studied them throughout his life, since first discovering them as a boy.

Ted had the idea of installing a monument to ancient oaks in the centre of London – where nature and our connection with it can so easily be forgotten – and initiated the Bronze Oak Project. He joined forces with Factum Arte who recorded 5,000 photogrammetric digital images of the Signing Oak and stiched them together to create a 3D template of the tree. A miniature bronze replica was cast and was presented to Queen Elizabeth II by Ted on her 90th birthday at the Royal Academy of Arts in October 2016.

Ted's ultimate aim is to create a life-size replica and install it at a central London location – either Parliament Square or the Tower of London – to celebrate and promote the cultural and historic importance of Britain's ancient trees.

These thousand-year-old oaks represent a biological continuity dating back perhaps only seven generations to the last ice age. They are not only of historic interest but are also a valuable part of our cultural heritage.
Ted Green, 2016

ABOVE: The miniature bronze replica of the Signing Oak on display at Saville Garden, 2018

OPPOSITE: The reverse side of the Signing Oak, 2018

Bagshot Heath Surrey, Berkshire, Hampshire

I took the coach-road, over Bagshot-Heath, and that great forest, as 'tis call'd, of Windsor: here is a vast tract of land, some of it within seventeen or eighteen miles of the capital city; which is not only poor, but even quite steril, given up to barrenness, horrid and frightful to look on, not only good for little, but good for nothing; much of it is a sandy desert, and one may frequently be put in mind here of Arabia Deserta.
From *A tour thro' the whole island of Great Britain* by Daniel Defoe, 1724

Bagshot Heath sprawls across the Surrey, Berkshire, Hampshire border to the south west of Windsor Forest. Poor sandy soil provides the substrate for a landscape characterised by heather, gorse, grasses and bracken with patchy stands of Scots pine and birch, supporting a distinct fauna including all six species of British lizard (adder, grass snake, slow worm, smooth snake, common and sand lizard).

Originally found in glades and clearings naturally grazed by wild animals, lowland heathland expanded in the Neolithic period when early drovers cleared trees to graze cattle, inhibiting regrowth. More treed areas are remembered in place names such as Bending Oak, Straight Oak and The Oaks, as are cattle grazing at Cow Moor.

Bagshot Park, currently the residence of the Earl and Countess of Wessex, was originally built as a hunting lodge for Charles I between 1631 and 1633. The park still hosts a clutch of veteran oaks, the largest measuring 7.5m (24.6ft) around its hollow bole.

The current domination of Scots pine came about in the early 19th century following enclosure of common land, used for centuries by locals to gather turf and bracken to fuel their homes. Ancient common rights to collect fuel are still retained at the Fuel Allotments in Frimley and Poors Allotments on Old Dean Common.

Wildfires are frequent on Bagshot Heath and, with the decline in grazing, parts of the heath are gradually reverting to woodland.

Returning to an area of the heath I knew as a child 35 years previously, I was struck by dense growth yielding it unrecognisable and demonstrating the transient and changeable nature of landscape.

Looking north-east across Bagshot Heath towards London, 2019

The Golden Farmer and Legend of the White Hart
Camberley, Surrey

I once lived at the Maultway on Bagshot Heath – an old drovers' road used anciently to herd sheep from Berkshire and Surrey to markets at Guildford and Blackwater. On a roundabout where the Maultway meets the Portsmouth Road and the Great South West Road (A30) stood a pub called The Jolly Farmer. The legend of the Golden Farmer (where the pub gets its name) tells the tale of William Davis – a farmer by day but highwayman by night – who robbed travellers on their way to and from London. A master of disguise, he once held up his own landlord, relieving him of the rent he had given him earlier.

Famed for paying his debts in gold – from where he received his nickname – after a 40-year career Davis was eventually shot during a coach heist in 1690, and taken to London where he was hanged. His corpse was publicly displayed for all to see on a gibbet near the pub (remembered by the aptly named Gibbet Lane). Davis' gold was never recovered and is rumoured to be buried nearby.

Close to The Jolly Farmer, a plaque attached to a roadside boulder recalls the legend of the Basing Stone. Whilst hunting in Windsor Forest, Richard II (1377-1399) wounded a stag which subsequently turned on him. The King was saved by a majestic white hart which saw off the wounded stag. Eternally grateful, Richard ordered that four hostelries be constructed in the forest. Today, only one survives – a 16th-century coaching inn standing 5km (3 miles) to the west at Frimley.

The fact that Richard bore a white hart on his coat of arms reveals the significance of the animal in medieval England. The tale resembles closely the legend of Herne the Hunter previously mentioned, and a similar story featuring David I of Scotland who, in 1128, was said to have been saved from a charging stag after begging God for mercy. The beast vanished, its antlers turned into a cross.

The mythical white hart appears as a lucky charm in Arthurian mythology, and was appropriated by Christianity to represent Christ.

YATELEY COMMON

Yateley Common

Yateley, Hampshire

Yateley Common stands between the village from where it takes its name and the busy A30 London road on the same Bagshot sands as Bagshot Common, whose character it shares. Yateley derives from 'gate at the forest clearing', describing its origins as a western gateway to Windsor Great Forest.

Hall Place, a 13th-century manor house, once stood in the village, yet the common has evolved since the Mesolithic, providing resources for commoners and historically managed by manorial courts. Its open-aspect landscape is the result of hundreds of years of grazing, the removal of wood and turf for fuel, and of grass, furze and bracken for bedding.

Once the haunt of highwaymen who lurked for prey on the Reading road, local legend has Parson Darby, curate of Yateley, hung for his crimes from a yew tree at Darby Green in 1841. Historical evidence is scant, but he is remembered in the Yateley Morris Dancers' 'beast' – a wooden horse disguised in highwayman's clothing.

Parts of the common were enclosed and later developed for housing, and in 1941 the RAF cleared Hartfordbridge Flats to install Blackbushe Airport. The poet John Clare's lament for his beloved heathland in Northamptonshire – devastated by enclosures in the early 19th century – is reflected in Yateley Common's surviving fragments.

Currently the 193ha (477 acre) Yateley Common Country Park is managed to promote diverse habitats, including heathland, woodland, scrub, open-grown trees and grassland. This enables its biodiverse wildlife to prosper – for which it is designated as a SSSI and an SPA. Viviparous lizards, adders, a variety of butterflies and birds (including nightingales) and roe deer are common, as are a wealth of wild flowers and native trees, including oak, sallow and Scots pine.

Ye commons left free in the rude rags of nature,
Ye brown heaths beclothed in furze as ye be,
My wild eye in rapture adores every feature,
Ye are dear as this heart in my bosom to me.

From *The Village Minstrel* by John Clare, c1820

ABOVE: Yateley Common, open woodland, 2019

OPPOSITE: Evidence of scrub clearing to prolong the open heathland character, 2019

BELOW: Roe deer on the run, Yateley Common, 2019

Odiham Deer Park Hampshire

While not a Royal Forest as such, Odiham was noted as a Royal Manor in 1086, having been seized from Harold by William following the Norman Conquest. Saint Edward's Oak, an ancient tree that blew down in the 13th century, suggests that the Confessor hunted there earlier still.

Odiham certainly appears to have been a favoured haunt of King John, who visited regularly. Equidistant between Windsor and Winchester, a stop at Odiham split a two-day ride in half, and provided ample opportunity for the hunt. This explains why John built a castle there around 1207, taking possession of Robert the Parker's land and mills for the purpose. A parker was 'keeper of the deer park', his importance to the king reflected in the Forest Charter of 1297, which exonerated them from killing poachers. John was at Odiham Castle when summoned by the Barons to seal Magna Carta beneath the Ankerwyke Yew in 1215.

At that time the deer park was well stocked with open-grown oak, a wood pasture landscape that provided cover and grazing for deer, a good supply of timber, and underwood for winter fuel.

In 1276, six oaks were used to construct a springald (a giant, wheeled crossbow), others provided timber to build Eton College. In 1358, ships were assembled in large pits dug on site, and were then taken apart and reassembled at Southampton. Westminster Hall's hammerbeam roof, rebuilt in the late 14th century, is of Odiham oak, along with oak-framed houses in Odiham dating from 1300.

Odiham remained a royalty demesne until 1603, when, following the death of Elizabeth I, it was granted to John, who was Earl of Mar, later accused of felling 2,000-3,000 of the best trees. In 1630, the 208ha (513 acre) park contained 600 deer, and in 1646, 1,032 oaks. Yet felling continued, hastened by a hunger for agricultural land and the pressures of the Civil War.

Today's open fields are testament to those demands, yet some vigorous veteran ash, oak and hawthorn survive in the hedgerows.

Take in the county of Kent twenty workmen for cleaving boards called shippeborde for the making of the king's ships called La Nawe Seynte Marie and Le Christopher in the park of Odiham co. Southampton.

From *The Patent Rolls* by order of Edward III, 1358.

ABOVE: King John's Castle, c1900
BELOW: King John's Castle, 2019
OPPOSITE: Veteran ash, oak and hawthorn surround a watering hole at Odiham Deer Park – once used by deer, now grazed by cattle, 2019

Frenchman's Oak

Odiham Common, Hampshire

Lands at the first was granted unto them by the Kings Majestie this land has freedom of common in the waste for all kinds of cattle commonable and crop of all kind of underwood of the Kings Woods to make their hedges with.
From *A Presentment of Customs of Odiham*, 1589

Odiham Deer Park was kept to stock royal game for the hunt and, from the early 13th century, as a royal stud to rear horses as well; as a result it was largely out of bounds to the general populace.

Odiham Common, on the other hand, also privately owned, at least gave cattle grazing and underwood rights to freesuitors and freeholders – but not to everyone. Sheep were allowed only between March and September, two to an acre, to prevent overgrazing with their deeper 'bite', detrimental to regeneration.

Originally known as Holmhurst, meaning wooded hill in the marsh – indicating a wooded area – the 115ha (284 acre) common, consisting of wood pasture and meadow land, was designated an SSSI in 1992 on account of its rare flora and fauna. In wet weather, the common's marshy character is still evident.

Trees remained the property of the lord of the manor, recorded in 1822 as including oak, beech, ash, elm, chestnut, lime, sycamore, birch, walnut, fir, aspen, poplar, alder, larch, field maple and hornbeam. Some large, veteran pollard oaks remain at the eastern edge of the deer park where it adjoins the common.

In 1947, Frenchman's Oak, a 4.5m (14.75ft) ancient lapsed pollard oak *(Quercus robur)*, dropped a large branch exposing its hollow trunk, which was subsequently filled with plastic and covered in zinc sheeting in an effort to protect it. It was named to mark the limit that Napoleonic Prisoners of War, billeted in Odiham, could walk under the terms of their parole; a gentleman's agreement under which they promised not to escape.

The Jubilee Oak, a 4.65m (15.25ft) veteran oak pollard stands nearby, named for Queen Victoria's jubilee and adorned with a cast-iron bench. Both trees stand close to the London road, a milestone between them declaring it is 40 miles to the capital.

ABOVE: Frenchman's Oak, 2019

BELOW: The author sitting beneath the Jubilee Oak, 2019

The Mildmay Oaks

Hartley Wintney, Hampshire

Following the Battle of Trafalgar in 1805 – where Napoleon Bonaparte was defeated by the British Navy, – Admiral Collingwood made a plea to the nation to plant more oaks for future shipbuilding, to help sustain the country's naval dominance.

As Vice Admiral under Horatio Nelson during the battle, which took place off Spain's south west coast, Collingwood was pivotal in effectively denying Napoleon his aim of absorbing Britain into his expanding European Empire.

Heeding the call was Lady Mildmay, of the Manor of Hartley Witney, who in 1807 employed her steward to plant out row upon row of oaks at Hartley Row in the 'wastes' of former common land.

By the mid-19th century, the Industrial Revolution had enabled Isambard Kingdom Brunel to build the SS *Great Britain* – the first entirely wrought-iron ship. And by the 1880s steel had become the de-facto material, ending over a 1,000 years of wooden ship building in Britain.

Skills learnt from Viking settlers had been passed through generations. In medieval times, shipwrights wandered the countryside, selecting oak boughs that exhibited the right proportions and properties for their specific purpose, often cutting just one limb for a ship's bough or stern. The rest of the tree was often left to grow on.

As a result, the Mildmay Oaks were never harvested as intended. Some 200 years later, around 400 mature oaks *(Quercus robur)* still stand tall, many from the original planting – the largest measures 4.1m (14.5ft) in circumference – their decaying hollows providing habitat for bats, woodpeckers and invertebrates.

They reflect the oaks of old Hartley Witney (meaning clearing in a deer wood), remembered in a 13th-century text which complains of 'damage to Thomas's pasture and pannage (acorn fodder) by Stephen's pigs'.

What I am most anxious about is the plantation of oak in the country. We shall never cease to be a great people while we have ships and we cannot have ships without timber... I plant an oak wherever I have a place to put it.
Admiral Collingwood in a letter to Lord Radstock, 1807.

ABOVE: The Mildmay Oaks, c1900
BELOW: The Mildmay Oaks, 2019

EVERSLEY FOREST

Queen Elizabeth's Oak

Elvetham Hall, Hampshire

Now birds record new harmony,
And trees do whistle melody:
Now everything that nature breeds,
Doth clad itself in pleasant weeds.

From *The Honourable Entertainment given to the Queen's Majesty at Elvetham*, 1591

Queen Elizabeth I was a frequent visitor to the Royal Manor of Odiham, and it is likely she participated in the hunt there as she did elsewhere across the country. In 1591 she set off from Odiham to Elvetham Hall, six miles to the north east near Hartley Wintney.

First mentioned in the Domesday Survey in 1086, by 1234 Elvetham was in the hands of the Sturmy family from Wolf Hall in Wiltshire. Sir William Sturmy was granted a royal licence to create a deer park of 121ha (300 acres) there in 1359. A century later the estate passed into the hands of the Seymour family through marriage. The short-lived Queen Jane was born there in 1509, and it was there that she met her future husband Henry VIII.

It was Jane's nephew, Edward, Earl of Hertford, who had invited Queen Elizabeth to visit Elvetham in 1591. Edward had been confined to the Tower of London after marrying Lady Catherine Grey without royal permission and fathering a child, a penal offence (as potential claimants to the throne). He was released in 1572, fined £15,000 for 'seducing a virgin of the blood royal', and the child was declared illegitimate.

So Edward was keen to curry favour with Elizabeth, and for three days he entertained her and her retinue of 500 in some style at Elvetham. Royal apartments and a crescent lake with three islands were constructed especially for the visit, and lavish foods, poems, sports, songs and plays were presented to the queen.

By all accounts Elizabeth was so impressed with the proceedings that she forgave Edward and, according to tradition, planted an oak tree in the gardens facing the manor house to commemorate the occassion. A large oak *(Quercus robur)* measuring 8.15m (26.75ft) around its solid trunk is testament to the story and carries her name. Its towering form is unusual for a maiden oak of such antiquity, which, against the odds, managed to keep its head on its shoulders, much like Edward.

ABOVE: Elvetham Hall fireplace from 1856 depicting Elizabeth's visit in 1591

BELOW AND OPPOSITE: Queen Elizabeth's Oak, 2019

CRANBORNE CHASE

Kingston Lacy Beech Avenue
Dorset

The Kingston Lacy Estate was inherited by William John Bankes from his father in 1835. An active member of parliament and confidential military assistant to the Duke of Wellington, he immediately set about putting his own stamp on the estate. That same year he planted an avenue of cedar of Lebanon *(Cedrus lebani)* leading north to the manor house. The trees have grown to a considerable size and stand at around 6m (19ft) in girth.

His pièce de résistance, however, and one of his first actions, was to have an avenue of beech trees *(Fagus sylvatica)* planted either side of a 3km (2 mile) stretch of the family-owned turnpike road leading to the estate from the west. As a birthday gift to his mother, Frances, Bankes planted 365 trees on the north side of the road – one for each day of the year – and 366 on the other – for leap years. The trees were well chosen, as beech is often described as 'Mother of the Forest', 'Madonna of the Wood', or the 'White Lady', due to its gracious form.

In 1841, Bankes was exiled after being caught in a clandestine liaison with a guardsman at St James' Park, and his tenure at Kingston Lacy was terminated. The beech trees, however, lived on and, over 180 years later around 200 remain. Now in the care of the National Trust, 70 of the trees were removed in 2013 due to decay, and were replaced with hornbeam *(Carpinus betulus)* – similar to beech in appearance but generally hardier. The young trees were planted slightly further from the road to preserve the avenue.

The busy road connecting Wimborne to Blandford has a long history, standing as it does in the shadow of Badbury Rings – an Iron Age hill fort in use since the Bronze Age. The site was held by the Durotriges, a Celtic tribe who put up fierce resistance against Roman occupation. Later, it was the location of an important crossroads in the Roman road system.

Kingley Vale West Sussex

Tradition would seem to contain nothing incredible when it asserts that the yews on Kinglye Bottom, near Chichester, were on their present site when the sea-kings from the north landed on the coast of Sussex.
From *Longman's Magazine*,
J A Farrer, 1883

Britain is lucky to possess a large number of ancient and veteran yew trees, chiefly in its churchyards, sometimes as lone trees in fields and hedgerows, but rarely in woodland groves of any number.

This was not always the case, with many being cleared to make way for agricultural and livestock farmers wary of the trees' poisonous effects on their herds. However, one such yew wood survives in Kingley Vale, an SSSI, nestled in the chalk downs of Sussex. It was designated one of Britain's first National Nature Reserves in 1952 and remains one of Europe's most important ancient yew woods.

Local tradition holds that the yew trees were planted as a memorial to a Saxon battle against the Danes, who were said to have been buried either beneath the trees or in the burial mounds on the downs above. Interestingly, in support of the legend, the Anglo-Saxon Chronicle describes a battle against the Danes in 894: 'the townsmen of Chichester put them to flight, slew many hundreds of them, and took some of their ships'.

It is a wonder that the wood survives at all, having being used for military operations since the mid-19th century, through the Boer War and both world wars. Individual yew trees were used for target practice, and Spitfires from nearby RAF Tangmere destroyed around 100 trees from the air during a five-week-long exercise. Some of the yews are still pitted with bullets.

Estimates put the age of the oldest yews between 500 and 700 years, the largest measuring 5.65m (18.5ft) in circumference near the ground. John Lowe's measurement from 1895 of 4.69m (15.4ft), reflects the yew's slow growth. While Kingley Vale's oldest remaining yews may not date to the time of the Vikings, their magical, dark, sinuous presence is reward enough for a visit, safe in the knowledge that the yew wood as a whole could easily predate that era.

Forest of the Weald

Hampshire, Surrey, Sussex, Kent

Bare slopes where chasing shadows skim,
 And, through the gaps revealed,
Belt upon belt, the wooded, dim,
 Blue goodness of the Weald.
From *Sussex* by Rudyard Kipling, 1902

ABOVE: The Picnic Tree, Haywards Heath, c1910
BELOW: Beech border trees at Broadstone Warren, 2018
OPPOSITE: Ashdown Forest – heath, wood and field, 2018

The great forest known by the Romans as Silva Anderida (after the Saxon shore fort where Pevensey Castle now stands) has seen human occupation since at least the Mesolithic. According to the Anglo-Saxon Chronicle, in 893 the forest stretched from Hampshire through Surrey and Sussex to Kent for some 193km (120 miles), running between the North and South Downs for some 48km (30 miles). To the Saxons it was Andredes Weald – a mosaic wilderness of open-grown trees, woodland, grassland and scrub – largely uninhabited apart from the seasonal labour of drovers, woodmen, iron-workers and swineherds. The high number of Wealden towns and villages ending in 'den' (Tenterden, Horsmonden, Cowden, etc) comes from the traditional practice of pannage, whereby each autumn pigs were turned out to eat acorns and beech mast in forest 'dens'.

When the Normans arrived, the Weald was England's largest area of wood and heathland, notable for its absence of settlements, according to the Domesday Survey of 1086. It was the Normans who really exploited local sandstone for iron – an activity already in practice in the Iron Age and continued by the Romans. The landscape and close proximity to London also saw six Royal Forests established for the hunt, namely Ashdown, Worth, Waterdown, Dallington, St Leonards and Arundel. This practice continued into Henry VIII's reign, although the forests passed between Royal and private hands several times. The Norman's favourite chase animal, the stag, is remembered in town names such as Hartfield.

Tree clearance expanded slowly at first, with the common right to graze animals within enclosures of small agricultural clearings. Some of the Weald's wide, curved hedgerows left behind stand as some of Britain's most ancient woodland remnants. The Jute Law of Gavelkind in Kent – which divided estates equally between a dead man's sons – ensured numerous smallholdings prevailed over large baronial manors, for centuries.

FOREST OF THE WEALD

*Jove's oak, the warlike ash, vein'd elm,
the softer beech, Short hazel, maple plain,
light asp, the bending wych, Tough holly,
and smooth birch must altogether burn
What should the builder serve, supplies the
forger's turn; When under public good base
private gain takes hold, And we, poor woeful
woods, to ruin lastly sold.*

From *Polyolbion* by Michael Drayton, 1612

ABOVE: Monument to A A Milne and Shepard, 2018
BELOW: The mixed, open landscape of Ashdown Forest, 2018

Ashdown Forest East Sussex

Ashdown, largest of the Wealden forests, sits on the High Weald, a hard sandstone ridge rolling into softer clay valleys, central to the rise of the area's iron industry. Coppiced wood provided a sustainable source for charcoal burning, which in turn fired the kilns of the iron works.

Ashdown's proximity to London ensured its status as a royal hunting forest shortly after the Conquest, and by 1283 4,000ha (10,000 acres) had been enclosed to contain its deer, with 34 gates allowing access for commoners to exercise their rights to graze, collect windfall wood, furze and bracken for bedding.

During the late Middle Ages, highwaymen and outlaws were notorious, and reports of poaching had reached significant levels. Henry VIII passed acts controlling the cutting of wood and timber, as huge amounts were needed to supply the iron industry, the Weald having become England's primary supplier. Henry was also concerned for the future production of warships. His flagship, the *Mary Rose*, is estimated to have used 600 large oaks in its construction, representing a woodland of around 16ha (40 acres). Whole standard trees were used, whereas coppicing wood for charcoal was by nature a sustainable system. Overgrazing prevented regeneration and to a great extent shaped the landscape into heath.

Ashdown was disafforested by Charles II, and came under the control of Richard, Earl of Dorset, who met with fierce resistance from commoners infuriated at losing their forest rights. In 1683, following a long-running dispute, around a third of the forest was awarded to the commoners, the other two-thirds to the lord of the manor, an arrangement which still defines Ashdown Forest.

The Commons Act of 1876 saw a board of conservators established to manage the forest as an amenity, secure existing rights of common, and conserve it as an AONB.

A A Milne's classic Winnie the Pooh stories were set in Ashdown Forest. Milne bought a Sussex retreat at Hartfield, an easy walk into the forest. His son Christopher wrote: 'Anyone who has read the stories knows the forest and doesn't need me to describe it. Pooh's Forest and Ashdown Forest are identical.'

The Thomas à Becket Yew
Capel, Kent

The chancel remains nearly in its original state and possesses evident claims to antiquity... The churchyard contains one of the largest yew trees in the country.
From An historical, topographical and descriptive account of the weald of Kent by Thomas Downes W Dearn, 1814

ABOVE: The death of Thomas à Becket drawn in 1911
BELOW: Thomas à Becket's Yew, 2018

An ancient yew *(Taxus baccata)* sits in the churchyard at Capel, near Paddock Wood, in the High Weald's hop-growing country on the southern side of the Medway Valley. The 8.23m (23ft) girthed tree – the same as it measured in 1897 – is simultaneously in the throes of decay and regeneration, typical of its species. Long past hollowing, its fragmented stems throw beautiful patterns and shapes when seen close at hand. A smaller yew of 4m (13ft) stands to the south of the church.

The 12th-century church is dedicated to the saint and martyr Thomas à Becket, Archbishop of Canterbury, murdered gruesomely in 1170 at Canterbury Cathedral by the sword of four knights who apparently misinterpreted Henry II's vocal exasperation with the holy man. Becket had refused to sign Henry's Constitutions of Clarendon – an act which sought to reduce the power of the Church – straining their previously good relationship, an act for which Becket paid the ultimate price.

Legend has Becket preaching beneath the great yew at Capel, sited just over the halfway point on the pilgrimage route between Chichester and Canterbury cathedrals.

In 1639, lightning struck the western tower of the church at Capel, which had to be rebuilt as all the woodwork and the southern half of the building were destroyed and three of the bells were melted.

In 1868, a series of wall paintings depicting biblical scenes and thought to have been painted between c1200 and 1250 were uncovered on the church's north wall. Having been plastered over in the mid-16th century, they provide a window on how colourful medieval churches were before the Reformation.

As part of his penance for Becket's murder, Henry was forced to fund and found several monasteries, including one in Selwood Forest.

The Domesday Oak
Brenchley, Kent

The name Brenchley, from Branca's Leigh, meaning 'a clearing in the forest', hosts one of the Weald's oldest trees, the Domesday Oak *(Quercus robur)* named after a belief that dates it to the Survey of 1086. Measuring almost 10m (33ft) around its hollow, heavily burred and mossy trunk, Domesday grows in a private garden, nestled in a carpet of snowdrops and light snow on my visit.

While it may be contemporary with the Norman invasion, it almost certainly predates the 16th-century timber-framed manor house standing beside it, and the development of the 12th-century village.

Henry VIII took Brenchley for himself in 1526, as a base from where he could hunt the forest, granted it to Cardinal Wolsey until his demise in 1539, then gave it to Paul Sydnor who is thought to have built the house.

Wat Tyler, a leader of the Peasants' Revolt who died for his cause in 1381, may have lived in the parish – one timber-framed cottage bears his name – while Siegfried Sassoon, one of England's foremost First World War poets, was born there.

In 1945 part of the oak split. Concrete was poured into the hollow (a remedial practice discouraged today), some of which can still be seen, although moss and lichen disguise it well. Sixty years later, another limb dropped – itself the size of a mature oak – a scene witnessed by builders renovating the house right beside the tree. The fallen timber was cleared, and reappeared for sale in the form of Domesday chopping boards.

I stopped in the village to enquire about the oak at the local butchers – whose premises happened to have once been a royal hunting lodge – and they let me copy their wartime photograph of the tree (right). They asked if the old man, hidden within the hollow, was still there. Alas he had gone, it may have been too cold for him in the freshly fallen snow.

This parish is for the most part skirted with woodlands, which as well as the hedge-rows still contain no inconsiderable portion of fine thriving oak.

From *An historical, topographical and descriptive account of the weald of Kent* by Thomas Downes W Dearn, 1814

ABOVE: The Domesday Oak, 1944
OPPOSITE: The Domesday Oak, 2018

Savernake Forest Wiltshire

Savernake Forest lies to the south east of Marlborough covering an area of around 1,600ha (4,000 acres), just a tenth of its medieval extent but, remaining heavily wooded, it is the most important ancient tree site in Wiltshire.

King Athelstan mentions 'the woodland called Safernoc' in a Saxon charter of 934, but the name itself is likely to be from the Celtic 'Savern' (applying to a river) and the Saxon 'ake' (meaning oak). A road running north to south through the forest, attests to the presence of the Romans.

In 1087, 21 years after the Battle of Hastings, William granted Savernake to the knight Richard Esturmy for his part in the Conquest. Almost 1,000 years later, it remains the only privately owned forest in England, handed down through continuous family links, validated by ownership of a Norman hunting horn which is still blown whenever a monarch enters the forest.

Much loved by medieval kings for the hunt, Savernake was enclosed and stocked with red deer, with park pales that would wax and wane through the centuries. Today red, roe, fallow and muntjac deer roam the forest.

Henry VIII was particularly partial, and on several occasions hunted with his friend John Seymour, forest warden based at the family seat of Wolf Hall – where Henry met his third wife Jane Seymour. Jane died shortly after giving birth to Henry's only son, the future king, Edward VI. She lies buried in the church at Great Bedwyn.

Poaching occurred frequently, as recorded in historic court records, until park pales at Tottenham House – the manor house which replaced Wolf Hall – saw its decline.

In 1939, most of the forest was leased to the Forestry Commission for 999 years, under the proviso that 'the old forest would be regenerated by natural means', due to concerns it would be overrun by coniferous plantations. Today the commission is addressing those concerns by haloing the ancient oak pollards and releasing them from overshading. Their primary function at contemporary Savernake is to revive the oak wood pasture and associated fauna in the SSSI, including 116 species of lichen, some of which are found only in ancient forests.

How soothing sound the gentle airs that move
The innumerable leaves, high overhead,
When autumn first, from the long avenue,
That lifts its arching height of ancient shade,
Steals here and there a leaf!

From *Avenue in Savernake Forest* by William Lisle Bowles (1762-1850)

ABOVE: Henry VIII and Jane Seymour who met and courted in Savernake Forest.

BELOW: The Grand Avenue c1915 – Britain's longest beech avenue – created by Lancelot 'Capability' Brown in the 1740s

OPPOSITE: Rare lichen and fungi on a fallen oak

ABOVE: Tottenham Park, 1818
BELOW: Chichester Cathedral, 1890
OPPOSITE: The Cathedral Oak, 2015

The Cathedral Oak Savernake Forest

Savernake's virtually unbroken line of ownership spanning almost a thousand years, has left a wealth of ancient trees in the forest, some of which are thought to date back to the Saxon Charter of Safernoc in 934.

Thousands of veteran beech trees adorn the forest, but historically oak was the dominant species. Over 100 ancient and several hundred more veteran oaks remain – mostly pollards – living chronicles of Savernake's working past.

Many of the ancient oaks have been named since at least Victorian times. The King Oak, recorded in J G Strutt's *Sylva Britannica* in 1850; the Queen Oak; and the Duke's Vaunt, documented as standing 10m (32.8ft) in circumference, and said to be a favourite of Edward Seymour, the first Duke of Somerset (c1500-1552), all now reduced to rubble.

At the northern edge of Savernake, however, stands the Cathedral Oak *(Quercus robur)*, an ancient pollard measuring 10.15m (33.3ft) around its hollowing bole. One of the three largest-girthed living oaks in the forest, it is not hard to imagine how the tree acquired its name, due to a medusa-like crown which once threw more than 12 major branches to the heavens, like the pillars of a cathedral. Pagan Britons worshipped under 'consecrated groves' (described by Tacitus when Suetonius massacred the Druids on Anglesey in AD61). When Christianity arrived, worship sometimes continued outside, often beneath the branches of landmark trees, or gospel oaks as they were known. Once congregations moved inside, church pillars appeared to represent the trunk and spreading limbs of great trees, the grander the building the more spectacular the effect.

Throughout its life, the Cathedral Oak could have been systematically worked for firewood – its branches cut at regular intervals, promoting regrowth, whilst at the same time stimulating the tree's longevity.

The tree has not been pollarded for many a year, and has inevitably dropped some of its top-heavy branches. Re-pollarding after such a time could prove fatal, so the Cathedral Oak is likely to descend into fracture gracefully over time, much as its other famed companions have done.

ABOVE AND BELOW: The King of Limbs, 2018

The King of Limbs

Savernake Forest, Wiltshire

'An expression of wildness and mutation.'
Thom Yorke

'Rhythm is the king of limbs! The rhythm dictates the record. It's very important.'
Ed O'Brien, interview in *La Semana De Frente*, 2012

In the north west of Savernake stands the Big Belly Oak, probably its best-known tree and, measuring 11.15m (36.5ft) around its bulbous waist, it certainly lives up to its name.

At the southern end, near the approach to Tottenham House (where Wolf Hall used to stand), is the King of Limbs *(Quercus petraea)* – the ultimate of Savernake's triumvirate of giant living oaks.

As its name suggests, the tree has a mass of sprawling limbs, a result of lapsed pollarding and a feature shared by its cousin the Cathedral Oak. It stands in a ride amidst a coniferous plantation, shaded out by non-native larch, once dominated by an open landscape of oak wood pasture. It is no surprise then to find the King of Limbs standing amongst many of its own fallen limbs, just one of which would dwarf many a full-grown tree.

The cavernous hollow trunk, measuring 10.18m (33.39ft) around and supporting three huge limbs, still cuts an impressive figure of a giant in decline, clothed in moss and lichen, refusing to give in.

It seems that cult band Radiohead were suitably impressed by the King of Limbs, naming their 2011 album after it and, adorning the original cover with tree limbs illustrated by singer/guitarist Thom Yorke, created with long-time collaborator Stanley Donwood.

The band spent three weeks recording their previous album, *In Rainbows*, at Tottenham House, finding time to sojourn in the forest, and evidently discovering the King of Limbs.

Harewood Forest

Hampshire

Harewood, named after the magical hare that still abounds there, used to mark the southern extent of Savernake Forest and the boundary with Chute Forest; today it stands some 32km (20miles) away, near Andover, in the Test Valley.

At 650-700ha (1,600-1,730 acres), it is Hampshire's second largest ancient woodland (after the New Forest), is privately owned and is known to have been worked as coppice since the 13th century. Today it still earns its keep as a working woodland.

In 1825 a 21m (70ft) tall monument was erected by Colonel William Iremonger to commemorate a legend at 'Dead Man's Plack'. The story goes that in 963, having heard of a beautiful lady named Elfrida, the Saxon King Edgar sent his trusted earl, Ethelwold, to meet and assess her suitability as his bride. Ethelwold was stunned by Elfrida's beauty, sent word to the king that she was unworthy, and promptly married her himself. On hearing of this treachery, Edgar invited Ethelwold to hunt in Harewood Forest, murdered him with his javelin, and took Elfrida as his queen.

From 1943 Harewood was used by the RAF to store 40,000 tons of munitions for the war effort. A network of concrete tracks was built for the purpose, and remain in use today for walking and forestry.

In 1962 the A303 dissected the forest from east to west, virtually cutting it in half. Since then, coniferous plantations have expanded, and the forest is used for other business activities, including piggeries and a chicken farm. Roe deer roam freely.

The closing of tracks previously open to the public has prompted the founding of groups such as 'Friends of Harewood Forest', who aim to keep ancient rights of way open for the general public.

For he fell so desperately in love with her the moment he saw her, that, dissembling his indignation, he sent for the earl into a wood at Warewelle, called Harewood, under pretence of hunting, and ran him through with a javelin.
From *Chronicle of the kings of England* by William of Malmesbury, 1125

ABOVE: The Monument at Dead Man's Plack, 1911
BELOW: Harewood Forest, 2017

Stonehenge and the King's Barrow Beeches Wiltshire

Often cited as Britain's most important ancient monument, the complex ceremonial landscape at Stonehenge has dominated Salisbury Plain both physically and culturally for over 5,000 years.

A chalk downland covering an area of 780km² (300 miles²), the plain is the largest expanse of unimproved grassland in north west Europe. Scattered with hawthorn and small woodland stands, the landscape is sustained by grazing, and the population is sparse, in spite of the presence of the MOD.

In Neolithic times the plain was well populated, and generally thought to have been one of Britain's early deforested areas, as people turned from hunter-gatherer to a more settled farming-led lifestyle. Pollen and snail records suggest a densely wooded landscape gradually cleared for crop farming, and while this undoubtedly occurred, archaeological excavations reveal quite a different picture.

On the banks of the River Avon, 3km (2 miles) east of Stonehenge, bones of auroch, red deer and wild boar dating to 10,000BC were uncovered. Natural grazers of Britain's wildwood before domestication, these animals helped shape the landscape.

Aurochs were formidable beasts. Twice the size of modern cattle (their domesticated descendants), athletic and aggressive, they could run up to 55kmh (35mph). A successful auroch hunt – no mean feat – could provide food for 100 people, rewarding the hunters with valuable food and veneration from their peers.

When enlarging the visitor car park at Stonehenge in 1966, archaeologists discovered three post holes cut into the chalk bedrock between 6500 and 8500BC. They appeared to support pine posts about 2.35m (7.7ft) in circumference, at a time when the species was still native. A fourth hole is thought to have marked the location of a living tree.

Hard is the life when naked and unhouzed
And wasted by the long day's fruitless pains,
The hungry savage, 'mid deep forests, rouzed
By storms, lies down at night on unknown plains
And lifts his head in fear, while famished trains
Of boars along the crashing forests prowl,
And heard in darkness, as the rushing rains
Put out his watch-fire, bears contending growl
And round his fenceless bed gaunt wolves in armies howl.

From *Salisbury Plain* by William Wordsworth, 1793-94

ABOVE: Summer Solstice celebrations at Stonehenge, c1920
BELOW: New King's Barrow Beeches, 2017

Between these two sites stand the King's Barrows, a line of Bronze Age round barrows built of turf layered on the crest of a ridge running from north to south, bisected by a Bronze Age ceremonial avenue which leads from the River Avon to the Stonehenge monument.

A recent theory suggests that the pine posts may have had a practical as well as ceremonial use, by marking out the migratory passage of aurochs and helping direct them into a confined space where they could be trapped and more easily slaughtered.

In Britain, aurochs were extinct by the Iron Age, but they survived in Poland until 1627. Favouring woodland cover in winter, Polish aurochs grazed a more open landscape in the warmer months, helping sustain an open wood pasture landscape as opposed to dense woodland. All the evidence points to a similar landscape at Stonehenge. The significance of auroch hunts to Neolithic people may well have spawned the later monuments for which Stonehenge is famed.

A stand of ancient beech trees *(Fagus sylvatica)* flank the New King's Barrows, framing the ridge and offering far-reaching views across the downs and towards the Stonehenge monument. Further trees stood on the barrows themselves but were blown down during the Burns' Day storm of 1990.

Thought to have been planted for aesthetic and territorial reasons – the trees mark the boundary of the Amesbury Estate – the larger trees probably date to the early 18th century, but some, measuring up to 7m (23ft) around, could be older still. Many have previously been pollarded, a practice not repeated for many years and resulting in 'top heavy' trees liable to failure. So to prolong their longevity a program of light crown reductions suggested by Brian Muelanar was implemented by the National Trust.

The twisted, gnarled, lichen-covered forms of the ancient beech trees present a stunning natural memorial to the ancient kings buried beside them, and to the time-honoured stones in the vale below.

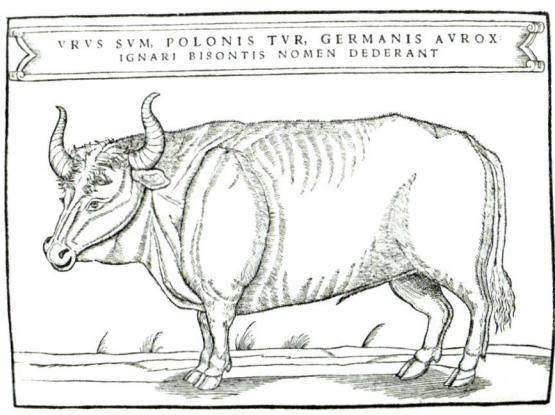

ABOVE: Auroch by Sigismund von Herberstein, 1556
BELOW: Ancient pollard beeches at New King's Barrow, 2017

Clarendon Forest Wiltshire

In medieval times a great belt of forest ran from Savernake in the north all the way to the New Forest on the south coast. Somewhere in the middle lay Clarendon Forest, including the smaller Buckholt and Melchet.

First mentioned in a writ of 1072 during the reign of William the Conqueror, excavations in the 1930s at the ruins of Clarendon Palace revealed earlier buildings, providing evidence of Clarendon in use as a royal hunting forest by the Saxon elite prior to the Conquest. In those days it was known as Penchet – 'the end of the wood'.

Kings from William I to Henry VI – who exhibited his first signs of 'madness' there (residing as a near recluse for almost a year following a breakdown) – frequently visited over a 600-year period. Then, in 1606, James I granted the entire forest to the Earl of Pembroke.

A survey of 1273 depicts the boundaries of Clarendon to be much the same as those of the contemporary private estate of Clarendon Park. At that time, however, exploitation of the largely oak woods of the forest had begun in earnest. Construction of the new Salisbury Cathedral in the early part of the century and the city that grew up around it, were built largely from generous timber grants bestowed by Henry III and Edward I.

The 13th century also saw deer leaps established with park pales to mark the forest boundary and contain its deer. Some of the banks and ditches are still clearly in evidence, and host some fine veteran trees (opposite).

By the 14th century, Clarendon still retained a large stock of wild boar, saw its last wolf killed, and suffered numerous reports of swans being poached from the River Avon, its western boundary.

By 1650, the forest still contained almost 15,000 timber trees, mostly oak, around 500 fallow deer and several rabbit warrens. Some deer remain, and a fine selection of veteran trees stand in wood pasture around the 18th-century manor house; but most of Clarendon Forest's current woodland is densely planted coniferous crop.

It was on his return from hunting in this forest that Edward the Martyr was murdered by order of his mother-in-law, with the view of securing the throne to her son Ethered.

From *Remarks on Forest Scenery* by William Gilpin, 1834

ABOVE: Ancient beech on the park pale at Clarendon, 2017
BELOW: Veteran oak avenue at Clarendon Manor, 2017

Clarendon Palace Wiltshire

With a castle stronghold at Old Sarum only 5km (3 miles) to the west, and capital city Winchester 32km (20 miles) to the east, Clarendon Forest was well placed for Norman kings to quench their thirst for the hunt.

William the Conqueror was the first of them to visit, and it is likely that he prepared there for his invasion of Scotland. At that time his Clarendon residence was merely a hunting lodge, built on an earlier Saxon site. It was Henry II – the last king to consider Winchester capital of England – who initiated the transformation of Clarendon from hunting lodge to magnificent Royal Palace, built from Clarendon timber. It grew to become the second largest building in England after the great Hall of Westminster.

In 1164 Henry summoned the bishops to Clarendon palace to sign the infamous 'Constitutions of Clarendon' – a paper defining ecclesiastical privilege, deliberately prepared to commit the bishops to terms. Thomas à Becket, Archbishop of Canterbury, refused to sign, an act regarded as treacherous by Henry, his former friend, the dispute eventually leading to Becket's assassination by sword in 1170.

Henry had the 'Assize of Clarendon' ratified at the Palace in 1166. The document was responsible for initiating trial by jury, as opposed to trial by ordeal or battle.

Clarendon Palace became centrepiece to the largest deer park in medieval England. Further excavations in the 1960s, 70s and 80s revealed richly decorated royal apartments, chambers, kitchens, courtyard, chapel, salsary (for butchering fallow deer), and a great hall built by Henry III around 1230 – the focus of the Royal Palace – all set in the heart of Clarendon Forest.

Following Charles II's execution, Clarendon was seized by parliament, and the palace gradually fell into ruin. In 2017, masons from Somerset-based company Minerva Stone worked to conserve the remains, under the watchful eye of the resident llamas.

The habitation of kings is levelled with the dust and all the proud revelry of the court has given way to the hooting of the owl and the croaking of the raven.
John Britton, 1801

ABOVE: Minerva Stone renovating Clarendon Palace, 2017
BELOW: Veteran oak and beech on the park pale, 2017

The Tythe Barn Bradford on Avon, Wiltshire

During the sixth and seventh centuries, Bradford on Avon was at the frontier of Saxon Wessex – the River Avon and Selwood Forest forming a geographical and political boundary – until the Battle of Peonnum in 658 enabled expansion west to the River Parrett.

In 1001, Ethelred II (The Unready) gifted the Manor of Bradford to medieval England's richest nunnery at Shaftesbury as a refuge for nuns along with the remains of his assassinated half-brother Edward the Martyr for burial at Shaftesbury.

Shaftesbury Abbey established Barton Grange to farm the surrounding lands, and built a large limestone tythe barn, to store their 'tythes' – the entitlement to a tenth of the property's agricultural produce. The barn, 51m (168ft) long and 9.5m (31ft) wide, retains a magnificent raised cruck roof, constructed from pairs of oak 'crucks' – large, curved timbers that rise from the ground to meet at the apex.

The building style pointed to 14th-century construction, but it was not until 1993 that dendrochronology (tree ring analysis) of surviving oak timbers confirmed a construction date of the 1330s.

The cruck blades were formed from whole and split timbers selected from naturally curved tree trunks, which were shown to have been felled between 1334 and 1379, from trees no older than 150 years. None of the timbers were seasoned. In medieval times timber was selected as required, felled and worked green, when it was easier to shape, especially in the case of hardwoods like oak.

In 1546, following the Dissolution of the Monasteries, Henry VIII granted Bradford Manor to Sir Edward Bellingham of the Privy Council. The property changed hands several times until 1914, when the Hobhouse family – owners since 1850 – passed ownership of the barn to the Wiltshire Archaeological Society, who commissioned repairs, with further work undertaken on the roof by the Ministry of Works in the 1950s.

The barn remained in use until 1974. Its oak timbers still support around 100 tons of stone tiling, as they have for almost seven centuries. It is now in the care of English Heritage.

To the wood that goes into Broughton, back to the seven pear trees, forth by Ælfnode's border to Æthelwine's border at Chalfield, from his border to the border of Ælfwine the Hoarder, forth by his border to Ælphwine's border at Broughton, back to the pear trees.

Grant by King Ethelred II detailing Bradford Manor boundary in 1001.

ABOVE: Bradford on Avon's Tythe Barn, c1910
BELOW: Tythe Barn roof timbers still in place, 2018

Salisbury Cathedral Wiltshire

When Bishop Richard Poore decided to relocate his Norman cathedral from Old Sarum – a strategically placed Iron Age hill fort subsequently occupied by all of Britain's various invaders – he effectively founded the new city of Salisbury.

The clergy was under pressure from the military – with whom they shared the site at Old Sarum – as the small, overcrowded town could not cope with a growing population and an inadequate water supply.

Legend has the bishop firing an arrow to decide where the new cathedral should be built. Landing over 3km (2 miles) away – said to have hit a deer that carried it further than it would ordinarily fly – the arrow came to rest in water meadows on the eastern bank of the River Avon (which were conveniently owned by Poore himself). And there a new cathedral was built. Foundation stones were laid in 1220, and the cathedral, which practically floats on its shallow, watery foundations, was eventually consecrated in 1258.

Salisbury is famed for its medieval spire – at 123m (404ft) the tallest in Britain – but originally the cathedral was topped only with a short lantern tower. The spire came later, constructed around 1330, reflecting the church's desire for status, and proximity to God. Defying the laws of physics, many predicted the spire would collapse, adding an additional 6,397 tons (6,500 tonnes) of weight which caused the supporting pillars in the cathedral directly below to buckle.

Within the spire itself, 332 steps above the ground, stands a large and impressive network of oak scaffold, traditionally thought to have been left in place following the spire's construction. Dendrochronology, documentation and structural analysis, however, suggest that the scaffold was added half a century later, probably erected to repair damage caused in a storm in 1362, providing restraint for the capstone and acting as a future maintenance aid.

Much of the oak used to construct the scaffold and cathedral (thought to be in the region of 1,000 trees) was sourced locally from the forests of Clarendon, Chippenham, Chute and Melksham, with some hauled all the way from Dublin.

ABOVE: Salisbury Cathedral c1920 – cedars of Lebanon remain in the cloisters

BELOW: Oak scaffold spire timbers still in place, 2018

King Arthur's Round Table

Winchester, Hampshire

King Arthur, legendary fifth-century Romano-British warlord, hero of Welsh poetry, chivalrous leader in medieval romance and literature – 'the once and future king' – delights and confounds in equal measure.

Defying all attempts to prove his 'real' existence – historical evidence is scant at best – the Arthurian legends remain deep rooted, continuing to inspire as they have for 1,500 years. Places bearing Arthur's name abound in Cornwall, Wales and Scotland where memories of Celtic Britain persist, maintaining its core mythological cycle.

Yet at Winchester, one piece of the Arthurian puzzle was long held to prove his existence. Arthur's Round Table, central to the legend of the Knights of the Round Table, essentially established a template for the chivalric age: the very fact that the table was round, not rectangular, meant that no one man was above any other and all who sat around it were seen as equal.

Constructed entirely from 121 pieces of English oak *(Quercus robur* and *Q. petraea)*, the table measures 17.25m (56.5ft) in circumference and weighs a hefty 1,200kg (1.2 tonnes). It has hung on the wall of Winchester Great Hall – last surviving building of Winchester Castle, seat of the Norman kings and founded in 1067 – since at least the 1460s.

Sir Thomas Malory, who wrote *Le Morte d'Arthur* in the 15th century – a hugely influential portrayal of Arthurian romance in its time – certainly believed the table was authentic, leading him to identify Winchester as Camelot – Arthur's legendary court and castle.

It was not until 1976, when the round table was removed for renovation, that radio carbon dating, dendrochronology and carpentry techniques suggested its construction took place between 1250 and 1280, from trees felled after 1236, in the reign of Edward I – possibly commissioned by the king for a great tournament or 'round table' held in 1285 or 1290.

The table remained unpainted until 1522, when the design was applied by order of Henry VIII, who had Arthur's image painted after his own likeness, thereby cementing his claim as rightful heir to the throne, directly descended from Arthur himself.

Arthur won all the north, Scotland... Also Wales... he overcame them all, as he did the remnant, through the noble prowess of himself and his knights of the Round Table.
From *Le Morte d'Arthur* by Malory, 1465

BELOW: King Arthur's Round Table, c1925
OPPOSITE: King Arthur's Round Table, 2018

When every morning brought a noble chance, And every chance brought out a noble knight. Such times have been not since the light that led The holy Elders with the gift of myrrh. But now the whole Round Table is dissolved Which was an image of the mighty world.
From *Idylls of the King* by Lord Tennyson, 1885

Grovely Forest Wiltshire

Grovely Wood (formerley Grovely Forest) is one of the largest mixed woodlands in southern Wiltshire, and stands on a high chalk ridge rising between the Wylye and Nadder river valleys, a few miles north west of Salisbury.

The Iron Age fortifications of Hanging Langford Camp at the wood's western edge and Grovely Castle to the north are testament to the area's prehistoric occupation. Grim's Ditch – an Iron Age earthwork thought to be over 2,000 years old – is still clearly visible and marks the northern extent of the wood.

The Roman road from Venta (Winchester) via Old Sarum (Salisbury) in the east runs straight through the wood, and doubtless follows an ancient ridgeway track as it continues west towards Charterhouse. The route of the road is still the main carriageway through the wood.

By 1086 Grovely became one of the smaller Norman Royal Forests, under Roger, the King's forester, but when viewed together with Cranborne Chase and the New Forest must have provided an extensive run for the royal hunt. By the 13th century Grovely's bounds enclosed an area of some $50km^2$ (20 miles^2) and, 100 years later, were subject to the authority of the Warden of Clarendon Forest.

In 1547, following the Dissolution of the Monasteries, Grovely was granted to the Earl of Pembroke, and it remains part of the Wilton family estate to this day. The forest contained 14 named coppices in 1603, an indication of the value of its worked underwood. Many of these are still maintained under their original names such as Ebsbury Copse and Powten Stone. That same year, a Charter of the Forest Court of Grovely granted rights to local villagers to common pasture and pannage, to gather dead wood, take boughs, and fell a load of wood annually. One buck was given to them every year by the forest ranger to feast on.

Tales told of an apparition of the 'Burcombe Woodsman', who was hanged from a tree for poaching in Grovely, recall the harsh punishments of Forest Law in response to taking the king's deer.

Oak Apple Day
Great Wishford, Wiltshire

Right: Oak bough house decoration at Great Wishford, 2016

The wood gathering and grazing rights asserted at Grovely in 1603 were at various times challenged by the Wilton Estate. In 1825, four villagers from Barford St Martin were arrested while gathering wood and imprisoned. One of those arrested, 19-year-old Grace Reed, contested the charge. The courts found against the Wilton Estate, upholding the villagers' right to gather wood or 'estovers'. However, Barford's right was lost in 1970, when the Parish Council, having misunderstood the document's significance, failed to register it.

One village however, Great Wishford, has never lost its right and continues with zest to uphold it. Every year on 29th May, Oak Apple Day, the villagers gather at dawn having been woken by a 'rough band'. They make their way up an ancient sunken lane a mile or so to Grovely Wood where green boughs of oak are cut and carried back to the village, along with any oak apples (growth balls caused by gall wasps on oak trees) that can be found, to be worn later.

The villagers then deck their houses with the boughs, saving the largest, which is hauled to the top of the for the 13th-century church tower. Known as the Marriage Bough, it is thought to bring luck to those marrying in the coming year.

After breakfast at the Royal Oak pub, the villagers make their way to Salisbury Cathedral and gather in Cathedral Close with traditional banners. They then proceed to the lawn by the west door where four women dressed in traditional costume perform two dances around bundles of oak wood that they have been carrying to the sound of an accordion.

The procession is then led to the high altar by the Dean and Chapter of the Cathedral where they are welcomed and read their forest rights from the charter. The tranquillity of the setting is then shattered by the villager's shout of 'Grovely, Grovely, Grovely and all Grovely', which asserts their right to gather wood.

The charter insists on only two 'Grovelys' in the shout, the third is added for good measure, 'all Grovely' confirms the rights over the whole wood, whereas villagers from Barford were restricted to their side of Grim's Dyke.

The retinue then withdraws to Great Wishford, where a parade, fête, maypole dancing and general revelry continues.

The tradition surely dates to pagan times, and was originally held at Whitsun, but was moved to Oak Apple Day sometime after the restoration of the monarchy in 1660 – the occasion which it celebrates. Many Mayday festivities countrywide were moved to the 29th May and incorporated oak apples and boughs. This was a reference to the Royal Oak that Charles II climbed in order to hide from the Parliamentarian troops at Boscobel, following his defeat at the Battle of Worcester in 1651.

The Monarch's Way – a 990km (615 mile) footpath that approximates Charles' route of escape to France after the battle – runs straight through Grovely Wood, further cementing the Oak Apple Day connection.

GROVELY FOREST

The lords, freeholders, tennants and inhabitants of the Manor of Great Wishford, or so many of them as in ancient time would used to go, in a dance, to the Cathedral church of our blessed lady, in the city of New Sarum in the county of Wiltshire, and there made their claim to the custom to the forest of Grovely in these words; 'Grovely, Grovely, Grovely and all Grovely!'

Item 17, *Charter of the Forest Court of Grovely*, 1603

THIS PAGE: Oak Apple Day, Great Wishford, 1946 (above) and 2016

GROVELY FOREST

The Witching Trees

Grovely Wood, Wiltshire

Historically, Grovely Forest was known as a 'damp oak wood', remembered in Great Wishford's continued traditions on Oak Apple Day. One time Lord of the Manor Sir Richard Grobham holds the dubious credential of slaying the last English wild boar in 1624.

While some oak woods remain, following the Second World War, as with many woodlands across the country, the Forestry Commission established large tracts of Douglas fir and Norway spruce at Grovely Wood. Today these account for 85% of its tree cover, while only 3% of ancient native woodland remains. The Commission aims to rectify this and improve biodiversity by reverting to a more natural landscape. The site is, however, a top spot for moths and butterflies, including the elusive tree-top dwelling purple emperor.

Mature beech trees are common at Grovely, with some fine trees lining the Roman road through the wood. Just south of the Roman road amongst thick groves of spruce stand four large beech trees with their own unique story.

In 1737 an outbreak of smallpox killed 132 people in the town of Wilton. Four sisters named Handsel who had recently moved to the area from Denmark, were accused of witchcraft by locals who blamed them for the deaths. Forcibly taken to Grovely Wood, the sisters were bludgeoned to death and buried a safe distance apart so that they could not conjure black arts against their assailants.

A tree was said to have been planted to mark each of their graves, and three veteran beech trees *(Fagus sylvatica)* measuring 5-6m (16-19ft) in girth stand tall. The fourth fell in a storm around the year 2010, its huge trunk and stump lying where it fell. The largest of the quartet, hollowing, twisted and gnarled, is often decorated with offerings and gifts left in its hollow, a practice remembered from time out of mind, honouring the memory of the unfortunate sisters, while perhaps recalling a more distant pagan custom.

ABOVE, BELOW AND OPPOSITE: The Witching Trees, 2016

Selwood Forest

Somerset, Wiltshire

The ancient forest of Selwood – from the Saxon *Sealhwudu* or 'Sallow Wood' (named after the willow that used to proliferate in its marshy vales and in some areas still does) – once stretched from Bruton in the west to Warminster in the east, and from Frome in the north to Shaftesbury in the south, covering an area some 16x48km (10x30 miles), according to John Leland, antiquary to Henry VIII, who travelled there in 1540.

As with most forests, Selwood consisted of a mixture of wooded and more open treescapes, marsh and field, and coupled with the high contour of the land running north to south, Selwood provided a natural geophysical border to the west. The British knew it as Coit Mawr – The Great Wood – and it is the site of several important historic battles.

In AD47, following the Roman invasion, Emperor Vespasian fought a battle at Penselwood in the south of the forest before leaving for Rome, having sworn the defeated King of the Britons to perpetual fealty.

Often described as a 'dense forest of damp oakwood', Selwood Forest was at least in part responsible for delaying western Saxon advancement on the British in the sixth century for up to 100 years, sited as it was on the British western frontier.

In 658, the Saxon King Kenwalh finally defeated British resistance at the Battle of Peonnum at Kenwalh Castle in Penselwood (Selwood Hill). The Iron Age hill fort is still known locally as Kenny Wilkin's Castle.

Two centuries later Selwood provided refuge for King Alfred and his men for two nights before England's defining Battle of Ethandune near Bratton in 878. After gathering support from the men of Somerset, Wiltshire and Hampshire against the marauding Danes, Alfred met them at Egbert's Stone, possibly near Alfred's Tower on Kingsettle Hill (although other sites contend for that honour). They rested the following night at Iley Oak, an

SELWOOD FOREST

Alfred rode to the stone of Egbert, in the eastern part of the wood called Selwood, which means in Latin Silva Magna, the great Wood, but in British Coit mawr...

At dawn the next morning the king moved his camp thence and came to a place called Iglea, and there encamped one night.

From *The Life of King Alfred* by Asser, 893.

ABOVE: Longleat House, 1818

BELOW: Robin Hood's Bower – likely site of Iley Oak, planted with monkey puzzle trees in 1966, 2016

OPPOSITE: Longleat's oldest tree – the Longleat Yew – 8.54m (28ft) in girth, 2016. It stands in the village of Temple, named after the Knights Templar of Templecombe who held the village in the 13th century, following their return from the Crusades. It measured 8.9m (29ft) in 1878.

ancient meeting place for the Warminster Hundred or Council thought to have been at Robin Hood's Bower, an ancient earthwork in Southliegh Wood. The next day they proceeded towards Ethandune where they utterly defeated the Danes. Iley Oak remained a meeting place for the Hundreds until 1652, and was subsequently used by non-conformists for secret meetings.

Claims have been made that the rotting stump of the Iley Oak remains at Robin Hood's Bower. Two large tree stumps can be seen, but they are most likely giant sequoias, removed around 1966 when the sixth Marquis of Bath planted the bower with monkey puzzle trees. In fact, Iley Oak – first mentioned in Asser's *Life of Alfred* in 893 – is likely to be a corruption of *Iglea* or *Aclea*, meaning a clearing amongst the oaks, as opposed to the name of one specific tree (*Ac*-oak, *Lea*-clearing).

By 1086, Selwood came under Norman Forest Law, primarily enclosed to protect the king's deer for the royal hunt, making life very difficult for the local populace in the process. Selwood remained under Forest Law until the disafforestation in 1630, when large parts were turned over to arable and pastoral farming.

From that period on, the area's fortunes were owed largely to a thriving wool trade, and substantial areas of wood pasture – where open-grown trees had been sustainably worked for centuries – were utilised for sheep farming. Although this practice is not conducive to the longevity of veteran trees, it is nonetheless largely responsible for the present day's surviving remnants. Wood pasture at Longleat is still part managed by sheep grazing on a field rotation basis.

Ancient trees from the medieval period are still extant. They are living links to Selwood Forest's history, notably in the grounds of manorial estates such as Longleat, Marston, Mells, Orchardleigh, Berkley, Ammerdown and Stourhead. Previously parts of the Royal Forest, sold by kings to favoured subjects in times of need to raise funds, and they have since been allowed the time and space to thrive.

ABOVE: The Elephant Beech, c1965

BELOW: The Elephant Beech on the first school run after the felling – young child asks "What have they done to the tree?" 2016

The Elephant Beech

Frome, Somerset

Around 685, St Aldhelm resolved to start a mission in Selwood Forest and built a church beside a spring on a hill above the River Frome. He arrived on midsummer's eve with six monks intent on converting to Christianity the native pagans who were apparently 'living in a state of wickedness' at Woodlands, 5km (3 miles) to the south of the town. (The name lives on in the still-wooded East and West Woodlands.)

It is likely that the abbot was prompted by Caedwalla, King of Wessex, who was keen to establish a hunting lodge in the forest, but first sought to remove the threat from hordes of robbers, said to have 'kept the inhabitants of the area in a constant state of terror'.

A church dedicated to St John has stood on the site ever since, and has benefited more recently from a copper beech tree planted around 1865, when William Bennett restored the church and surrounding yard.

The oldest tree in the town centre, with a trunk measuring 5.15m (16.9ft) in circumference and standing 30m (98ft) tall with a glorious crimson canopy, the Elephant Beech's days were numbered once it was found to host a Ganoderma bracket fungus, which caused internal decay to the trunk.

Specialist ancient tree arboriculturists suggested the tree's life could be prolonged with a programme of works. Had the tree grown in a field or wood, or even been 18m (20 yards) further away from Blind Alley, which runs beside it, it may have been saved. But on Friday 24 June 2016, after 11 years of monitoring, Mendip District Council had the tree felled following consultation with the health and safety officer.

Around 3.6m (12ft) of stump was retained for biodiversity – ancient trees host myriad life-forms not supported by younger trees – and as a monument to its former glory.

Much of the timber was retained by Frome Town Council and a section now hangs in Frome Museum.

Frome town centre's last ancient tree has been lost, relegated to Selwood Forest's long history, but the spring remains, flowing through the town via an ancient leat as it has done for centuries.

ABOVE: A large section of the Elephant Beech was moved to a playground at Frome Cheeseshow field – a natural and substantial climbing frame, with other sections placed as benches in several green spaces. The spalted texture is caused by fungal colonisation as the wood decays, 2018

RIGHT: The Elephant Beech the night before it was felled, replete with woven offerings and a note pleading for its salvation. Seen in golden sunlight 23rd June 2016

BELOW: Face of 'The Old Man of Froome' in the trunk, 2016

Birch Tradition

Frome, Somerset

The once-widespread tradition of hanging birch branches in church at Pentecost (to celebrate the descent of the Holy Spirit upon the Apostles) is still maintained at St John's Church in Frome.

Each May, permission is sought to top young birch trees at Longleat, and hang the cut branches along the entire length of the church on either side of its naves.

First recorded in 1836 and thought to represent the renewal of life, the tradition probably reflects much older pagan fertility rites and Freya, Norse Goddess of fertility. The maypole, centrepiece for fertility rites and dances, was traditionally made from birch, as were the heads of besom brooms, still used in the 19th century for 'jumping the broom' at wedding ceremonies.

Beating the bounds – another ancient custom whereby communities walked the boundaries of the parish and literally beat them with birch branches – occurred around the same time of year. It is likely that after Whitsun celebrations the branches at St John's were used for that very purpose as well.

Most beautiful of forest trees – the Lady of the Woods.
From *The Picture, or the Lover's Resolution* by Samuel Taylor Coleridge, 1802

ABOVE: Ancient birch at Longleat, 2016
BELOW: Birch branches in St John's Church c1900 and 2016

The Bounds of Selwood
Wiltshire, Somerset

The punishment, pecuniary or corporal, of forest offences, is outside the jurisdiction of the other courts, and solely dependent on the decision of the King.

Before maps were easily accessible and with a largely illiterate population, it was necessary for landowners, parishes and royal forests to physically mark boundaries on the ground with stones, trees and embankments, to ensure everybody knew precisely where the limits lay.

Important for territorial reasons, it also helped settle disputes between neighbouring owners and tenants whose grazing livestock often strayed, and to prosecute poachers intent on helping themselves to the king's game and firewood.

Around Selwood and many other forests, at great effort and expense, large embankments were dug for demarcation. An outer ditch and inner rampart also helped keep game within the bounds, making it difficult for the animals to escape.

The practice of beating the bounds appears to date back to at least Saxon times when it was known as 'ganging': communities would walk the bounds and beat boundary markers with birch wands, along with anybody else who happened to be in the way. Still commonly used in the north east with its original Old English meaning, 'to go', the word has developed over the centuries to mean a large rough gathering, or more simply: a gang.

By Norman times Forest Law was upheld with a heavy hand, delivered by foresters and verderers who were often despised by local people for abusing their positions of privilege. Punishments were harsh, and could include penalty of death, but that did little to deter desperate would-be offenders.

Between 1217 and 1300, five actual perambulations – whereby the bounds of the forest were walked and recorded – show a continual reduction in size of the forest, which was gradually eaten away by enclosure and agriculture, and as a result of protestations by local people trying to eke a living.

In 1257, forest pleas held at Ilchester list the names of 21 men of Frome charged with poaching, each was fined around 12d. In 1613, the Leversedges of Frome and Sir Thomas Thynne of Longleat were deemed to have caused over £5,000 worth of damage by killing royal deer, felling 3,000 trees, taking underwood and spoiling pasture. Forest law became an instrument for raising money, and would continue until the disafforestation in 1630, when the royal forest was once again reduced to a status of 'ordinary ground'.

BELOW: A 4.75m (15,6ft) girthed beech tree stands on forest bounds at Rough Cliff. These bounds are within Selwood Forest, marking internal boundaries to Witham Friary – church lands exempt from Forest Law.

SELWOOD FOREST

Capability Brown at Longleat

Longleat, Wiltshire

The park is about 16 miles in circumference and five miles across, and includes within it the only remaining part of the original forest of Selwood.

From *A Short History of Frome Selwood*, c1885

Following the Dissolution of the Monasteries, in 1540 Sir John Thynne snapped up the Longleat Estate (from 'long-leta', signifying long stream) for the princely sum of £53. Longleat was formerly home to brethren of the Priory of Black Cannons who had established a monastery there by 1235. The manor house subsequently built by Thynne has remained in the family ever since.

Successive lords of the manor initiated the planting of tree groves and avenues on the estate, providing a continuity of planting which survives to this day.

In 1754 the celebrated landscape gardener 'Capability' Brown was called upon to re-fashion the grounds in his own particular style. He allowed trees and shrubs to flourish, and added lime and elm trees on the lower slopes and beech to the higher ground to enhance the sweeping views from the house.

With the exception of elms – devastated by Dutch elm disease in the 1960s and 70s – a large number of the trees survive, although Longleat fell victim to the Great Storm of 1987 and lost many large, fine beech trees on the high ground at Heaven's Gate.

LEFT: Beech trees at Heaven's Gate, Longleat c1925, taken by Frome photographer Aldhelm Ashby

ABOVE: The same stand of trees in 2016

Heaven's Gate and Bishop Ken

Longleat, Wiltshire

Born in 1637, Bishop Ken was appointed Bishop of Bath and Wells in 1684. The appointment was commended by Charles II, although Ken had previously amused and displeased the King in equal measure by refusing lodgings to his mistress Nell Gwynne on 'moral grounds'.

Four years later Ken refused to publish James II's *Declaration of Independence,* and was committed to the Tower on a charge of high misdemeanour, but was later acquitted.

He did however lose his Bishopric, and for the next 20 years took lodgings at Longleat, where he wrote many hymns, including his famous *Morning Song* and *Evening Song.* These were said to have been inspired by the panoramic views across Selwood Forest from Heaven's Gate.

Ken died in 1711 and was entombed in the churchyard at St John's Church in Frome.

A great number of tourists mount the hill towards the house and spread their fare on nature's table cloth, the green grass, beneath the trees at "Heaven's Gate"; where a magnificent expanse of scenery is open before them, whilst at their feet lies the mansion with its lake and deer park, through which roam 700 or 800 head of deer.

From *A History of Longleat,* 1882

LEFT: Bishop Ken depicted in stained glass at St John's Church, Frome, 2016

FROM TOP: Views from Heaven's Gate, Longleat 1882, c1905 and 2016. Little visible change through 134 years.

The Lion of Longleat

Longleat, Wiltshire

The largest-girthed and possibly oldest living oak on the Longleat Estate stands in wood pasture at the southern edge of the 'Grove' in the old deer park, which has existed at Longleat since at least 1579 (according to Saxton's map of that year, which clearly defines the circular park pale). Deer parks have proved to provide a good environment for ancient oaks by affording them the time and space required to reach their full potential, growing through the three stages of youth, maturity and decline. More ancient oaks are found in deer parks than anywhere else in Britain.

I call the oak 'The Lion of Longleat' (the safari park lions can often be heard roaring nearby). Lions may be king of the jungle, this oak is surely king of Longleat Forest.

Putting an age on Britain's ancient trees is a tricky business. Without a known planting date, the fact that native trunks hollow out makes accurate ageing by counting annual growth rings impossible. The Lion of Longleat is completely hollow from tip to root – bats and barn owls fly from its trunk and tree creepers feed from its bark. It is host to a bees nest, an array of fungi and myriad invertebrate creatures – few of which harm the tree. The oak is truly a biodiversity hotspot.

In 2014 I found its girth to measure 8.17m (26.8ft). By 2017 it had grown to 8.20m (26.9ft) – enlarging in circumference by 3cm in just three years. That equates to an average yearly growth ring width of 4.7mm. If taken as an average yearly growth rate for the life of the tree, that would make the Lion of Longleat around 575 years old, meaning it started life around 1442, before the Dissolution of the Monasteries, placing it firmly at a time when Longleat still belonged to the Black Cannon Priory. It is an ancient, monasterial oak.

Given that tree growth rings fluctuate depending on environmental conditions (a nearby felled oak showed growth rings varying from 2-7mm), 575 years could be a fairly conservative estimate.

In 2015 I grew a tree from an acorn collected from the Lion of Longleat. It was planted close to its parent in 2017, signifying in a small way, a revival of the Forest of Selwood.

As the lion is king of beasts, and the eagle, king of birds, the oak is the king of the forest, most noble and puissant of trees, largest and strongest, eternal emblem of grandeur, strength and endurance, of force that resists as the lion is of force that acts.

From *The New Book of Trees* by Marcus Woodward, c1920

ABOVE: Red deer hind at Longleat
OPPOSITE: The Lion of Longleat, 2017
BELOW: Offspring planted close to parent tree, 2017

SELWOOD FOREST

The Marston Yew

Marston Bigot, Somerset

South of Frome, due west of Longleat, lies the estate of Marston Bigot, a small but well-preserved manorial remnant of Selwood Forest, recorded in Domesday as having three square miles of woodland.

On the lawn below the mid-17th-century Manor House stands an ancient yew *(Taxus baccata)*, 8.90m (21ft) in circumference, larger even than Longleat's giant of the species at Temple.

At first glance the tree appears solid, but on closer inspection the trunk reveals itself to be hollow, with substantial internal root and branch regrowth typical of the species. These regenerative properties are part of the reason why the Church assimilated ancient yews from former pagan sites into its churchyards, to signify eternal life in the hereafter.

This begs the question, why does the Marston Yew survive on a garden lawn? Many ancient yews are preserved in churchyards, sometimes in ancient woodland, but rarely in a garden. And this tree is no exception: a church did indeed stand near the tree as early as the 12th century, granted to the Abbey of Cirencester between 1160 and 1173. Shown on a print from 1739, the building was described by Edmund Rack as a 'mean edifice' in his Survey of Somerset c1785. This may explain why Edmund, Seventh Earl of Cork and Orrery – lord of the manor – had it removed and built a new church further from the house between 1787 and 1789. The demolition also had the effect of opening up extensive views across the vale of elm and oak wood pasture towards the Wiltshire Ridge. Thankfully for the yew, Edmund seems to have inherited his parents regard for trees, evidenced in a letter written by his mother to his father in 1744: 'As to the trees, I cannot cut them down, it is like taking away a dozen of your best heads and honestest hearts from amidst your House of Lords.'

The current view owes much to landscaper Stephen Switzer's 'gradual transition from finished art to wild nature' between 1724 and 1745, and further remodelling by William Gilpin, including the creation of Marston Pond, in the 1820s.

The Pleasure Grounds are naturally beautiful... and contain some grand specimen trees, including a magnificent Turkey Oak and one of the finest English Yews in the West.
From *Watson and Lees Sale Catalogue*, 1905

In the churchyard is a fine old yew 23ft in circumference 4ft above the ground.
From *Edmund Rack's Survey of Somerset*, c1785

ABOVE: Marston House, 1818
BELOW: The ancient Marston Yew, 2016

Black Dog Wood

Berkley, Somerset

A dog with burning eyes haunts… Black Dog Woods… anyone who sees it will be dead by Christmas.

From *Wilts folklore & legends* by Ralph Whitlock, 1992

To the north east of Frome lies the village of Berkley, meaning birch clearing – a tree still in abundance there, and obviously cleared to make way for Berkley House. The grounds are still laid out to wood pasture with a good number of veteran and ancient oaks, many showing signs of pollarding, having been worked for most of their lives.

To the south east of the house stands Black Dog Wood, richly wooded to this day with native oak, birch, ash and beech with hazel and holly understory, although the hazel coppices and pollard oaks struggle for light as the ungrazed forest floor reverts to wildwood.

A large vetetran yew tree 4.8m (15.7ft) in girth marks the Somerset/Wiltshire border, and stands beside earthworks denoting the same. The tree is plotted on early OS Maps (1843-1893) and is said to be 1,000 years old (unconfirmed). However, unusually for an ancient tree, the trunk appears not to be hollow, so an annual ring count could conceivably be made with an increment borer.

Formerly known as Gibbet Wood and Prickets Wood, Black Dog Wood is said to have been named after the tale of a maiden whose hand in marriage was sought by two suitors. They decided to settle the matter by duel in the wood. One of the men was shot dead. The victor was then attacked and mauled to death by the dead man's black dog. The maiden, distraught by proceedings, took her own life. She was buried nearby at Dead Maids crossroads.

Another story sees the 'black dog' as accomplice to a local highwayman, who conducted his business on Black Dog Hill, which runs through the wood, and had his dog attack passing stage coach drivers so he could relieve the passengers of their belongings.

ABOVE: County border yew, Black Dog Wood (with white dog), 2016

The Witches of Selwood

Somerset

Pendle in Lancashire is perhaps best remembered for its Witch Trials of 1612 where 12 'witches' – 11 of them women – were tried for committing murder by witchcraft. The trials resulted in the deaths of ten of the women, who were hanged on the moor.

While perhaps less well known, Selwood Forest was long held to have a deep connection with demonology, and was inclined toward the unrestrained persecution of its witches. Those 'living in a state of wickedness' when St Aldhelm arrived c685 to deliver them from their heathen practices, were doubtless living 'the old ways', using incantations alongside herbs and medicines to heal. The practice appears to have survived in part into the 17th century, fuelling a campaign of persecution that became entrenched following the Civil War.

Between the 15th and 18th centuries, witch trials saw around 500 people either hanged or burnt to death. Thousands more were harmed or tortured. Victims were predominantly women, invariably poor and often old, convicted by spurious and circumstantial evidence.

Trials are recorded for witchcraft, with covens alleged to have been discovered in wooded groves at Stoke Trister and Brewham. Bewitchments were reported at Bruton, Kilmington, Wincanton and most famously at Beckington, where one young victim, Mary Hill, declared she had thrown up 200 crooked pins over a fortnight. The accused, Elizabeth Carrier, was subjected to three swimming tests in the River Frome – ordeal by water – but each time found not guilty due to lack of evidence.

Others were not so lucky. In 1730 one accused of witchcraft lost her life in a fatal witch swimming in the same river at Frome, an outcome that, by the laws of the time, proved her innocence.

All the nation are already physicians. If you ail anything, everyone you meet, whether a man or a woman, will prescribe you a medicine for it.
Nicholas Culpepper, 1649

ABOVE: Manifestations of the Devil from *Saducismus triumphatus or Full and plain evidence concerning witches*, 1681
OPPOSITE: The Magic Tree, 8m (26ft) girth oak, Bruton, 2016

These miserable wretches are so odious unto all their neighbours, and so feared, as few dare offend them, or deny them anything they seek.
From *The Discoverie of Witchcraft* by Reginald Scot, 1584

Stourhead Sweet Chestnuts

Stourton, Wiltshire

*Close-grain'd chestnut, wood of sov'reign use,
For casking up the grapes' most powerful juice.*
From *The Garden* by René Rapin, 1665

Above: Stourhead House, 1818
Below: Ancient sweet chestnut tree, 1844

At the southern edge of Selwood Forest sits the Stourhead Estate, historically exempt from Forest Law but geographically absorbed by it.

The Stourton family owned the estate for 500 years, John Stourton being granted a licence to empark deer in 1474, before selling to Sir Thomas Meres in 1714. Three years later Meres' son John let it go to Henry Hoare, the son of a wealthy banker, for £14,000.

Henry 'the good' immediately set about transforming the estate. By 1725, the year of his death, he had demolished the near-derelict Stourton Manor and had a fashionable Palladium Villa built in its place. He also damned the River Stour to create a lake with vistas. The estate remained in the family, with each successive generation adding something of their own identity to the property.

Described as 'a living work of art' when first opened in the 1740s, Stourhead is famous for its folly temples, grottos, commanding views across the lake and collection of exotic plants and trees. In 1946, Sir Henry Hugh Arthur Hoare – the last member of the family to own the property – gifted the house, gardens and 100ha (247 acres) of woodland to the National Trust.

Lining the driveway to the house stands a row of five ancient sweet chestnut trees *(Castanea sativa)*. The largest has a girth of 8m (26ft), all are hollowing pollards, twisted and gnarled and have lost limbs, but appear healthy and strong. Two more of similar stature stand in the adjacent field, most likely planted by the Stourton family at around the same time in the 17th century.

A large, attractive tree, the sweet chestnut yields good timber – favourable for palings, gates and casking wine – its fruit a delicacy for princes on the continent, but only fit to feed to swine and stuff turkeys in Britain according to John Evelyn, the celebrated 17th-century writer and gardener.

Six Wells

Stourton, Wiltshire

Just to the north of Stourhead house and gardens is Six Wells Bottom, a natural sweeping valley running from Alfred's Tower down to the estate. At the top of the southern bank of the valley rises Park Hill Camp, now heavily wooded with coniferous plantation but once an Iron Age hillfort – a Celtic stronghold before the domination of the Saxons.

At the upper end of the valley is Six Wells Pump, originally part of Bristol's water system but removed by act of Parliament in 1766 was rebuilt at the source of the River Stour by Henry Hoare in 1768. As the name suggests, there were once six springs at the pump, as depicted on the Stourton coat of arms, but now only one remains, flowing through the valley and eventually reaching the sea at Christchurch, 96km (60 miles) away.

Here stands the fir to Hoare's all-fost'ring hand
Debtor for its sublimity – the pride
From *A ride and a walk through Stourhead* Anon, c1780

Either side of the pump stands a veteran tree – an oak on the north side and an ash on the south, in all probability planted at the time of the pump installation. The oak measures almost 5m (16.5ft) in girth, and is heavily burred from prolonged grazing by Exmoor horn sheep. Limousin cattle also graze in the valley from spring to autumn.

The ash measures only 1.75m (5.74ft) around and is heavily decayed, with bark remaining only on its southern side, meaning it stands at just a fraction of its former size. The National Trust have planted young trees near the veterans for continuity.

BELOW: Six Wells Bottom – pump to the left, oak to the right, 2016

Last Tree Dreaming

Stourhead, Wiltshire

In February 2013, a 25m (82ft) tall oak tree weighing 11 tonnes fell during a storm in Turner's Paddock on the Stourhead Estate where it had been standing for around 250 years. The paddock was so named after JMW Turner, who painted *View over the lake at Stourhead* there in 1798.

Local visual artist Barry Cooper noticed that the fallen oak appeared in Turner's painting as a young tree and, struck by its significance, set about creating a community project to celebrate the tree and the wider Selwood Forest.

Barry approached the Stourhead Estate, who agreed to donate the oak to Frome College, and he assembled a team to apply for funding. They were successfully awarded £40,000 from the Heritage Lottery Fund to involve Frome's young people in the tree's historical and ecological heritage. Barry named the project 'Last Tree Dreaming'.

The team arranged to relocate the tree trunk, transporting it on the back of a flat-bed lorry the 20km (9 miles) journey from Stourhead to Frome, where it was set down in the playing field next to the school.

Over the next two years, students and youth and community groups from the local area carved personal and aspirational carvings into rectangular recesses in the trunk, prepared by wood sculptor Anthony Rogers.

On 31 August 2016 the tree was erected in the playing field beside the college – a major feat of engineering – where it will remain for 50 years, after which it will be laid down and allowed to decay naturally, giving the children and grandchildren of the original carvers a chance to see their forebears' artworks.

To complete the project, Barry envisions a 24km (15 mile) walk starting in Frome, running through the heart of Selwood to Stourhead where the journey began.

ABOVE: Last Tree Dreaming in-situ, 2017
BELOW: The author's carved acorn, 2017

The Sweet Track

Shapwick Heath, Somerset

ABOVE: The Meare Heath Track, 2017
BELOW: The Sweet Track, 2017

In 1970, Ray Sweet, a peat worker, stumbled across some buried timber while cleaning ditches on the Somerset Levels. Subsequent excavation and analysis revealed that Ray had discovered the remains of an ancient Neolithic trackway that had laid preserved in the wet peat land for almost 6,000 years.

The Neolithic saw communities move towards a more settled lifestyle – these were early farmers who utilised both wet marshland, pasture and wooded upland resources. The 2km (1.24 mile) long Sweet Track (named after its discoverer), was built on reed-swamp that separated Westhay Island from Polden Ridge to the south, and was part of a network of trackways that connected settlements on drier land.

Carbon dating and dendrochronology revealed that the Sweet Track was made from timber cut in the winter/early spring of 3806-3807BC and constructed soon afterwards. Nothing more than stone and flint hand axes, wooden wedges and mallets were used, illustrating a good understanding of carpentry.

Sharpened alder and hazel pegs, obliquely driven into the peat, supported 3m (9.84ft) length rails of oak, ash and lime, secured in place by vertical pegs. The size and shape of the pegs suggest that they were harvested from a worked coppice, providing early evidence of woodland managed by people.

Some of the oak planks were shown to have been split from 400-year-old trees 3m (9.84ft) in girth.

Maintenance was undertaken on the track for only ten years. It was probably abandoned as water levels rose, consuming it into its peaty preserve.

Of the many Neolithic trackways found in Britain, more than half are in Somerset and, while the Sweet Track assisted purely local travel, a jade axe head found nearby – originating from the French Alps – indicates a much wider travel network.

King and Queen Oaks

Hazelgrove, Somerset

ABOVE: The King John Oak painted by a member of the Mildmay family in 1849
OPPOSITE: The King John Oak, 2016
BELOW: The Queen Elizabeth Oak, 2016

To the south of Selwood Forest lies Cadbury Camelot, a 7ha (18 acre) hillfort – legendary stronghold of King Arthur – shown by Leslie Alcock's excavations in the 1960s to have been redefended following the departure of the Romans after 383. This was the case for many of the 70 or so hillforts spread across the Somerset hills. Cadbury Camelot sits next to the parish of Queen Camel, which by the 11th century belonged to Earl Godwin, the most powerful man in England. He gave it to his wife Countess Gytha as dower – a share for life of her husband's estate – and according to tradition it was there that she heard of her son Harold's death at Hastings in 1066. Soon after William the Conqueror seized the manor for himself.

Two royal deer parks were established and in 1633 reported as ancient by Gerard, who described 'a grove of oaks of remarkable girth' at Hazlegrove, the northernmost of the two parks. A manor house was built there when Sir Walter Mildmay acquired Hazelgrove between 1556 and 1558. Near the house stand two relic oaks *(Quercus robur)* – the King John Oak, an ancient but healthy giant measuring 10.7m (35ft) around, and the Queen Elizabeth Oak, slightly smaller at 9.24m (30.3ft). It is not unlikely that these trees date back to the reigns of their royal namesakes.

A plan of the Manor of Queen Camel from 1795 shows an avenue of elm trees lining the driveway to the house. The trees are marked on early Ordnance Survey a century later, but by the 1950s they had succumbed to Dutch elm disease.

American servicemen, treated at Hazelgrove House when used as a hospital during the Second World War, planted an American red oak *(Quercus coccinae)*. The tree appears to have lacked the tenacity of its native cousins and stands moribund among the chestnuts, limes and native oaks.

In 1947 a preparatory school leased the house and then bought it outright in 1952, hopefully providing safe haven for its most venerable vegetation.

"Hazlegrove House lies to the north of the hamlet"; to quote Phelps, the county historian, it "stands on a gentle elevation surrounded by a park-like lawn well clothed with fine timber." From Country Life, 1929

Blackmore Forest Dorset

Arable lands are few and limited; with but slight exceptions the prospect is a broad rich mass of grass and trees, mantling minor hills and dales with the major. Such is the Vale of Blackmoor.
From *Tess of the D'Urbervilles* by Thomas Hardy, 1891

Blackmore Forest encompassed much of the area now known as the Blackmore Vale. It is thought to be named after a hamlet in the heart of the forest and is notable for one notorious resident: John Clavel a 17th-century, poet, lawyer, doctor and highwayman.

Described by Leland as stretching from Yeovil in the west to Shaftesbury in the east, Blackmore Forest was bordered by Gillingham Forest to the north and Cranborne Chase to the east, comprising an almost continuous band of forest running from Windsor to Selwood.

Blackmore is still recognisable from Hardy's description (above), similar to how it may have appeared a thousand years before. Woods it most certainly did have, both coppiced and timber, mostly owned by the powerful landowners at Cerne Abbey.

Its first mention as a Royal Forest appears in 1215 when King John demanded deer for the royal table, and while kings rarely hunted in Blackmore, a story involving Henry III remains writ large in local folklore. Having 'run down' several deer whilst hunting in the forest, Henry spotted a milk-white hart and, struck by its beauty, spared the beast. Thomas de Linde, a local landowner present at the hunt, ignored the King's mercy and slew the deer at Pulham. De Linde received the King's wrath in the form of a severe fine payable annually to the King's exchequer, a tax subsequently referred to as White Hart Silver. The story is remembered on pictorial tiles in Holwell Church, now a private residence.

Records show abbots and commoners alike frequently disregarding Forest Law to fell trees for profit or to poach game. They were prepared to suffer heavy fines for the privilege, which in effect became just another revenue stream for the Crown.

Ancient bluebell woodland at Piddles Wood and fine wood pasture at Minterne and Stock Gaylard estates endure as living remnants of Blackmore Forest's sylvan past.

BLACKMORE FOREST

Stock Gaylard
Dorset

At the eastern edge of Blackmore Forest sits the Stock Gaylard Estate, formerly a Saxon village owned by William of Eu in 1086, according to the Domesday Survey of that year.

In 1268, a license to empark deer was granted, marking it as one of the earliest medieval deer parks in Dorset. A herd of around 150 menil fallow deer still roam the 32ha (80 acre) deer park today, enclosed by a wrought-iron fence erected in the 1880s.

An old folk belief still held by some locals claims that rain is imminent if the deer gather close to the southern edge of the deer park, and sunny weather if they gather in the middle of the park. Not so daft when you consider that the interior displays open grown wood pasture, whereas the southern edge is more densely wooded and provides the deer with better shelter from the rain.

The name Stock Gaylard derives from 'stock', meaning log – a reference to the estate's plentiful woodland in historic times – and a corruption of 'Coylard' – the family name of its ancient lords.

In 2012, the park was designated an SSSI (Site of Special Scientific Interest). The fact that it avoids the use of inorganic pesticides and fertilisers makes it a perfect environment for the ancient oaks, as well as the invertebrates, animals, birds, lichens and fungi that they support.

Every year in August the estate opens its gates to the public to celebrate the annual Oak Fair. The event caters for those interested in woodcraft, timber, conservation and the countryside and has done since 2005. Activities include traditional woodcrafts and woodland pursuits such as timber house building, falconry and heavy horse logging – still active in places inaccessible to modern machinery.

Within the ancient forest now called the Vale of Blackmore or Blake more, is Stock, where William de Cantilupe is recognised as the possessor of the park in the thirty-second of Henry III.
From *Deer and Deer Parks* by Evelyn Shirley, 1867

ABOVE: Wood pasture in the deer park, 2014
BELOW: Menil fallow deer in the deer park, 2017

The Crusader Oak

Stock Gaylard, Dorset

Mark yonder wood high tow'ring on the right
How rich with green of every tint and hue !
The pine's deep gloom, the chesnut's lighter shade
And the huge branching oak that dark and full
O'erhangs and sombres all…

From *Brent Knoll* by Henry Farr Yeatman, 1817

The most famous oak on the Stock Gaylard Estate is an ancient, hollow pedunculate oak *(Quercus robur)*, standing 7.5m (24.6ft) in girth and thought to be around 700 years old. Known as the Crusader Oak, the tree is named after Sir Ingelramus de Waleys who was lord of the manor in the 13th century. A Templar Knight, de Waleys was killed on crusade whilst fighting in Jerusalem around 1275. His dismembered body is said to have been carried back to England on pack-horse and buried in St Barnabas Church, which stands on the mansion lawns close to the house. De Waley is credited with founding the church, presumed to have been built on the site of an earlier Saxon monastic building.

In 1884 the church was restored in honour of the Reverend Henry Farr Yeatman, magistrate to the Assizes in Dorchester, and his wife, who resided at the manor from 1804. During renovation, workmen uncovered a chamber beneath a stone effigy of a knight. It contained the bones of a dismembered but complete skeleton, along with some shards of red leather, echoing the legend of De Waley's death and his return from the Holy Land.

The bones were once again laid to rest, this time in a wooden coffin, painted with a red Knights Templar Cross and returned to the chamber beneath De Waley's effigy.

Captain Harry Farr Yeatman, Henry's grandson, also died in Palestine whilst serving the Dorset Yeomanry in 1917. Buried in Jerusalem, a bronze memorial commemorates his life in the church opposite De Waley's effigy.

At first glance it may appear that the Crusader Oak has itself been in the wars – stag-headed branches, a gnarled leaning trunk and a multitude of holes and water pockets lend a battle-weary appearance. In its old age pollarding and natural retrenchment – a survival mechanism to help cope with senescence – it provides homes for a whole host of lifeforms including rare, threatened lichens found only on nutrient-rich tree bark, free from pollution and pesticides.

ABOVE: The Crusader Oak, 2017

Neroche Forest Somerset

Castle Neroche stands 265m (870ft) above sea level dominating the skyline on the Blackdown Hills for miles around, affording views on a clear day across six counties.

Its name derives from the old English *nierra* and *rechich*, meaning 'place where hounds are kept', an unimaginative but apt description considering the castle was a Norman motte and bailey stronghold used as a lodge from which to hunt in the surrounding forest.

Gifted to Robert, Count of Mortain by his half-brother William the year after the Norman Conquest in 1067, Castle Neroche held a strategic position guarding main routes to the west and south. Robert lived at the castle for 20 years before moving east to Montacute.

During the Iron Age the hillfort had been known as Dunn Meten, remembered today in the name of the neighbouring village, Dommett, and which could mean 'meeting place of the horses', again referring to the hunt.

The Saxons also no doubt staged hunts at Neroche before the Norman invasion – King Ina of Wessex is known to have held a Royal Palace at South Petherton, to the east.

In medieval times Neroche covered an area larger than 2,000ha (5,000 acres); today it measures around half that size.

In 1627 the forest came into the hands of the Portman family, and remained part of their estate until 1944 when it was purchased by the Crown Lands Commission. Three years later it was leased to the Forestry Commission who retain responsibility for its upkeep today. As elsewhere, that decision inevitably saw large coniferous plantations replace native broadleaf trees. So today the Forestry Commission is actively thinning these to help revive native woodland, wildlife and biodiversity.

LEFT: View from Castle Neroche looking west over the Blackdown Hills across wooded remnants of Neroche Forest. The photograph illustrates the changing treescape that has developed over centuries – in the foreground sweet chestnut trees high on the hillside give way to larch plantation in the valley, before native broadleaves – oak, ash and beech – climb the hills beyond.

Samples of pollen taken from Bywood Farm in Dunkeswell at the western edge of Neroche suggest a landscape consisting of open grassland interspersed with oak woodland and a hazel understory some 9,000 years ago. The pollen study also revealed that deforestation started in earnest around 2000BC, as the population moved from a nomadic to a more settled agricultural lifestyle, a practice that continued apace throughout the Bronze Age and beyond.

An open-wooded landscape similar to that early scene can still be found in some areas today, revealing a continuity of wood pasture habitat stretching back to the early medieval period. In 2005 the Neroche Project set out to celebrate, enhance and reinforce the heritage of Neroche Forest. Part of their work involved surveying veteran and ancient trees within the forest. Almost 1,000 veterans of 25 different species were measured, photographed and recorded on a database, with 22 trees measuring over 6.27m (20.5ft) in girth, confirming their ancient status. Most of the trees were oaks – our most common long-lived tree – but there were also notable specimens of beech measuring over 5m (16.4ft) in girth, field maple (11 of the 19 surveyed were coppices), and the comparatively rare black poplar. One of these measuring 6m (19.68ft) in girth was growing on steep-sided stream banks, or 'goyles' as they are known in this part of the world. The area also has plentiful hazel coppice growing in the shade of the broadleaves.

The ancient trees of Neroche offer a snapshot of a time gone by, bearing clues to an historic landscape where trees were retained for their economic benefits, a sustainable source of firewood, timber, mast and cover for the hunt and grazing animals.

As that beneficial relationship has diminished in recent years, ancient treescapes are often neglected. At Neroche, many of the light-loving pollard oaks have lapsed and become overshaded with undergrowth due to a lack of grazers. The Neroche Project has reintroduced old-breed longhorn cattle to encourage regeneration.

ABOVE: Veteran beech trees line the ramparts of Castle Neroche
BELOW: Beech-lined walkway towards Castle Neroche, 2016

The Wellington Witches
Wellington, Somerset

Somerset folklore tells the tale of the Wellington witches, who were said to meet at Coven Wood near the Wellington Monument. In 1750 an unfortunate soul caught spying on the coven was entombed inside a hollow oak for eternity. Apparently his contorted face is still visible at the base of the tree, and it is certainly true that ancient oaks often appear to display 'faces' in their twisted, gnarled trunks. Interestingly, the story closely reflects a legend of Merlin who suffered a similar fate after falling hopelessly in love with Nimue, the Lady of the Lake. Similarly, in the 15th century, the Welsh hero Owain Glyndwr is said to have imprisoned his mortally wounded but treacherous cousin Hywel Sele within the Nannau Oak, and left him there to die.

In 1878, workmen discovered a secret room with no entrance in the attic of a house they were demolishing. The room contained six brooms, an armchair and a rope with feathers woven into it. The men immediately declared the rope a 'witch's ladder'. Precious little evidence remains as to the true purpose of the 'witch's ladder, but local folklore and similar traditions in eastern Europe ascribe its use to 'get away the milk' from neighbours' cows and for casting death spells. Modern wicca used the ladders to bind positive wishes. The Wellington Witch's ladder has hung in the Pitt Rivers Museum in Oxford since 1911.

Witch hunts, common in late medieval times when innocent victims were often punished with gruesome penalties, were partly a result of demonising the old pagan religion. Hounding people unjustly in more recent times invokes the same term.

LEFT FROM TOP: Veteran 6.15m (20ft) lapsed pollard oak at Staple Lawns
Ancient coppiced field maple at Piddle Wood
Remnant oak wood pasture at Piddle Wood, 2016

NEROCHE FOREST

The Piddle Oaks

Piddle Wood, Staple Fitzpaine, Somerset

Sir Hugh Portman purchased Staple Deer Park in 1595 for the sum of £80. It was stocked with fallow deer – introduced by the Normans – and enclosed by a ditch and bank to keep stock for the hunt. In 1627 Charles I disafforested Neroche to raise funds for his Navy. Large tracts of the forest were purchased by Hugh's son, William, and later passed on to his son, Henry. The land remained in the hands of the Portman family for 350 years until 1944, when crippling death duties forced the sale to the Crown Lands Commission.

At the northern edge of the old deer park in Piddle Wood stand around 25 ancient oaks. Most of them are lapsed pollards – open-grown wood pasture trees that have been worked for centuries. In fact, they were probably worked until the advent of the coal industry, which effectively replaced wood as fuel in the late 19th century.

Three of the largest oaks in the group were named after the three generations of the Portman family previously mentioned: the largest, a hollow, mossed, crumbling giant measuring 8.10m (26.5ft) in circumference was named after Sir Henry, its nearest neighbour measuring 7m (23ft) after Sir Hugh, and a third giant named after Sir William.

Important as hosts for biodiversity, including rare lichens, invertebrates and fungi, the venerable oaks at Piddle Wood are a living link to the ancient forest of Neroche, presenting a vivid glimpse of the medieval landscape. Nearby stands Wychwood, named after the wych elms that undoubtedly flourished there until the advent of Dutch elm disease in the 1970s.

Many of the pathways through Piddle Wood became overgrown with scrub and dense beech plantation, denying the oaks the light they crave, so the Forestry Commission are gradually haloing the grove to release the old sentinels and offer them a new lease of life.

ABOVE: Sir Henry, Piddle Wood's oldest, largest oak, 2016
BELOW: Sir Hugh, companion to Sir Henry, 2016

The Remedy Oak
King's Wood, Woodlands, Dorset

According to tradition, King Edward VI sat under this tree and touched for King's Evil. Plaque beneath the Remedy Oak

Just 3.2km (2 miles) from the site of the Monmouth Ash – where the Duke of Monmouth was found hiding following his defeat at the Battle of Sedgemoor in 1685 – is a venerable tree known as The Remedy Oak *(Quercus robur)*. It stands over the crossroads at Remedy Gate, central to large tracts of ancient woodland, including a medieval deer park. The 6.42m (21ft) girthed hollow tree – likely a fraction of its former size – commemorates a lost but once prevalent-belief of the healing powers inherent within the ruling monarch.

In July 1552, Edward VI – son of Henry VIII – left Hampton Court with a large entourage and toured Southampton, the New Forest, Christchurch and Poole before arriving at Woodlands where he camped for four days to rest and take in some hunting at the park.

The story goes that Edward sat beneath the Remedy Oak where he 'touched for King's Evil'. King's Evil was a disease known as scrofula – a swelling of the lymph nodes in the neck caused by tuberculosis – and people believing that it could be cured by the King's touch, would line up to meet him.

The practice had been popular throughout England and France since Saxon times. Edward the Confessor (1003-1066) performed the ceremony which was upheld until Queen Anne's death in 1714.

The custom recalls ancient beliefs in the restorative powers of oak: derivative tannins and astringent acids from its bark have been applied to sores and have treated throat conditions for centuries.

The Remedy Oak, although a shadow of its former self, still cuts an imposing figure. The tree has regressed naturally, been lopped and pruned, and lost one large branch to a passing lorry whose driver was looking for Romford – in Essex! Mossed with age, the tree supports lichens and tree ferns, and sits in a carpet of snowdrops, bluebells and wood anemones in springtime. In its final throes, it is helped upright with cables, and a descendent grows beside it.

Ironically, Edward the 'Boy King' died within a year of his visit to Woodlands aged just 15, probably struck down by tuberculosis – the King's Evil – the very disease for which he was believed to hold the cure.

ABOVE: The Remedy Oak, 2016
BELOW: The Monmouth Ash, 1855

The New Forest Hampshire

The New Forest survives as one of Britain's best examples of a traditional medieval forest both from a landscape and from a cultural perspective. On the one hand, woodland, wood pasture, grassland, heathland, scrub and bog are kept largely open by grazing, and on the other, an ancient system founded under Forest Law still survives in part with a Court of Verderers, responsible for upholding rights of the common.

Originally known as 'Ytene' – after the Jutes that had settled there – William I's 'New Forest' was created in 1079, expanding former Saxon hunting ground. Taking advantage of poor, infertile lands, the founding of the forest nevertheless necessitated the removal of houses, hamlets and even entire villages, often along with the people that lived there. Harsh Forest Laws set up to protect the King's deer included the 'putting out of eyes' for those convicted of poaching, and 'expeditation', which was the enforced removal of three claws from the paws of large dogs.

Two of William's sons died there: Richard, gored to death by a stag around 1072, and King Rufus, killed instantly by an arrow fired by Walter Tyrell, that glanced off an oak (although some believe it was an assassination).

By the 16th century, the royal hunt had declined, and timber became the forest's primary commodity. Some of Nelson's ships were built from New Forest oak at Buckler's Hard: 2,000 oaks were used in the construction of HMS Agamemnon, for example. In 1608, 200,000 oaks were recorded in the New Forest. Three years later, 1,800 were felled for the navy and, by 1783, only 20,000 remained.

The 1851 Deer Act prompted the removal of the forest's 8,000 deer. A century later, half that number remained. Today, native red and roe deer, along with introduced fallow, sika and muntjac, collectively number around 1,500.

Charcoal burning, coppicing and pollarding have all seen a decline, but are remembered in ancient trees such as the King and Eagle Oaks. Non-native Forestry Commission plantations are now the chief timber resource.

Round broken columns clasping ivy twined;
O'er heaps of ruins stalk'd the stately hind;
The fox obsene to gaping tombs retires,
And savage howlings fill the sacred quires.
From *Windsor Forest* by Alexander Pope, c1712

ABOVE: Harry Brusher Mills – New Forest snake catcher – Standing beside a charcoal stack ready for burning, 1905

BELOW: New Forest gypsies (1856) who roamed the forest from the 16th century. The last family was evicted in 1963

OPPOSITE: Ancient pollard oak at Bolderwood, 2016

Grazing

Of all Britain's ancient forests, the New Forest exercises the most active use of common rights across its substantial territory. Once bounded by Southampton Waters to the east, the Solent to the south, the Avon to the west and Wiltshire to the north, the forest is still sizeable, covering around 27,114ha (67,000 acres).

The New Forest Act of 1877 re-established the Court of Verderers, upholding ancient common rights attached to properties in the forest. They are: estovers, the right to firewood, pannage (see opposite); and pasturage, the right to graze livestock, and are still practiced in the forest today.

Grazing has continued to sustain the open outlook of the New Forest. Cattle, donkeys and sheep are grazed there, but for most visitors, it is the free-roaming ponies that truly embody the character of the living forest.

New Forest ponies have grazed the forest for at least 2,000 years – prior to its occupation by either Norman or Saxon nobles – and have helped shape it. In 1066, William the Conqueror shipped 2,000 of them across the Channel to Normandy.

Today around 5,000 ponies roam the forest. They are semi-feral, not truly wild, as they are owned by the commoners. Five Agisters, employed by the Verderers, monitor them.

The ponies are hardy and rarely require treatment as they self-medicate on forest fauna. But over the last 50 years the rise in tourism and the massive increase in motor cars has become a threat to the ponies. In 2018 alone, 63 animals, including 38 ponies, died as a result of road traffic accidents.

Right from Top: New Forest grazers: highland cow, 2017; donkey, 2018; New Forest ponies, 2019

THE NEW FOREST

Pannage

The boar, when he seeth unavoidable death, he singleth out one of the Huntsmen and will run upon him, with the greatest rage imaginable. From *The History of Brutes* by Wolfgang Franz, 1670

Another important element of forest life was the right of pannage, or 'common of mast'. Once widespread across Britain, pannage gave commoners the right to fatten swine, and it is still observed in the New Forest.

Each autumn, around 600 pigs are turned out to feed on fallen acorns and beech mast. Poisonous to ponies and cattle, pigs devour acorns in quantity, with the best ham said to come from those fattened on them.

Place names across the country ending in 'den' or 'dean' (meaning 'swine pasture') bear witness to the practice: Dibden in the New Forest, Neasden in London and the Forest of Dean are examples. According to the Domesday Survey of 1086, woodland was often valued in terms of how many pigs it supported.

By the 19th century, swineherds released as many as 6,000 pigs into the forest for pannage. Fed in the first to the sound of a horn, they were retrieved by the same means. So many hungry pigs left few acorns to regenerate the oaks, and pannage was reduced. In times of hardship, acorns were also ground into meal to make bread and, prior to farming, they provided a natural staple.

The New Forest once hosted wild boar that were peculiar to the region – a cross with those imported from Germany by Charles I in his effort to restore game to the forest. The Civil War helped curtail that process, and by 1686 they had been hunted to extinction. The only wild boar in the forest today are those farmed in captivity for meat.

LEFT FROM TOP: Swineherds beating acorns from oaks to feed pigs, from *Queen Mary Psalter*, 1310-20
Attending hogs, 1855,
New Forest pigs, 2016

The Boxer Tree

Eyeworth Wood, Hampshire

ABOVE: The Boxer Tree, showing Jimmy Downer's carving, 2018
BELOW: The Boxer Tree, recently fallen, 2019

Eyeworth Wood is an ancient woodland near Fritham. New Forest ponies graze there in the dappled shade of beech and oak, on an abundant understory of holly, hawthorn and hazel, and among a mass of decaying, fallen tree trunks rich in moss, lichen and fungi.

Eyeworth's picturesque tranquility belies its working history; it is a a landscape that has adapted to many changes of use, dictated by the needs of people over centuries.

Eyeworth Manor is listed in the Domesday Survey as belonging to the king. By the 16th century it was a hunting lodge; later, it housed the forest keeper, who was responsible for managing the surrounding forest, a position traditionally passed from father to son, along with generations of accumulated local knowledge.

By 1859 the lodge was producing gunpowder. It became Shultze Gunpowder Factory in 1869, the first to produce 'smokeless gunpowder'. Owned by Edward Schultze, a Prussian artillery captain, the powder was apparently used to fight the 1870 Franco-Prussian war.

Shultze became a major local employer. A hundred people worked at the site, which was chosen for its remoteness (gunpowder being a volatile material) and for its abundance of coppice woodland to provide the necessary charcoal. Eyeworth Pond was constructed to supply water and, along with adjoining streams, became heavily polluted, killing its fish. Today, a century on, it is a haven for wildlife.

In Eyeworth Wood stood a beech tree *(Fagus sylvatica),* which for 100 years displayed a carving of a bare-knuckle boxer. It is said to have been carved by Jimmy Downer, a Shultze employee, to commemorate his victory in a bare-knuckle fight. The veteran tree stood 3.68m (12ft) in girth, until the winter of 2018-19, when the Boxer Tree fell in high winds, leaving the carving and trunk to decay into the forest.

The Mary Rose Portsmouth, Hampshire

In 1510, just a year into his reign, Henry VIII commissioned the construction of two great warships. He was eager to assert himself as King, and exhibit naval might towards his contemporaries, like the King of France.

Henry named the larger of the vessels *Mary Rose*, after the Virgin Mary, her Mystic Rose, the Tudor Rose and possibly after his favourite sister.

Launched in 1511, it seems likely the ships saw their first action off the coast of Brittany at the Battle of Brest, where the French fleet was convincingly seen off.

Henry's favourite ship, the *Mary Rose* saw 34 years of service until 19 July 1545, when she sank during the Battle of the Solent off the coast of Southsea. It is unclear just why the ship sank. She may have heeled over in strong winds and taken water in through open gun ports, or through holes caused by French gunfire. Whatever the cause, within minutes *Mary Rose* sunk to a watery grave, along with most of her crew.

The whereabouts of the ship remained unknown until 1836 when she was discovered by pioneer divers. But it was not until 1982, 437 years after she sank, that the ship was raised to the surface following the largest underwater archaeological excavation ever undertaken.

While the port side of the *Mary Rose* was totally eroded, the starboard side lay preserved under silt. She was built largely of oak, carvel planks (set edge to edge) secured to an oak frame with trenails (wooden tree-nails). The keel was made from three huge, overlapping elm trunks. The whole construction used around 600 trees.

Dendrochronology revealed the timber came from trees cut between 1443 and 1540, with some of it sourced from as far afield as East Anglia. Other wooden artefacts found included oak chests, nit combs and long bows made from European yew.

In 2013, following painstaking preservation work, the salvaged hull was reassembled and displayed in a dry-dock museum at Portsmouth, just yards from where the ship had been constructed 468 years previously.

Two new ships to be made for us, £700, and the one ship to be of burden of 400 tonnes, and the other ship to be of burden of 300 tonnes.
By *Warrant of Henry VIII*, 1510

ABOVE: 'Great Ship of Henry VIII', engraving from 1865
BELOW: The preserved remains of the *Mary Rose*, 2018

OPPOSITE: Bennet's Cross, ancient granite marker and boundary cross, 2016

BELOW: Dartmoor ponies, 2017.

Dartmoor Forest Devon

Dartmoor is now desolate, and where the oak once grew, there is seen nought but the lonely thistle and the "feebly-whistling grass," yet that it was once, in part at least, richly clothed with wood cannot be doubted... Evidence is not wanting to prove what it has been, since in bogs and marshes on the moor, sometimes embedded twenty feet below the surface of the earth, are found immense trunks of the oak.
From *English Forests and Forest Trees*, 1855

Dartmoor could rightly be described as England's bleakest, most remote forest, while barely resembling a forest in the wooded sense at all.

From the Mesolithic until the Iron Age, Dartmoor appears to have been one of southern England's most densely populated areas. Stone circles, monuments and dwellings litter the landscape.

Then the climate cooled and the moor lay virtually uninhabited for over 1,000 years, until the arrival of the Saxons around AD700. Saxon kings claimed it as a hunting ground, and local people began to farm and graze livestock there.

The Normans, with their grand appetite for the hunt and scant regard for common people, applied Forest Law to the whole of Devon, until 1204 when King John disafforested the county except for Dartmoor.

While Dartmoor's upland granite tors, marsh and bog appear stark and barren, they once hosted wolves, wild cat and red deer – the very game that attracted hunters. It is these animals that suggest at least a partly wooded landscape in former times. Forest Law protected 'vert and venison', referring to the greenery that fed and sheltered the game.

Burning the moors helped drive away wolves. They were probably finished off around 1780, the same year the Duke of Bedford's stag hounds were ushered in from Woburn to eliminate the red deer, which they did in no uncertain terms.

By then, grazing herds of cattle and sheep vastly outnumbered the endemic Dartmoor pony, all but putting an end to any hopes of forest regeneration.

DARTMOOR FOREST

Sam and the Meavy Oak
Meavy, Devon

Dartmoor's most celebrated and probably oldest oak stands centre stage on the village green at Meavy. Stories abound around the Meavy Oak, twisting and weaving themselves into its history.

One tells the tale of Sam Gaskett, a poor 19th-century miner from Meavy, who used the hollow trunk of the tree to store peat turf, recalling the common right of turbary (the right to take turf for fuel) which is still upheld in Dartmoor.

One night, while collecting turfs from the tree, Sam saw that his pile had been disturbed. After cursing local youths for the disruption, he noticed a leather purse full of money on the ground. He took the treasure home and was told by his wife to return the purse to its rightful owner. Sam asked locally if anybody had lost any possessions near the oak tree but nobody claimed the purse, so it was put to one side.

Around this time Sam went back to school to learn how to read and write in order to improve his job prospects. Months later, work from the mines dried up, leaving him unemployed. He returned to the purse, telling his wife it was time to use the coins. Just then a stranger arrived at the door. The stranger explained how he had lost his purse in the oak tree some years before while sheltering from a storm. Sam explained how he had found the purse 'before school' (as, being illiterate, he was learning to read and write). To this the travelling gentleman replied, "Well Sir, you may keep it, for if you found it before school I would have been only a child." And, mounting his steed, the stranger rode away.

RIGHT: Formerly a gospel oak, the Meavy Oak (c1905 and 2017) most likely pre-dates the 13th-century church in whose shadow it stands. Charles II is said to have sheltered in its hollow during his escape from the Parliamentarians, hence the naming of the Royal Oak pub which stands beside it. Each June the Meavy Oak Fair is held on the green beneath its branches.

The Stumpy Oak
Hawsons Cross, Devon

A small, triangular, grassy road island at Hawsons Cross presents a double ancient monument, one of stone and one of wood.

The Stumpy Oak, a hollow pollard *(Quercus robur)* stands beside the Hawson Cross, a granite waymarker. The pair mark the route of the Monks' Path, an ancient trackway linking the medieval abbeys of Buckfast, Tavistock and Buckland. They were important beacons in a time before roads were constructed, when traversing the moor could be perilous.

It is difficult to know which of the monuments is older. The 3.5m (11.5ft) girth of the oak belies its age; its hollow trunk and advanced veteran characteristics confer more years than might be surmised on initial inspection. Oaks tend to grow smaller and more slowly on the moor due to altitude and climate, and are sometimes reffered to as 'chitjacks'.

At only 2.18m (7.15ft) tall and 79cm (2.5ft) across its arms, the cross is dwarfed in the shadow of the oak. For many years it stood at the entrance to Hawson Farm, but was restored and moved to its present, original location by the Dartmoor Preservation Association in 1952.

A young oak was recently planted beside the Stumpy Oak to succeed the old tree. While the act was surely performed with good intentions, I can't help but think that perhaps the longevity of old stumpy has been underestimated.

ABOVE: The Stumpy Oak and the Sturdy Oak, Hawson Cross, 2016

Sole relics of the wreath that crown'd the moor!
A thousand tempests (bravely though withstood,
Whilst, shelter'd in your caves, the wolf's dire brood
Scared the wild echoes with their hideous roar).
By Robert Southey, from *A description of Part of Devonshire*, 1836

Wistman's Wood Devon

Along with Black Tor Beare and Piles Copse, Wistman's Wood is one of only three remaining high-altitude, Dartmoor oak woods.

Reached via a one-mile hike north from Two Rivers, Wistman's Wood rises sharply up the east bank of the West Dart River. Covering an area of around 3.5ha (9 acres), at an altitude between 380 and 410m (1246-1345ft), it is one of England's highest-altitude oak woods.

In stark contrast to the open moor surrounding it, stunted, dwarf oaks (*Quercus robur*) replete with mosses, lichens and epiphytes clinging to twisted sinewy branches, grow among moss-covered granite boulders, which have protected the trees from grazing.

Certainly an ancient wood (written accounts survive from the 17th century onwards), opinion is divided as to whether Wistman's Wood is a relic from Dartmoor's prehistoric wildwood, or was more recently planted.

One account attributes its inception to Isabella de Fortibus, 13th-century Countess of Devon and one of the most landed and powerful women of her time. Yet a perambulation of Dartmoor Forest confirms the wood's existence two centuries prior to her tenure.

The trees themselves have proved difficult to date. An oak cut down in 1866 produced 168 growth-rings from a trunk only 72cm (28in) in girth, illustrating a very slow growth rate. More recently, larger trees have shown wider growth rings, so estimating their age is problematic. The largest oak I found on site measured 2.86m (9.4ft) around a hollowing trunk and is thought to be about 300 years old. A more comprehensive study is underway as I write.

The name Wistman's Wood could derive from one of several sources: the old English *wissen*, meaning 'wise' (referencing the Druids); Wealas, describing British inhabitants (later corrupted to Welsh – some 17th-century accounts refer to it as Welshwood); and the Devonshire *wisht*, meaning 'pixie-led or haunted'. If ever there was an enchanted wood, then surely this is it: a perfect haven for Dartmoor's elusive pixie.

It is small wonder then that Wistman's Wood has attracted more than its fair share of myth and legend. It is said to be the lair of adders and 'wisht hounds'. These demon dogs led by Old Crockern (spirit of Dartmoor) or by the Devil, could evoke a distant memory of Dartmoor's extinct wolves.

FOREST OF CORNWALL

The Forest of Cornwall
Cornwall

Crossing the Tamar Bridge into Cornwall, you become immediately struck by a changing treescape. Sessile is the dominant oak species, especially in woods. But here they grow differently: shorter, stunted, with Medusa-like twisting, winnowed branches, mossed with age, thickly encrusted with lichens and tree ferns, as are the abundant ash, beech, sallow, hawthorn and sycamore.

Almost the entire county was at one time designated as Royal Forest – a hunting ground for kings. Forest Law denied local people their previously held rights to graze, forage and hunt, and strong opposition eventually led to King John disafforesting the county in 1204.

The Darley Oak is often thought to be Cornwall's only ancient oak pertaining to the period, but other less well known contenders survive. Following the disafforestation, at least 18 deer parks were created in Cornwall – havens for veteran trees. Around 120 fallow deer still roam the deer park at Boconnoc, with Restormel Castle hosting several veteran oaks in its deer park. It is likely that these veteran oaks stood as young trees when the castle saw action in the Civil War, most being sessile or 'Cornish' oaks. Other ancient trees commonly survive on the banks of Cornwall's rivers, streams and ancient holloways.

The county's temperate climate and frostless valleys suit well the exotic trees planted during the 18th and 19th centuries in the county's many Victorian 'Great Gardens'. But the native trees appear to have a tougher time of it. Much like the oaks at Wistman's Wood on Dartmoor, they grow slowly, displaying a more stunted, twisted appearance than their more easterly relatives.

Slower growth suggests that trees such as the oaks growing almost to the water's edge along the Fowey river estuary at Lanhydrock, Tregrehan and elsewhere could be several centuries old, in spite of their smaller than expected trunk diameters.

ABOVE: Ancient dwarf oaks at Lanhydrock, 2017
BELOW: Ancient hollow, pollard ash at Seworgan, 2018
OPPOSITE: Ancient beech, oak and ash bluebell woodland at Bosahan Wood, 2018

Giant of olden time!
There in thy strength sublime,
A thousand winters thou hast braved the blast;
Thine ancient brethren gone,
Thou reignest here alone,
Last lonely remnant of the mighty past.

Anonymous, attributed to Rev H A Simcoe, 1834

The Darley Oak

Darley, Cornwall

Cornwall is not renowned for its large, ancient oaks as other parts of the country are. Its largest and most famous specimen appears at the eastern edge of Bodmin Moor, south of Launceston in a village called Darley Ford.

The Darley Oak stands in the front garden of a farmhouse built in 1733, yet could predate it by as much as 600 years, most likely planted when the Dingle family purchased the estate in the 12th century.

The tree is first mentioned as a 'great natural curiosity' in Harvey's book on the Parish of Linkinhorne in 1727, which proclaimed its circumference to be 11m (36ft), measured at 1m (3ft) from the ground. Apparently its hollow trunk provided a venue in which to house 'small pleasure parties' throughout the season.

Seven granite steps lead to the oak's hollow – aiding a young man who hid there to escape a press gang in the 18th century – hewn from the base granite outcrop just below the thin soil. A protective wall was erected around 1830 at the tree's base, which stands high above the surrounding driveways.

Local folklore grants a wish to those who pass through the hollow and complete a circle of the trunk. Similarly in Japanese culture circling certain sacred trees after prayer is held to grant a wish and add a year to your life. I have no doubt this recalls long lost ancient British beliefs. Claims that the Darley Oak had the power to cure boils and other diseases are a reminder of the high tannin and astringent medicinal properties of British oaks.

Darley was held by the Dingles until 1919 when the farm was sold to Samuel Hoare, with whose family it remains. In 1930, the tree was found to be 8.2m (27ft) in circumference. Tea parties were still held beneath it until the Great Storm of 1987, when a right-hand section of the tree – previously held firm by an iron bar – split apart from the left side and collapsed.

The remaining trunk, now measuring 6.4m (21ft), is still hugely impressive and, even now, is Cornwall's fattest oak.

ABOVE: The Darley Oak from *British and Foreign Trees and shrubs in Cornwall* by Edgar Thurston, 1930

OPPOSITE: The Darley Oak pre-leaf, spring, 2017

FOREST OF CORNWALL

Kings Wood

Pentewan, Cornwall

One of Cornwall's best loved ancient woodlands stands on ground rising from the Pentewan Valley between St Austell and the sea. A 58.52ha (144.61-acre) site, its ancient credentials are confirmed by its former life as a deer park in the Manor of Tewington, owned by Thomas, Earl of Lancaster in the 14th century. It is likely that Thomas took it from Piers Gaveston, Earl of Cornwall, after he had him beheaded in 1312. Piers was a favourite and possibly lover of King Edward II, who imposed the same fate on Thomas – his cousin – in 1322, and confiscated the land for himself.

In 1780, tin 'streaming' began in earnest along the St Austell River valley. During excavations at Nansladron – in Cornish the 'valley of thieves' – tree trunks from a submerged prehistoric wood, along with bones of extinct animals that lived there were uncovered, some as much as 15m (50ft) below the surface.

Today, Kings Wood is densely wooded with ash, beech, birch, alder, sweet chestnut and sycamore, and an understory of holly, sallow and hazel. Coniferous plantations were laid out in the 1960s and 70s, although some large veteran lapsed pollard oaks are scattered through the wood – reminders of a more open aspect during Kings Wood's days as a medieval deer park. The park pale – a high brick wall with overhang – is still visible at the higher aspects.

A large number of native wild flowers including bluebell, dog's mercury, bilberry, bugle, red campion, speedwell, wood forget-me-not, violet and foxglove are responsible for the wood's County Wildlife Site status. Flag iris – thought to be the template for the fleur-de-lis symbol beloved of medieval kings grows in its marshy lower reaches, and produces more nectar than almost any other British plant – a great food source for bees and other insects.

The wood... is known as the "King's Wood" – probably it was part of Earl Thomas's property which, on his attainder and execution, reverted to the King. I suspect it is called King's wood because the Commonwealth, just before the sale, had taken it over from the King.
From *An Account of St Austell* by J Hammond, 1897

ABOVE: Flag iris, 2019
BELOW: Ancient lapsed coppice birch, 2019

The Lost Oaks of Heligan
Pentewan, Cornwall

A manor house has stood at Heligan (from the Cornish *helygen* meaning willow tree), near Mevagissey, since at least the 13th century, and has been owned, worked and planted by the Tremayne family since they purchased the 400ha (1,000 acre) estate over 400 years ago. With the onset of the First World War, a 22-strong team of gardeners who tended the grounds found themselves uprooted from Heligan to fight in the trenches. Only six of them would return home.

Following the war, the house was rented out, the then owner preferring to live in Italy, and the gardens subsequently fell into decay and ruin.

The house was sold and converted into flats in 1973, but the gardens remained with the Tremaynes. Then, in 1990, Tim Smit and John Willis chanced upon the now-overgrown 'hidden gardens'. The discovery led to their complete restoration – a monumental challenge that became famously well documented. Since completion, the Lost Gardens have become celebrated as one of Britain's most popular botanical gardens.

In a field at the edge of the gardens, off the beaten track and largely unnoticed, stand ten veteran oaks that appear strangely unfamiliar in this region, along with some veteran sallow and holly and outgrown coppice trees.

Ranging between 3m and 5m (9.8ft and 16.4ft) in circumference, most of the oaks are hollowed and twisted, hosting lichens, ephyphites, invertebrates and, in one case, a nest of honey bees. One trunk is almost completely white with lichen – which only grows under clean air conditions – as if it has been painted. Several show signs of pollarding; these are working trees that have long earned their keep. Remnants of the estate's long, working history – they have survived the cutting of a shelterbelt of trees for the First World War effort, and the stationing of American troops in the Second. The oldest trees are likely to date back to the arrival of the Tremaynes at Heligan in the 16th century.

Their few parcels yet preserved, are principally employed to coaling, for blowing of Tynne. This lacke they supply, either by Stone coale, fetched out of Wales, or by dried Turfes, some of which are also converted into coale, to serve the Tynners turne.
From *The Survey of Cornwall* by Richard Carew, 1602.

ABOVE: Heligan Manor, c1910
BELOW: Veteran wood pasture oak, 2017

Helston Furry Day Helston, Cornwall

Every 8th May (or the Saturday before if it falls on a Sunday or Monday), the Cornish town of Helston celebrates Flora Day – a custom so ancient, that its origins are obscured in the mists of time. Previously known as Furry Day (after the Cornish *feur*, or 'fair'), it celebrates the dawn of spring, and the lush, green regrowth that accompanies it.

The day before the festivities, houses, doorways and shops are decked with branches and wild flowers, then, at 7am, the Town Band leads the first dance of the day around the streets of Helston. The dancers go in and out of open houses, driving out winter's darkness to usher in the lightness of spring. All the while they are playing the tune of 'The Floral Dance', immortalised nationally by Terry Wogan's 1978 rendition. The tune itself is said never to have been written down, and is always played from memory. The first dance is performed by around 80 couples.

At 8.30am, the *Hal-an-Tow* starts its first of several performance across the town. A Mummers' play, the *Hal-an-Tow* has an altogether more ritualistic flavour about it, reflecting its ancient origins. Revellers, dressed in Lincoln green robes adorned with verdure and waving sycamore branches aloft, tell a story of the town that includes the Spanish Armada, Robin Hood, St George and the Dragon and the town's patron saint St Michael getting the better of the Devil. As with other pre-Christian myths still practised, the tradition incorporates contemporary tales and deeds with each retelling, binding them into the story for future occassions.

Around 1,000 children dressed in white start the next dance at 9.40am, then at midday, the ancient Furry Dance commences. It was originally reserved for the gentry who hoped that by this time their servants would have had their fun and returned to work. At 5pm the final dance of the day invites all-comers to join in, but the early dances, and custom of wearing sprigs of lily of the valley, is reserved for Helstonians only.

With Hal-an-Tow! Jolly Rumble, O!
For we are up as soon as any day, O!
And for to fetch the Summer home,
The Summer and the May, O,
For Summer is a-come, O,
And Winter is a-gone, O.

The Hal-an-Tow, traditional

ABOVE: The Floral Dance, 1907
BELOW: AND OPPOSITE: Hal-an-Tow, 2018

St Michael's Mount

Mount's Bay, Cornwall

Rising majestically out of the sea in Mount's Bay, the historic landmark of St Michael's Mount shadows a secret revealed only once in a blue moon.

The Mount has been inhabited by people since at least the Neolithic, and doubtless imposed its dominance over the surrounding landscape as it does today. Reached by boat or via a causeway accessible only at low tide, the island's ancient Cornish name, *Karrek Loos yn Koos* which translates to 'grey rock in the woods' offers a clue to its former topography.

In February 2014, harsh storms hit Cornwall's southern coast, shifting gravel and sand to reveal large remains of oak and pine tree trunks, hazel thicket, cob nuts and acorns, that had laid submerged, preserved for eons, rarely exposed, and last seen 40 years earlier.

Carbon dating confirmed the trees to be between 4,000 and 6,000 years old, remnants of a marshland wood growing at a time when the sea levels were some 30m (100ft) lower than today, and finally submerged around 1700BC. Similar sunken forests have emerged on North Yorkshire, Pembrokeshire and East Sussex coasts.

Britain was cut off from mainland Europe by tsunami around 6100BC, securing its island status. But sea levels continued to fluctuate, illustrated by a tsunami caused by an earthquake in Lisbon, which battered the coast around Mount's Bay in 1755.

Cornish and Breton folklore remembers the lost land of Lyonesse, immortalised in Arthurian legend as the home of Tristan, Cornish hero and Knight of the Round Table. Said to have stretched from Cornwall to the Isles of Scilly, the Lyonesse stories could represent a lingering folk memory that recalls the very real flooding that swallowed the oak and pine forest at Mount's Bay, leaving the 'grey rock in the woods' standing tall.

Then rose the King and moved his host by night
And ever pushed Sir Mordred, league by league,
Back to the sunset bound of Lyonesse –
Where fragments of forgotten peoples dwelt,
And the long mountains ended in a coast
Of ever-shifting sand, and far away
The phantom circle of a moaning sea.

From *Idylls of the King* by Alfred Lord Tennyson, 1859-85

TOP: St Michael's Mount, 1878
ABOVE: Ancient preserved tree stump revealed in 2014
OPPOSITE: Mount's Bay at low tide, 2017

FOREST OF CORNWALL

This place was originally inclosed within a very thick wood, distant from the ocean six miles, affording the finest shelter to wild beasts... On the third of the Nones of November the sea overflowed the shore, destroying towns and drowning many persons and innumerable oxen and sheep.
From *Chronicon ex chronicis* by John of Worcester, 1099

Forest trees

Britain's native tree are defined as species which settled naturally in the moderately short period between the end of the last ice age (c10,000-12,000 years ago), and the time when Britain was separated from northern Europe (6200-6500BC), and became the island we know today.

Around 30 tree species are generally accepted (depending on precise definitions), a relatively small number when compared to a large country like the United States of America (which hosts around 100 species of oak alone compared to Britain's two).

Add to that a school of thought which includes sycamore (whose pollen deteriorates quickly and hence leaves little to historical record), subspecies and hybrids, and the picture can become distorted.

Included here are 20 common trees which feature most frequently in this book, listed for reference and as a rough guide to identity. These are the trees that have significantly helped shape Britain's ecological landscape for over 10,000 years – biologically, historically, culturally, economically and aesthetically.

Oak *Quercus robur/petraea*

300 years young, 300 mature, 300 in decay.
Britain's two native oaks – pedunculate and sessile – our largest and most important tree for wildlife, hosting at least 500 species. Built from oak, Britain's houses, ships, legend and history depend on it. The acorn fruits fed pigs at 'pannage' and provided flour for bread cakes.

Elm *Ulmus procera/glabra*

Once almost as common as oak, our two native species – English and Wych – were decimated in the 1960s/70s by Dutch elm disease. Previously an important timber tree, large elm beams are frequently visible in historic houses, where elm was often planted in grand avenues. Britain's National Elm Collection survives in Brighton.

Ash *Fraxinus excelsior*

Yggdrasil was the sacred 'Tree of Life' in Norse mythology – its branches reached to heaven and its roots descended to hell. Britain's only native of the olive family, ash produces the ultimate firewood, for which it was historically pollarded. The virulent ash dieback disease could see the decimation of our third most common tree.

Beech *Fagus sylvatica*

The word 'book' – from the Saxon *beoc* – derives from beechen tablets used for ancient writing, hence the 'leaves' of a book. Originally native to southern England, but now widely planted, its smooth grey bark and elegant spreading crown earned it the title 'white lady of the wood'. Pollarding greatly extends its life.

Yew *Taxus baccata*

Britain's longest-lived tree, once more commonly found in groves and woodlands, now surviving in churchyards where it often predates the church. A symbol of eternal life, revered since earliest times. Used in chemotherapy, every part of the tree is poisonous, except for the fleshy red aril eaten by birds who distribute the seeds.

Lime *Tilia cordata/platyphyllos/x europea*

Three native species, small-leaved, broad-leaved and common (a hybrid), a large stately tree often planted in parkland. Takes well to pruning, providing Britain's oldest coppices. Irresistible to bees, the flowers make a fine tea. Representing fertility in Greek mythology, Baucis and Philemon became lime and oak trees after death.

Birch *Betula pubescens/pendula*

The first tree to establish itself on unmanaged land, downy and silver birch have long symbolised renewal and regeneration. Associated with fertility, the 'lady of the woods' provided the village maypole, its bows 'beat the bounds', and jumping a birch-broom confirmed wedding vows. The rising sap makes a refreshing drink.

Field maple *Acer campestre*

Generally considered Britain's only native maple (if the disputed sycamore is left out of the equation), produces a small tree and leaves, responsible for much of our autumn colour. Found in woodland and hedgerows and anciently coppiced. Horizontal keys 'fly' in a helicopter-like fashion to propagate the seeds.

FOREST FLORA AND FAUNA

Hornbeam *Carpinus betulus*

Horn = hard and beam = *baum*, (old English for 'tree') describes the quality of its timber perfectly. Similar in appearance to beech, but smaller and more rugged. Famously pollarded at Epping and elsewhere, understory to oak, forming its own woods in the south east. Provided a tonic for exhaustion, its leaves were used to heal wounds.

Hawthorn *Crataegus monogyna/laevigata*

Two variants, common and midland, also known as may tree after the month it flowers (badge of the House of Tudor), giving way to crimson haws in autumn. An important hedgerow/woodland tree supporting 300 species of insect. A wreath was thought to protect a house from bad spirits – as long as it was not brought inside.

Holly *Ilex aquifolium*

An understory evergreen provides winter animal fodder, though tradition holds it bad luck to cut. It can grow into a large tree. Sharp-spined lower leaves protect against grazers, upper leaves are smooth. Red winter berries provide a vital food source for birds. The 'holy' tree's use as Christmas decoration predates Christian tradition.

Hazel *Corylus avellana*

One of the early trees to colonise Britain, in understory and hedgerow, universally coppiced to great effect, harvested rods have myriad uses. Best for water divining, forked wands cut on St John's Eve were thought to aid in the discovery of treasure. Nuts provide food for birds, squirrels and people, who carried them as charms.

FOREST FLORA AND FAUNA

Wild cherry *Prunus avium/padus*

The wild cherry, or gean, a woodland tree often planted, and bird cherry, found in damp woodland and on river banks, proffer snow-white blossom in spring, an important pollen source for bees. The summer cherries feed birds, animals and people, leading to its ancient name of merry tree – 'a cherry year, a merry year'.

Crab apple *Malus sylvestris*

The 'original' British apple (now 6,000 varieties), from Saxon *scrobb* or shrub. *An apple a day keeps the doctor away* is from the Norse custom of gifting apples to the gods to ward off old age. Sweetly scented pink May blossoms produce hard bitter fruits good for jam, jelly and wine. Wassailing ceremonies ensure a good crop.

Rowan *Sorbus aucuparia*

Also known as 'mountain ash', ancient examples grow in the Scottish Highlands. Bears creamy white flowers in May and orange/red berries in August, providing food for insects and birds, harvested for beer and jelly. The Celtic 'wizard's tree', often planted beside houses and in churchyards to protect against evil.

Whitebeam *Sorbus aria*

The 'white tree' – well named after the silvery undersides of its spring leaves and clusters of insect-pollinated white flowers in May. Scarlet berries in autumn provide late food for birds and animals edible as 'chess apples' when over-ripe and for making jelly. Several endemic variants around southern Britain.

Scots pine *Pinus sylvestris*

A pioneer coloniser following the last ice age, Britain's only native pine retreated to Scotland, forming expansive open Caledonian forest, where ancients survive, though much depleted. Now widely planted, harvested for ships' masts and telegraph poles and tapped for turpentine. Scent beneficial for respiratory complaints.

Willow *Salix alba/fragilis*

Britain's two willows, white (large and common) and crack (the familiar pollard) thrive on river banks and hybridise freely. Held as unlucky when sawn, but readily harvested for basketry, fencing and winter fodder. Salicin in the bark was chewed for pain relief as a precursor of aspirin. The tree of mourning.

Sallow *Salix caprea/cinerea*

The two 'pussy willows', goat (great sallow) and grey (common sallow) are shrub like, common in hedgerows, often coppiced. First willow to flower, its early spring blossoms – resembling cats paws – provide a banquet for bees, the rounded leaves beloved of grazers.
Timber used for clothes pegs and rake teeth.

Alder *Alnus glutinosa*

Thrives in water, otters frequently nest amongst exposed roots. Timber survives indefinitely in water, traditionally used for clog making. A symbiotic relationship with bacteria *Frankia aini* provides the tree with nitrogen and the bacteria with sugars, whilst enriching the soil. Coppiced for charcoal burning for superior gunpowder.

FOREST FLORA AND FAUNA

Forest animals

Prehistoric Britain was home to several large mammals, which were all rendered extinct by humans: aurochs in the first century BC; brown bear and lynx in the first century AD; wolves by the 13th century in England and 16th century in Scotland; wild boar in the 17th and wildcats in the 19th century.

Large predators were significant in controlling populations, thereby preventing overgrazing, a role now managed by people, though seldom effectively.

Reports by RSPB (State of Nature, 2016), WWF (Living Planet, 2018) and IPBES (Global Assessment, 2019) detail a 50-60% decline in Britain's native wildlife over the last half century. Intensive agricultural land management and climate change are listed as two defining factors, which is why conservation projects and landscape restoration is so important for the future of Britain's unique wildlife, for their benefit and ours.

Red deer *Cervus elaphus*

'Prime Beast of the Forest', with more rights than commoners under Forest Law, left alone for 14 days either side of midsummer's day – the 'fence month' – when young are born. 1.2m (4ft) tall at the shoulder, males (stags) grow antlers in spring for the autumn 'rut', when they secure harems of breeding hinds who produce single calves.

Roe deer *Capreolus capreolus*

The other of our two native deer – diminutive, shy and nocturnal – scarce from the hunt by the late 17th century, now widespread. Leave a distinctive low browse line on trees. Grow to 0.75m (2.4ft) at the shoulder, females (does), slightly smaller than males (bucks). Rut in late summer, two kids are born in May.

Fallow deer *Dama dama*

Introduced by the Romans, favoured by the Normans for the hunt, who reintroduced them in numbers, abundant by the Middle Ages, and now considered naturalised. Growing to 1m (3ft) at the shoulder, females (does), slightly smaller than males (bucks). Rut in autumn, with a single fawn born in June/July.

Wolf *Canis lupus*

Both feared and respected, an apex predator once common in Britain. A forest pack animal, man's prime competitor for deer, persecuted to extinction by the late 15th century in England and Wales and by the 18th in Scotland – where plans are underway to reintroduce them for red deer control and to allow forest regeneration.

FOREST FLORA AND FAUNA

Hedgehog *Erinaceous europaeus*

Once a gypsy delicacy, persecuted (unjustly) for 'sucking milk from cows', the nocturnal, spiny, omnivore hibernates each winter, sometimes beneath exposed tree roots in woodland. Once common in gardens, 'foraging corridors' (fence holes) between properties has a beneficial impact on their declining population.

Red squirrel *Sciurus vulgaris*

Nest in round, moss-lined twig dreys at tree forks, producing three to five kittens from one or two litters in spring and summer. Displaced by the bolder North American grey, introduced in the 1870s, which carries deadly squirrelpox virus. Now confined to a few hotspots in the north and on island retreats, despite conservation efforts.

Grey squirrel *Sciurus carolinensis*

Herbrand Russell released ten grey squirrels from New Jersey at Woburn Abbey in 1890, unaware they would number around 2,500,000 in the UK by 2018, at the expense of native reds, which number only 10,000-15,000. Culling has little effect, but an oral contraceptive produces positive results, and could redress the balance.

Pine marten *Martes martes*

Mostly nocturnal, agile and aggressive, nest and predate in trees. Single litter in spring of three to five kits. Hunted to near extinction both as a beast of the chase and as vermin by 1900. Successful reintroductions in Ireland and Wales suggest red squirrel populations may benefit as pine martens help reduce the distribution of greys.

FOREST FLORA AND FAUNA

Wild boar *Sus scrofa*

Animal of the hunt, once numerous in Britain's forest, hunted to extinction c1260 for Henry III's Christmas dinner. Survived in parks until 17th century. Reintroduced to the Forest of Dean and the Weald, where wallowing and rooting has increased biodiversity by opening up the ground. Ancestor of the domestic pig.

Wildcat *Felis sylvestris*

Britain's only native cat, solitary and nocturnal, living in woodland dens often in hollow trees. Persecuted to extinction by gamekeepers in England by 1853, they survive remotely in Scotland. Despite protected status, as few as 35 remain in the wild due to reduced habitat and cross-breeding with the smaller domestic cat.

Red fox *Vulpes vulpes*

Long persecuted as a 'pest' and hunted for fur, the world's most abundant predator survives in rural and urban environments. Said to mate when rain and shine coincide, vixens produce four to six kits in spring in underground 'earths'. 'Cunning, deceitful, associated with the devil', the beautiful red fox has suffered some bad press.

Badger *Meles meles*

'Brocks' occupy complex 'setts' often centuries old. Nocturnal, omnivorous, produce a litter of two to four in spring. Thought to bring good luck if seen behind you, bad luck if seen ahead. Protected since 1992, a UK 'cull' controversially rolled out in 2018 to prevent the spread of TB to cattle, contradicts much scientific evidence.

FOREST FLORA AND FAUNA

Pipistrelle bat *Pipistrellus pipistrellus*

Britain's most common and smallest bat, with a wingspan of 18-24cm (7-10in). One of 17 native bat species, roosts and hibernates in colonies in hollow trees and buildings. Produces one to two blind pups in summer, feeds nocturnally on insects and moths, using ultrasonic pulses for echo-location and navigation.

Wood mouse *Apadimus sylvaticus*

One of Britain's most common mammals, omnivorous, rarely lives more than a year, in which time they can foster up to seven litters. Largely nocturnal, agile, nimble tree climbers, sometimes re-use bird nests to store tree seeds and sleep, as well as in usual burrows. A sylvan animal, also happy to make residence in a house.

Dormouse *Muscardinus avellanarius*

Nocturnal, arboreal specialists up to 9cm (3.5in) long. Spherical nests, often in hazel coppice – nibbled hazelnuts a tell-tale sign – a staple with fruit, flowers and insects. A protected species, habitat loss since 2000 has seen numbers decline by a third. 900 have since been released across 12 counties, six where they were already extinct.

Adder *Vipera berus*
Grass snake *Natrix natrix*

Three native snakes – adder, grass snake and the rare smooth snake – are found in meadow, heathland and open woodland. Grass snakes favour wetland and lay up to 100 eggs, while adders, our only poisonous variety, have up to 20 live young in late summer.

Forest birds

The 13 species listed here offer an arbitrary selection from Britain's wide variety of forest birds. Some live primarily in woodland, and have developed distinctive territorial songs in the trees that provide cover, food and nesting bases from which to forage and hunt. Others venture across field, meadow and moor – part of the forest mosaic. All are non-migratory, resident year-round, their apparent fragility belying a tenacious resilience.

A mastery of flight, keen eyesight and an inherent wildness are key factors in their success, although a 20% decline in woodland bird numbers (around one in four of Britain's threatened bird species), over the last half century presents real cause for concern. There are success stories, however; in particular, certain birds of prey have seen marked population resurgence through reintroduction, conservation and protection programmes.

Goshawk *Accipiter gentilis*

Adapted to the forest hunt, esteemed by medieval falconers. Preys on large birds and rabbits. Almost extinct by the end of the 19th century, reintroduced, effective at grey squirrel control. Large flat nests in canopy close to tree trunks, lays three to five eggs in early summer. Wingspan up to 119cm (47in) for the larger females.

FOREST FLORA AND FAUNA

Raven *Corvus corax*

King of the corvids, esteemed in Norse and Welsh mythology, world's largest perching bird nesting in the highest trees. Persecuted as an 'ill omen', now recovering well. Highly intelligent, mates for life. Unmistakable deep, guttural 'pruk-pruk.' Acrobatic, appearing to fall through the air. Wingspan up to 150cm (59in).

Buzzard *Buteo buteo*

Britain's most common large bird of prey, numbers declined in the 1950s when myxomatosis decimated its favourite food – rabbit. Nests in treetops, soars in ascending circles scanning for prey, often in pairs. Makes high-pitched 'piew'. Frequently mobbed by crows. Wingspan up to 140cm (55in).

Kestrel *Falco tinnunculus*

Numbers declined in the 1950s and 60s, now recovered to become Britain's most widespread bird of prey. Builds no nest, lives in tree cavities and disused nests, or in buildings where it has become urbanised. Hovers before swooping for small mammals. Makes shrill 'kee-eee' call. Wingspan up to 76cm (30in).

Red kite *Milvus milvus*

Considered a Tudor scavenger (because it cleaned carrion from London's streets). Gave its name to the toy after its gliding flight. Persecuted into Wales by 1900, successfully reintroduced and now fairly widespread. Nests of sticks and mud in native woodland. Makes shrill 'weeou-weeou' call. Huge wingspan up to 185cm (73in).

FOREST FLORA AND FAUNA

Barn owl *Tyto alba*

Could aptly be named 'tree owl' after its preference to roost in hollow trees – a habitat in decline, as is the bird. Silent in flight, hunts day or night due to its water-porous feathers, and the need to keep dry. Pinpoints prey by sound in the dark. Makes an eerie 'shriek', long held to be a bad omen. Wingspan up to 95cm (37in).

Tawny owl *Strix aluco*

Most common native owl, roosts in hollow trees, more rarely in burrows. Beloved of wizards. Silent in flight, nocturnal, spies prey from a perch before swooping and swallowing it whole. The familiar hoot – 'ke-wick' followed by 'hoo-hooo' – is a winter call and response between male and female. Wingspan up to 105cm (41in).

Woodcock *Scolopax rusticola*

Ground-nesting, long bill probes for worms and insects. Good camouflage makes it hard to spot. Displays territorial 'roding' (breeding display flight) in spring/summer. Traditionally hunted by net, remembered in old place names like 'Cock Road' and 'Cockshoot'. Croaks and calls a high-pitched 'che-wick'. Wingspan up to 65cm (26in).

Jay *Garrulus glandarius*

Most colourful of the corvids, nests in trees and shrubs. Feeds on insects, small mammals and eggs, but mostly acorns – which it stores and buries in winter. Responsible for the spread and propagation of oak – individuals plant up to 1,000 trees a year. Makes a harsh 'skark' call, and is a keen mimic. Wingspan up to 60cm (23in).

FOREST FLORA AND FAUNA

FOREST FLORA AND FAUNA

Robin *Erithacus rubecula*

Distinctive red breast (from 'a drop of Christ's blood'), and plucky character ensure status as the nation's favourite bird. Fiercely territorial, feeds on insects disturbed by boar and pigs in the wood or on freshly dug garden soil. Nests in tree holes, banks and ledges. Sings sweet warble 'tic-tic' when alarmed. Wingspan up to 22cm (9in).

Woodpeckers *Picus viridis/Dendrocopos major/minor*

Green/yaffle/rain bird – largest, green with red crown; great spotted – once rare, now most common, black and white, red undertail; lesser spotted – smallest, black and white. Bore nest holes in trees. Feed on ants/insects, grubs, larvae. Wingspan to 42cm (16in)/39cm (15in)/26cm (10in).

Blackbird *Turdus merula*

A woodland bird, common in parks and gardens. Monogamous, jet-black males with orange bills and eye-rings, mottled brown females. Feed on fruit, berries, worms and insects. Females build round nests in shrubs, low trees or hedges – said to be fortuitous if near a house. Rich and varied flute-like song. Wingspan up to 38cm (15in).

Tree creeper *Certhia familiaris*

Lives up to its name– crawling up trees like a mouse, feeding on insects and spiders using its long, down-turned bill. Nests behind loose bark and tree cavities (the bird seen left is building its nest in a 750-year-old oak rich in invertebrates, a habitat it rarely needs to leave). Makes a shrill 'tsee' call. Wingspan up to 20cm (8in).

Forest flowers

Britain's ancient, deciduous woodland harbours a unique, rich and varied ground flora, absent from non-native plantations. From early spring, a colourful carousel presents itself, often carpeting large areas, with early flowers flourishing in dappled light that filters to the forest floor before trees come into leaf. Around 40 indicator species exist – the presence of ten or more of these offering strong evidence of ancient native woodland.

The snowdrop, Winter's timid child,
Awakes to life, bedew'd with tears;
And flings around its fragrance mild,
And where no rival flow'rets bloom,
Amid the bare and chilling gloom,
A beauteous gem appears!
Snowdrop Mary Robinson 1806

Snowdrop *Galanthus nivalis*

One of the earliest gauges of the coming spring, flowers from January to March. Aptly known as 'snow piercer', and 'fair maid of February', after a custom in which maidens wore bunches of the flower to celebrate St Mary's 'feast of purification' – their whiteness a symbol of purity. Often planted in churchyards.

Primrose *Primula vulgaris*

The 'first rose' flowers from February to May, heralding the advent of spring. Flowers can be added to salads, traditionally used in remedies for bronchitus, rheumatism and gout, and in love potions, their roots infused to alleviate headaches. Winter blooms forewarned of death, as did a single flower taken into a house.

Wood anemone *Anemone nemorosa*

Grows in great white, nodding drifts from March to May, signalling that spring has sprung. Also known as 'windflower' and 'smell fox', due to the musky smell of its leaves. The flowers – often tinged with pink – will only open each day if they have enough sunlight. All parts of the plant are poisonous.

FOREST FLORA AND FAUNA

Wood sorrel *Oxalis acetosella*

Widespread woodland plant, with white, solitary bell-like lilac-veined flowers from April to May. A second, self-pollinating flower appears in summer. The clover-shaped sharp-tasting leaves contain oxalic acid (hence the Latin name), and can be added to salads. A contender for St Patrick's shamrock illustrating the Holy Trinity.

Common dog violet *Viola riviniana*

Named 'dog' due to scentless flowers from April to June, distinguishing it from fragrant sweet violets. Second, self-pollinating flowers in summer. Leaves a food source for caterpillars. Also known as 'pig violets' and 'blue mice'. Worn around the neck, supposed to prevent drunkenness, and bring fleas into a house.

Yellow archangel
Lamiastrum galeobdolan

Part of the nettle family, stingless. Angelic but unpleasant smelling tiered flowers from April to June – during Archangel Michael Day – butter-coloured red-streaked lower lip acts as a bee landing pad. AKA 'weasel head', said to guard against evil spirits and protect cattle from spells.

Bluebell *Hyacinthoides non-scripta*

Flowers April to June in azure carpets with intoxicating bouquet (reintroduction of soil-ploughing wild boar suggests a patchwork cover may previously have prevailed). Britain hosts over 50% of the world's bluebells, now threatened by the freely hybridising Spanish variety. Bulbs made 'fletching' for arrows.

FOREST FLORA AND FAUNA

Ramsons *Allium ursinum*

Part of the lily family – also known as wild garlic, buckrams, wood or bear's garlic – often carpets the woodland floor, sometimes at the exclusion of all other plants. Swathes of star shaped white flower heads appear in late spring. Broad elliptical leaves emit a strong scent of garlic, and can be used in cooking and salads.

Lords and ladies *Arum maculatum*

'Cuckoo-pint', 'adder's root', 'snakeshead', 'devils and angels', 'Adam and Eve', and 'cheese and toast' are just some of its many names, most have sexual connotations. A spadix flowers from April to May, its warmth and smell attract flies into the spathe, which pollinate the plant. Poisonous berries turn from green to red in autumn.

Red campion *Silene dioica*

Abundant on woodland edges, hedgerows and grassy cliff edges, taking its scientific name from the wise, old, drunken Greek god of woodland – Silenus. The second part of its name refers to it being dioecious – each plant has only male or female flowers, between May and August, each needing the other to reproduce.

Foxglove *Digitalis purpurea*

Rather than a literal name, foxglove appears to be a corruption of Anglo-Saxon 'fairy bells', a name still used in Somerset. Flowering from June to September, the whole plant is poisonous, a fact picked up on in the late 18th century by William Withering, who discovered its potential to treat mild heart conditions.

FOREST FLORA AND FAUNA

Garlic mustard *Alliaria petiolata*

Commonly known as 'Jack-by-the-hedge', and sometimes 'hedge garlic' or 'poor mans mustard', as its name suggests, can be used to flavour fish, lamb and salad, its leaves release an odour of garlic when crushed. A member of the cabbage family, clusters of small white flowers show between April and June.

Wood forget-me-not
Myosotis sylvatica

Named after a German knight, who drowned when he fell into a river under the weight of his armour picking flowers for his lady, immortalised by poet Samuel Taylor Coleridge. Myosotis means 'mouse ear', describing the sky blue flowers borne between April and July.

Bugle *Ajuga reptans*

A syrup made from bugle was historically regarded as a cure-all – a remedy for anything from stab wounds to broken bones, ulcers to hangovers. Spreading chiefly by rhizomes, it bears two-lipped blue flowers between April and June, tiered between dark green oval leaves often flushed with bronze.

Early purple orchid
Orchis mascula

One of Britain's earliest-flowering, most common orchids, especially in woodland. Purple-lobed flowers appear between April and June, enticing pollinating insects into an upper hood. Known as 'long purples' in the west country, the 'amorous cup' was anciently used in love potio.

FOREST FLORA AND FAUNA

Forest fungi

The importance of fungi to a functioning forest cannot be underestimated.

Emerging around 470 million years ago, fungi paved the way for trees to develop about 100 million years later. They help break down dead animal and plant remains, generating a nutrient-rich soil where plants thrive. They colonise non-functioning heartwood in trees, helping break it down, in turn returning nutrient rich compost back to the tree itself.

Their fruiting bodies – toadstools and mushrooms – are a common sight on the forest floor in the autumn and winter months, but they are only part of the story.

Beneath the ground, thread-like hyphae known as mycellium can cover vast areas, and connect to fine strands of tree roots. Unable to photosynthesise, the mycellium take sugars and nutrients from the tree, in return supplying mineral nutrients and water. Known as mycorrhiza, this symbiotic relationship benefits both tree and fungi. Sometimes called the 'wood-wide-web', it also provides a network whereby stronger trees support weaker ones, distributing nutrient support via the network.

FOREST FLORA AND FAUNA

Oak bracket/weeping conk

Ganoderma bracket

Amethyst deceiver

Chantelle mushroom

Chicken of the woods

Chicken of the woods

Parasol mushrooms

Fly agaric

Porcelain mushroom

Scarlet elf cap

Candlesnuff fungus

Shaggy inkcap

Mycorrhiza on oak roots

Turkey tail

Honey fungus

Chalara ash dieback fruiting bodies

Violet click beetle

Stag beetle (male), 1758

Insects (invertebrates)

With a huge diversity that includes around 20,000 species, Britain's insects are essential for any functioning habitat. They provide food for a vast array of animals including birds, bats, hedgehogs and other insects.

Essential pollinators – bees, hoverflys, butterflys, wasps and others – are indispensible for the regeneration of forest flora, from the mighty towering canopy oaks down to the delicate, diminuitive, wood sorrel of the forest floor.

Insects are also important contributors towards a healthy soil, helping break down decaying matter into a nutrient-rich compost.

Dor beetle

Stag beetle (female)

Wood Decay specialists

Certain beetles' life cycles depend entirely on the decaying wood of veteran trees and, along with fungi, they are responsible for breaking it down, creating hollow trees in the process.

Stag beetle larvae develop in decaying wood on which they feed, other beetles favour breeding under bark.

Some species are found only in decaying wood of the British oak, with some so rare, that they are limited to one single location.

Woodlouse

Orb web spider

The Moccas beetle, for example, is found only at Moccas Park, where it lives in open-grown oaks. Its existence at all suggests a once wider colonisation when its habitat was commonplace. Fossil records reveal that the now-rare Windsor weevil was once widespread across southern Britain and substantiate the case for an historic, open forest landscape as opposed to a dense, closed-canopy. Habitat loss and the use of pesticides and insecticides constitutes a major threat to insects survival, and to all the benefits that they bring.

Red cardinal beetle

Soldier beetle

FOREST FLORA AND FAUNA

Hoverfly

Silver washed fritillary

Orange tip butterfly

Speckled wood butterfly

Honey bee

Scorpion fly

Meadow brown butterfly

Peacock butterfly

Horsefly

Red admiral feeding on oak sap

Small copper butterfly

Ringlet butterfly

Hover fly

Cinnabar moth

Small magpie moth

Willow beauty moth

SPONSORS

My sincere thanks go to the following for showing faith in Britain's Ancient Forest – Legacy and Lore and supporting and valuing the project by sponsoring production of this book.

Julian Hight August 2019

Barrell Tree Consultancy
Field House, Ashford Road
Fordingbridge, Hants SP6 1BD
t: 01425 651470
www.barrelltreecare.co.uk

info@barrelltreecare.co.uk   twitter.com/JeremyDBarrell

It is common for tree professionals to be so obsessed with the technical details about trees that they often don't see the bigger picture, missing great opportunities to engage with the wider public. Ordinary people are not that interested in the complexity of tree management, but they are interested in stories. Tales of the ancient forest, gallows trees, and trees associated with kings and queens, stir the imagination and rekindle basic instincts dulled through the modern lack of contact with Nature. Tree stories are so much more interesting than the technical stuff! As the ravages of the climate crisis bite, at no time in human history was there ever a greater need for ordinary people and politicians to engage with the idea that trees are good, and we need more of them.

Julian's new book sets the scene perfectly; society needs these stories as the psychological mechanism to reconnect with Nature and begin to turn the tide of destruction before it is too late.

HERITAGE TREE SERVICES
PROFESSIONAL ARBORICULTURE
• Inspect   • Maintain   • Replant

Unit 5, The Beeches, Stoke Row
Henley on Thames RG9 5RB
t: 01491 681185
www.heritagetreeservices.co.uk
admin@heritagetreeservices.co.uk

We recognise the vulnerability, fragility and potential for irreversible errors in ancient 'Jewel in the Crown' veteran trees. If not preserved through correct management, they will not succeed into longevity. Accurate evaluation of ancient and veteran trees, together with principles and procedures to prolong their lives, formulating flexible, long-term management programmes, cannot be undervalued. Continuity of habitat and associated species is combined with specialist inspections to produce detailed assessments of individual communities of trees and their physiological environments.

The Garden Cafe and Next Door
Natural, organic, local and fairtrade produce
16 Stony St, Frome, Somerset BA11 1BU
www.gardencafefrome.co.uk

Catch 22
Facilities management recruitment
Warnford Ct, 29 Throgmorton St, London EC2N 2AT
www.c22.co.uk

Select bibliography

Ancient Tree Forum, Ancient and other veteran trees, The Tree Council (2013)

Barnes, Ian, Historical Atlas of the Celtic World, Cartographica Press (2009)

Birds of Britain, Readers Digest (1981)

Book of British Birds, Drive Publications (1974)

Collins Gem Trees, Harper Collins Publishers (1980)

Cotterell, Arthur, Norse Mythology, Sebastian Kelly (1998)

Davies, Norman, Europe – A History, Pimlico (1997)

English Forests & Forest Trees, Ingram, Cooke & Co (1853)

Evelyn, John, Sylva Vol 1, A Discourse of Forest Trees (1670)

Ever Changing Woodlands (the), Readers Digest (1984)

Farjon, Aljos, Ancient Oaks in the English Landscape, Royal Botanic Gardens, Kew (2017)

Flegg, Jim, Oakwatch, Pelham Books (1985)

Folklore, Myths & Legends of Britain, Readers Digest (1973)

Hinde, Thomas, Forests of Britain, Victor Gollancz (1985)

Hight, Julian, Britain's Tree Story, National Trust (2011)

Hight, Julian, World Tree Story, Julian Hight (2015)

History Box (the), Hermes (2001)

Hoskins, W G, The Making of the English Landscape, The Folio Society (2005)

Illustrated Guide to Britain, AA, (1976)

James, Tanya, Along the Wild Edge, Neroche Landscape Partnership (2011)

Johnson, Hugh, The International Book of Trees, Mitchell Beazley Publishers Ltd (1973)

Johnson, Owen and More, David, Collins Tree Guide, Harper Collins Publishers (2006)

Jones, Mel, Sheffield's Woodland Heritage, Sheffield City Libraries (1989)

Lacey, Robert and Danziger, Danny, The Year 1000, Abacus (2000)

Lowe, John, The Yew Trees of Britain and Ireland, Macmillan and Co. (1897)

Marren, Peter, Woodland Heritage, David & Charles (1990)

McGarvie, Michael, The Book of Frome, Barracuda Books (1980)

McGarvie, Michael, The Bounds of Selwood, Frome Society for Local Study (1978)

Miles, Hugh & Jackman, Brian, The Great Wood of Caledon, Colin Baxter Photography (1991)

Muir, Richard, Ancient Trees Living Landscapes, The History Press (2005)

Neville Havins, Peter J, The Forests of England, Robert Hale (1976)

Packenham, Thomas, Meetings with Remarkable Trees, Patchwork Landscape (the), Readers Digest (1984)

Perceval, P J S, London's Forest, J M Dent & Co. (1909)

Pocket Trees, Dorling Kindersley Ltd (1995)

Rackham, Oliver, Woodlands, Collins (2006)

Roberts, Jonathan, Mythic Woods, Weidenfeld & Nicolson (2004)

Rotherham, Ian D, Sherwood Forest, Amberley (2013)

Rotherham, Ian D, Ancient Woodland, Shire (2011)

Schama, Simon, A History of Britain, BBC (2000)

Scott, Katie and Willis, Kathy, Botanicum, Big Picture Press, (2016)

Shelmerdine, J M, Woodstock, Samson Press (1951)

Spence, Lewis, The Mysteries of Britain Senate (1994)

Spencer-Jones, Rae and Cuttle, Sarah, Wild Flowers of Britain and Ireland, Kyle Cathie Ltd (2005)

Strutt, Jacob George, Sylva Britannica (1826)

Trees and Shrubs of Britain, Readers Digest (1981)

Trees, Dorling Kindersley (1992)

Trees, Timbers & Forests of the World, Leisure Books (1978)

Whitlock, Ralph, Historic Forests of England, Moonraker Press (1979)

Wilkes, J H, Trees of The British Isles in History & Legend, Frederick Muller Ltd (1972)

Wild Flowers of Britain, Readers Digest (1981)

Wildlife of Britain, Dorling Kindersley Ltd (2008)

Wilkinson, G, Woodland Walks, Book Club Assoc. (1985)

Wohlleben, Peter, The Hidden Life of Trees, William Collins (2015)

Wood, Michael, In Search of the Dark Ages, BBC (1981)

Woodward, Marcus, New Book of Trees, A M Philpot (1920)

World Atlas of Archaeology, Mitchell Beazley (1988)

About the author

Julian's passion for trees started early, as he grow up near woodland which had a profound effect on him. He travels widely, camera in hand, to document historic ancient trees, present regular talks, including an appearance as judge on Channel 4's Tree of the Year TV programme. Chair of Wessex Ancient Tree Forum, a verifier for the Ancient Tree Inventory, Julian has launched the Reviving Selwood Forest project to sustain heritage trees in Somerset and campaigns for ancient trees and woodland. Britain's Ancient Forest is Julian's third book, following Britain's Tree Story (*National Trust, 2011*) and World Tree Story (*self-published, 2015*).

For further information visit:
www.britainsancientforest.co.uk

Useful websites

In the course of my research, I trawled myriad websites, to numerous to mention. The following proved invaluable:
www.ancienttreeforum.co.uk
www.ati.woodlandtrust.org.uk (ancient tree inventory)
www.woodlandtrust.org.uk
www.ancient-yew.org   http://info.sjc.ox.ac.uk/forests

Picture credits

All images © Julian Hight, or in public domain, except for the following, for which I gratefully acknowledge permission: pg 29: The Bruce Yew ©Edward Parker; pg 75: Seahenge ©Wendy George/Thornage Hall; pg 92: Salcey Oak, pg 111: Moccas Oak – J G Strutt 1840 ©www.panteek.com; pg 95: Gog c1900 ©Pamela Carter; pg 102: Brimmon Oak 1905 ©Mervyn Lloyd Jones, 2016 Tracey Williams; pg 162: Darley Oak 1930 ©Tim Kellett; archive pics pg 220, 222, 225: © Frome Museum www.fromemuseum.wordpress.com; pg 266: Furry Day 1900 ©Graham Matthews www.helstonhistory.co.uk; pg 268: Stump ©Peter Sjöstedt Hughes; pg 284: raven ©Louise Hight; pg 281, 282, 286, 289: pine marten, fox, badger, wood mouse, jay, woodpecker ©Karen Capindale. Licensed under CC BY 3.0 - pg 73: Horn Dance c1900 ©Stone, 2006 ©Simon Robinson; pg 75: Waylands Wood 2008 ©Colin Viney; pg 279: wolf ©Gunnar Ries; pg 282: boar ©Richard Bartz; wildcat ©Aconcagua; pg 283: pipistrelle bat ©Lisa Jarvis; woodmouse ©Hans Hillewaert; dormouse ©Zoë Helene Kindermann; goshawk ©Nigel Wedge; ©Fepan Pestaña; pg 286: woodcock ©Ronalde Slabke.

Above and beyond

For invaluable support: Charlotte Woodall, Martin and Dominique Hayes, David Hight, Greg Bedford, Vince Parker, Jon Evans, Felicity Laughton, Ted Green, Jill Butler, Rita – my travelling companion and all the fabulous people I met on my travels around Britain.

Roll of honour

The following pledged via an Indiegogo crowdfunding campaign, whose support hleped production of this book:

Hayley Allen
Colin Ashley
Margaret Burr
Sara Butler
Tim Carey-Yard
Andy Clark
Olivia Clifton-Bligh
Kevin Cutler
Pat Feeney
Rachel Griffin
Sean Harding
Dominique Hayes
Grania Hayes
David Hight
Louise Hight
Tim Kellett
Elizabeth King
Robert Knott
Otteran Langrell
Colin Lawton
Bethany McNaught
Janet Millar
Crysse Morrison
Ben Norwood
Andy Nunns
Vince & Gina Parker
Robert Penlington
Claire Phillips
Katie Rossi
Maureen Sexsmith-West
Marion Sidebottom
Craig Skipper
Luke Steer
Gareth Thomas
Amanda Vesty
Matthew Walters
Sheila Wiggins
Louise Woodall
Woods

Index

Acorn	13
Adder	281
Adelaide, Queen	87
Adelaide's Oak	87
Alder	108, 275
Aldermaston Court	166-167
Aldworth Yew	164
Alfred, King	216
Amesbury Banks	148
Amethyst deceiver	295
Ankerwyke Yew	6, 7, 10
Arden, forest of	88-89
Arthur, King	208-209, 236
Arthur's Round Table	208-209
Ash	271
Ashdown Forest	192
Ashton Court	134-137
Athelstan, King	197
Babes in the Wood	78
Badger	280
Bagot's Park	72
Bagshot Heath	176-177
Bagshot Park	176
Bale Oak	77
Barn owl	284
Bear	21
Beating the bounds	222-223
Beech	31, 271
Beetle: Dor, Red cardinal, Stag, Violet click	49, 296
Beggar's Oak	72
Birch	18, 272
Bishop Ken	225
Black Death	10
Black Dog Woods	229
Blackbird	287
Blackmore Forest	238-241
Blenheim Park	126-131
Blenheim, Beast of	127
Bluebell	289
Boudicca	148
Bowthorpe Oak	60
Boxer Tree	252
Bradgate Oak	86
Bradgate Park	84-87
Bradford on Avon Tythe Barn	206
Brighton	272
Brimmon Oak	102
Bristol Whitebeam	141
Broadstone Oaks	119
Bronze Oak Project	175
Brown, Lancelot 'Capability'	12, 46, 62, 111, 126, 130, 224
Buck Stone	119
Bugle	291
Burnham Beeches	158-163
Butler, Jill	166
Butterfly: Meadow brown, Orange tip, Peacock, Red admiral, Ringlet, Silverwashed fritillary, Small copper, Speckled wood	297
Buzzard	283
Cadzow	32
Caesar, Julius	148, 158
Cage Pollard	162-163
Caledonia, great wood	18-33
Candlesnuff fungus	295
Casivellaunus	148
Cathedral Oak	198
Cawdor	21
Celts	9
Chalara ash dieback	14, 273, 295
Charcoal burning	13, 192, 249
Charles I, King	118, 142, 155, 176, 246
Charles II, King	14, 64, 93, 171
Charnwood Forest	82-87
Charter of the Forest	10, 142, 170
Chatsworth Park	44-47
Chicken of the woods	295
Civil War	64, 120, 142, 160, 170, 181, 251, 260, 280
Clarendon Forest	204-205
Common dog violet	289
Coppice	11
Copt Oak	82
Cornwall Forest	260-269
Cowper, William	94-95
Cowper's Oak	94
Crab apple	274
Crusader Oak	241
Cwm Byddog	108-109
Darley Oak	260, 262-263
Dartmoor Forest	254-259
Dean, forest of	118-123
Deer: Fallow, Red, Roe	21, 56, 62, 70, 84, 96, 113, 118, 134, 277
Dendrochronology	74, 86, 107, 151, 164, 207, 208, 235, 253
Devil's Pulpit	122
Domesday Oak	136-137, 194
Domesday Survey	10, 11, 44, 60, 82, 125, 146, 160, 166, 184, 190, 228, 252
Dormouse	281
Druid's Oak	160
Druids	13
Dukeries, the	54-55
Dutch elm disease	273
Early purple orchid	291
Edgar and Ethelwold	201
Edmund I, King	132
Edward I, King	29, 142, 208
Edward II, King	264
Edward the Confessor	151, 160, 171
Edward VI, King	247
Elephant Beech	220-221
Elizabeth I, Queen	13, 44, 152, 156, 181, 184
Elizabeth II, Queen	176
Elm	271
Enclosure	12, 146
Epping, forest of	146-149
Essex, forest of	142-149
Ethelred, King	125
Fairmead Oak	149
Fattest Oak	135
Field maple	272
First World War	12, 127, 194, 265
Fly agaric	295
Forest Law	5, 8, 10, 44, 49, 60, 64, 82, 96, 118, 122, 142, 168, 170-171, 211, 223, 232, 238, 255, 260
Forest of the Weald	190-195
Forestry Commission	12, 21, 26, 97, 214, 249
Foris	5
Foxglove	290
Francis Mundy	64
Frans Vera	8
Frenchman's Oak,	182
Fungi	26, 49, 292-293
Gallows Tree	31
Ganoderma	295
Garlic mustard	291
George VI, King	97
Glen Affric	23
Glyndwr, Owain	101, 114
Gog and Magog	95
Golden Farmer	177
Goshawk	282
Gospel Oak	68
Grass snake	281
Gray's Beech	162
Grazing	250
Green, Ted	175
Greendale Oak	55
Gregynog Oak	104-105
Grey, Jane	86
Grey squirrel	279
Grimsthorpe Park	62-63
Grovely Forest	210-215
Hadrian, Emperor	38
Hal-an-Tow	266
Harewood Forest	201
Harold, King	166, 236
Harry Potter Tree	130
Hawthorn	273
Hazel	273
Hazelgrove	236-237
Heaven's Gate	225
Hedgehog	279
Heligan, oaks	265
Helston Furry Day	266-267
Henry Hoare	232
Henry I, King	40, 126
Henry II, King	42, 126, 193, 205
Henry III, King	10, 96, 118, 142, 151, 170, 194
Henry VIII, King	10, 82, 149, 155, 170, 192, 197, 253
Herne the Hunter	172

Herne's Oak 172	Lime 274	Orb web spider 296	Seahenge 74-75
Hethel Old Thorn 79	Lion of Longleat 226-227	Pannage 13, 251	Second World War
High Peak, forest of 44	Loch Lomond 29	Parkland 12	12, 26, 265 43, 71, 91, 94,
Holly 275	Longleat 218-219, 224-225	Piddle Oaks 246	155, 160, 189
Honey bee 297	Longleat Yew 219	Pine marten 281	Sele, Howel 101
Honey fungus 295	Lords and ladies 292	Pipistrelle bat 282	Selwood Forest 216-233
Hornbeam 275	Lynx 21	Pollard 11, 96, 102, 103,	Seymour, Jane 149, 197
Horn Dance,	Lyonesse 268	113, 144, 148-163, 246	Shaggy inkcap 295
Abbots Bromley 73	Macbeth 28, 31	Primrose 290	Shakespeare 14, 88-89
Horsefly 297	Magna Carta	Queen Elizabeth's Oak 184	Shambles Oak 54
Hoverfly 297	6, 7, 10, 14, 126, 170, 181	Rackham, Oliver 8, 10	Sherwood Forest
Inchlonaig 29	Major Oak 5, 50	Raglan Castle 120-121	5, 13, 48-59
Ingelramus de Waleys 241	Margaret, Queen of Anjou	Ramsons 292	Shinto 13, 68
Inveraray Castle 31	35	Rannoch, Black Wood of	Signing Oak 174-175
Irton Oak 42-43	Marston Yew 228	26-27	Six Wells Bottom 233
Jack O'Kent's Oak 116-117	Mary Rose 253	Raven 285	Snowdonia, forest of 101
Jacob G Strutt 66, 68, 72	Mary, Queen of Scots, 26, 33	Red campion 292	Snowdrop 290
Jay 286	Meavy Oak 256	Red fox 282	St Aldhelm 220, 230
Jenny Lind Tree 162	Mendelssohn's Tree 162	Red kite 285	St George's Park 70-71
John Leland 82, 216	Merlin 21	Red squirrel 21, 281	St Michael's Mount 268-269
John White 14	Mildmay Oaks 183	Remedy Oak 247	Staple Hill Oak 132
John, King 10, 50, 79, 118,	Milking Oak, the 93	Repton, Humphry	Staverton Park 96-99
126, 170, 181, 238, 255	Moccas Park 110-113	12, 111, 134	Staverton Thicks 98-99
Jubilee Oak 182	Moccas Oak 111	Rewilding 13	Stock Gaylard 240-241
Kentchurch Court 114-117	Moth: Cinnabar, Small	Richard II, King 177	Stoggle 11
Kesteven, forest of 60-63	magpie, Willow beauty	Richmond Park 154-155	Stonehenge 202-203
Kestrel 285	297	Robert Kett 80	Stoneleigh Abbey 88
Kett's Oak 80-81	Mushroom: Chantelle,	Robert Southey 139	Stourhead 232
Kielder Forest 34	Parasol, Porcelain 295	Robert the Bruce 29, 150	Stumpy Oak 257
King and Queen Oaks	Mycorrhiza 294-295	Robin 289	Sunken Hundred, Borth
236-237	Nannau Oak 100-101	Robin Hood 35, 49, 52	106-107
King George VI Oak 97	Needwood Forest 64-73	Robin Hood's Bower 218	Sweet Track 235
King Oak 128, 156	Neroche Forest 242-245	Romans 9, 13, 18, 21,	Swilcar Oak 66
King of Limbs 200	New Forest 13, 248-252	38-40, 46, 190, 216, 236	Sycamore 31, 38, 272
King's Evil 247	Newton, Sir Isaac 60	Rowan 276	Tawny owl 286
King's Wood 264	Norman Conquest	Royal Forest 10, 54, 64, 71	Teddy Bear's Picnic 119
Kingley Vale Yews 188-189	5, 49, 56, 103, 168	Royal Oak 155	Tennyson, Alfred, Lord 164
Kingston Lacy Beech	Normans 9, 10, 12, 82, 84,	Rufus, King 249	Thetford Forest 76
Avenue 186-187	91, 118, 190, 246, 255	Salcey Forest 90-95	Thomas à Becket
Kingswood Forest 132-141	Norse 34, 78	Salcey Forest Oak 92	126, 193, 205
King's Barrow Beeches	Oak 40-43, 273	Salisbury Cathedral 207	Thomas à Becket Yew 193
202-203	Oak Apple Day	Sallow 277	Tintern Abbey 122-123
Knepp Castle 13	14, 93, 212-213	Savernake Forest 196-200	Tottenham Oak 150
Last Tree Dreaming 234	Oak bracket 295	Saxons 9, 34, 49, 56, 62,	Tree creeper 289
Leigh Woods 138-140	Odiham common 182	70, 73, 118, 190, 216, 240	Tree of the Year
Lichen 22, 26, 38, 42, 46,	Odiham deer park 180-181	Scarlet elf cap 295	38, 60, 102, 104, 144, 150
49, 77, 83, 104, 108, 156,	Old Knobbley 144-145	Scorpion fly 297	Trysting Tree 40
194, 197, 200, 203, 240, 241,	Old Oaks, the 152-153, 165	Scots pine	Turkey tail 295
246, 247, 252, 259, 260, 265	Old Oak, Clun 103	18-26, 76, 176-177, 277	Turley Chestnut 64

Tutbury Elm 64	Wild cherry 276	Witches of Selwood 230-231	Woodcock 286
Victoria, Queen 12, 160	Wild Edric 103	Witching Trees 214-215	Woodlouse 296
Vikings 9, 21, 31, 34	Wildcat 282	Wolf 21, 49, 70, 84, 279	Woodpecker 289
Wallace Yew 26	Wildwood 8, 9	Wood anemone 290	Woodstock 125,
Wallace, William 28	William the Conqueror	Wood forget-me-not 293	Woolaton Hall 56
Waltham Blacks 171	5, 10, 118, 166, 168, 204, 249	Wood mouse 283	Woolaton Oak 59
Warkworth Hermitage 36-37	Willow 277	Wood pasture 5, 9-12, 14,	Wordsworth, William
Waylands Wood 78	Windsor Great Forest	32, 37, 43, 46, 49, 52, 60, 62,	14, 122
Wellington Witches 245	168-175	64, 66, 71, 72, 88, 92-96, 104,	Wychwood Forest 124-131
Westminster Abbey 54, 151	Windsor Great Park 5	111, 113, 116, 120, 127, 134,	Yateley Common 178-179
Westminster Hall 181, 205	Winfarthing Oak 77	139, 140, 144, 155, 158, 166,	Yellow archangel 291
White Hart, legend 177	Winnie the Pooh 192	168, 170, 171, 181, 182, 197,	Yew 37, 274
Whitebeam 276	Winston Churchill 128	200, 203, 204, 218, 228, 229,	Yggdrasil 273
Wild boar	Wisht Hounds 259	238, 240, 246, 249	
21, 49, 70, 84, 118, 282	Wistman's Wood 258-260	Wood sorrel 291	

The End

www.britainsancientforest.co.uk